Dangerous Counsel

Dangerous Counsel

Accountability and Advice in Ancient Greece

MATTHEW LANDAUER

The University of Chicago Press
Chicago and London

The University of Chicago Press, Chicago 60637
The University of Chicago Press, Ltd., London
© 2019 by The University of Chicago
Published 2019
Printed in the United States of America

28 27 26 25 24 23 22 21 20 19   1 2 3 4 5

ISBN-13: 978-0-226-65401-0 (cloth)
ISBN-13: 978-0-226-65379-2 (paper)
ISBN-13: 978-0-226-65382-2 (e-book)
DOI: 10.7208/chicago/9780226653822.001.0001

Library of Congress Cataloging-in-Publication Data

Names: Landauer, Matthew, author.
Title: Dangerous counsel : accountability and advice in ancient Greece / Matthew
    Landauer.
Description: Chicago ; London : The University of Chicago Press, 2019. | Includes
    bibliographical references and index.
Identifiers: LCCN 2019009194 | ISBN 9780226654010 (cloth : alk. paper) |
    ISBN 9780226653792 (pbk. : alk. paper) | ISBN 9780226653822 (e-book)
Subjects: LCSH: Greece—Politics and government—To 146 B.C. | Political
    consultants—Greece. | Government accountability—Greece. | Democracy—
    Greece. | Despotism—Greece. | Comparative government.
Classification: LCC JC73 .L25 2019 | DDC 320.938—dc23
LC record available at https://lccn.loc.gov/2019009194

♾ This paper meets the requirements of ANSI/NISO Z39.48-1992 (Permanence of
Paper).

Contents

Acknowledgments

This project has benefited from the advice of many over the years—although, of course, responsibility for the finished product is mine alone. For conversations and comments, I wish to thank in particular Danielle Allen, Ryan Balot, Shadi Bartsch, Eric Beerbohm, Susan Bickford, Jonathan Bruno, Agnes Callard, Daniela Cammack, Federica Carugati, Josh Cherniss, Chiara Cordelli, Prithvi Datta, Mark Fisher, Jill Frank, Adom Getachew, Sean Gray, Kinch Hoekstra, Sean Ingham, Seth Jaffe, Demetra Kasimis, Tae-Yeoun Keum, John Lombardini, Melissa Lane, Harvey Mansfield, Patchen Markell, Liz Markovits, John McCormick, Christopher Meckstroth, Yascha Mounk, Joe Muller, Sankar Muthu, Eric Nelson, Michael Nitsch, Josh Ober, Jennifer Pitts, Sabeel Rahman, Nancy Rosenblum, Arlene Saxonhouse, Melissa Schwartzberg, Joel Schlosser, Matthew Simonton, Lucas Stanczyk, Christina Tarnopolsky, Andrea Tivig, Don Tontiplaphol, Richard Tuck, Lisa Wedeen, James Wilson, Carla Yumatle, Bernardo Zacka, Linda Zerilli, and John Zumbrunnen. In addition, audiences at Harvard, Stanford, Oxford, the University of Chicago, and conferences around the country have listened to various iterations of the arguments in the book, providing sharp questions, helpful feedback, and encouragement.

My fellow political theorists and political scientists at the University of Chicago—students and professors alike—as well as those studying ancient ethics and politics in other departments, have provided an ideal intellectual community to finish writing the book. Final edits to the manuscript were completed while I was a Laurance S. Rockefeller Visiting Faculty Fellow at the Princeton University Center for Human Values. I thank Katie Dennis for her invaluable editorial assistance and comments at this stage.

Two anonymous reviewers from the University of Chicago Press provided in-depth comments on the entire manuscript, spurring me to make a number of additions to the argument. Chuck Myers, Jenni Fry, Holly Smith, and Alicia Sparrow expertly shepherded me through the editorial process. I thank Pam Scholefield for creating the index.

Sections of chapters 2 and 3 are based on my article "The *Idiōtēs* and the Tyrant: Two Faces of Unaccountability in Democratic Athens," published in *Political Theory* 42, no. 2 (2014): 139–66. An earlier version of chapter 5 appeared as "*Parrhesia* and the *Demos Tyrannos*: Frank Speech, Flattery and Accountability in Democratic Athens" in *History of Political Thought* 33, no. 2 (2012): 185–208. Figure 1, Frontispiece to Hobbes' translation of Thucydides' *Eight Books of the Peloponnesian Warre* (1629), is printed with permission of the Princeton University Library. Figure 2, "Demos personified and crowned by the goddess *Dēmokratia*," is printed with permission of the American School of Classical Studies at Athens: Agora Excavations.

My mother, Hollis Landauer, and my sisters, Melissa and Rachel, have provided encouragement and support. I have told them to stop asking me when the book is coming out—I am glad to be able to say to them, "Now." Emma Saunders-Hastings is my closest adviser and partner in all things, and this book would not exist without her help. It is my father Michael Landauer's fault that I am a political scientist (he gave me his copy of Laswell's *Politics: Who Gets What, When, How* when I was in high school), and I dedicate this book to his memory.

Introduction

I. Picturing Political Debate

In the frontispiece to Hobbes' translation of Thucydides' *Eight Bookes of the Peloponnesian Warre* (1629), one can find, underneath towering portraits of Pericles of Athens and Archidamus of Sparta, two comparatively tiny depictions of political decision-making in action (see figure 1). Both pictures highlight the role of speech in the decision-making process. On the right, under the caption *hoi polloi*, "the many," we see a throng of citizens, gazing up raptly at a single speaker.[1] The scene is meant to illustrate the workings of a democratic assembly. On the left, we have *hoi aristoi*, the (self-styled) "best men," conversing around a table. If hoi polloi represent Athens, then this council of hoi aristoi must take place in Sparta.

The images are political caricatures, meant to provoke judgments about the relative quality of political discourse depicted in each scene. We can imagine the orator haranguing the crowd below, whipping them into a frenzy with the force of his words, manipulating and deceiving them. In contrast, we see the men at the table debating calmly and rationally: witness the two in the corner, consulting a book and each other, preparing to share their findings with the rest of the group. We are meant to see the superiority of decision-making and political discourse among the few "best" over decision-making and discourse among the many.

Yet setting aside their ideological slant, we can also see that the images depict a basic structural difference. The image of hoi polloi depicts a single speaker set off from a crowd. In one sense, his singularity is purely incidental; if we were to let the scene run its course, we could readily imagine other speakers eagerly taking their turn to persuade the audience. However, it is also an essential part of the structure of this kind of decision-making that

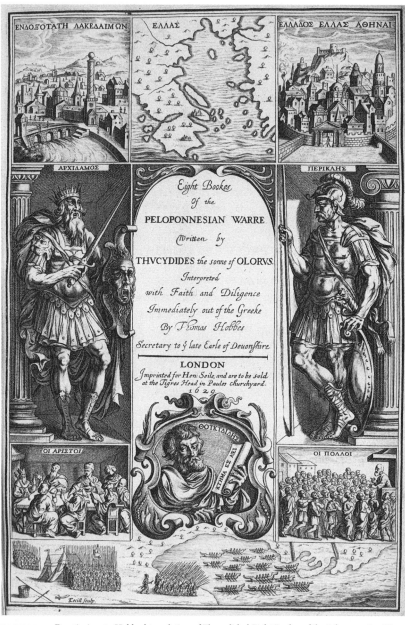

FIGURE 1. Frontispiece to Hobbes' translation of Thucydides' *Eight Bookes of the Peloponnesian Warre* (1629)

the speaker is alone on the platform, facing an audience of *nonspeakers*. The engraving illustrates the bifurcation of decision-making in the assembly into two complementary roles: that of (a succession of) persuasive speakers and an audience that listens, judges, and decides. Communication flows primarily in one direction—from the speaker's platform down to the audience below.[2] Nonetheless, the audience is not passive, for they ultimately have the power to decide on the issues put before them. At the end of the speeches, it is they who vote on what is to be done. The orator can only attempt to persuade and advise them.

In contrast, no single figure among hoi aristoi occupies the position of the orator. If we were to unpause the action depicted in this image, we would find ourselves in the midst of a lively debate. Decision-making in Athens relied on a division of labor between speaker and audience, but the roles at this table are much more fluid. The picture of hoi polloi has two nodes, speaker and audience; by contrast, the lines of communication at the table flow freely and in multiple directions. Each man, we are meant to see, is participating in the discussion, speaking and listening in turn.

If the role of speaker is distributed across the group of hoi aristoi, what of the power to decide? There is a man at one end of the table with a crown and scepter, but the accoutrements of royal power should not mislead us—if the scene is meant to represent Sparta, then the king is not the sole decision-maker.[3] Rather, what we have here is a depiction of the deliberations of a ruling council. If each member of hoi aristoi speaks and listens, each also has a vote in the decision. In this idealized image, hoi aristoi deliberate and decide together as speakers-cum-decision-makers.

It is important to stress again that these images are tendentious, simplified, and polemical. In ancient Greece, both democratic and oligarchic discursive practices naturally departed from the models suggested by the frontispiece in various ways (as I will discuss further below). But the Hobbesian frontispiece accurately captures a core insight driving the argument of this book: political discourse in the ancient world was conditioned by institutions and regime type and thus must be understood comparatively. In that spirit, the presence of a regal figure among hoi aristoi also invites speculation. After all, classical political thought, from Pindar and Herodotus to Aristotle and beyond, recognized three basic regime types: rule by the many, by the few—and by one.[4] If these images are meant to stand as illustrations, however tendentious, of the decision-making process in two of the three classical regime types, what kind of image would neatly capture decision-making in autocracies?

Perhaps the image of hoi aristoi could be pressed into double duty and serve to illustrate the process of a king taking counsel from his advisers. After all, there is already a little king in the image, to shepherd us along to this point of view. Yet the resemblance between a king in council and the idealized deliberations of hoi aristoi is only superficial. Rather, in a number of fundamental respects, the Greek understanding of autocratic decision-making closely paralleled their understanding of democratic decision-making. Both rule by the many and rule by one—democracy and autocracy—evinced the same bifurcation of decision-making into complementary roles: decision-maker (whether collective demos or individual ruler) and adviser. Moreover, given the overwhelming power of the decision-maker in both regimes—ordinary citizens voting together in the assembly and popular courts in a democracy, monarch or tyrant dictating in an autocracy—the relationships between decision-maker and adviser in the two regime types shared a number of key features. Throughout the period in which Athenian democracy flourished (roughly 508 to 322 BCE), philosophers, historians, dramatists, and rhetoricians, thinking through the problems of both autocratic and democratic decision-making and investigating the relationship between advisers and rulers in both regime types, found each regime useful for thinking about the other.

My central argument can be summarized as follows. I identify the *sumboulos* (adviser) as an important figure in Greek conceptions of both democratic and autocratic politics. Athenian orators are best understood—and understood themselves—as the accountable *sumbouloi* of the Athenian demos. This identification casts them not as codeliberators with their fellow citizens but rather as participating in an activity—giving political advice—that had long been a matter for theoretical reflection and found expression across political contexts. The figure of the *sumboulos* is not restricted to democracy; he appears in discussions and analyses of advice in autocratic contexts from Herodotus' depictions of the Persian court down to Isocrates' letters to Macedonian regents and Cypriot kings.

Oligarchic regimes, too, made use of *sumbouloi*, but in what follows, I focus primarily on democracies and autocracies. The distinctive role of *sumbouloi* in these regime types follows from the structural similarity between the two, to which I already alluded briefly above. The Athenian demos, gathered together in the assembly and in the popular courts, was understood in the fifth and fourth centuries to have competencies and powers akin to those of an autocratic ruler. In particular, both the demos and the autocrat were recognized as unaccountable rulers able to hold others—including their advisers—to account.[5] Given the way in which power asymmetries structured the relationships between *sumbouloi* and decision-makers in both democracies and autocracies, both practicing orators and theoretically inclined observers—dramatists, historians, philosophers—came to see that the problems and opportunities associated with having (or choosing) to speak to the powerful were comparable across regimes. The issues at stake in the demos-adviser relationship could be compared fruitfully to those in the autocrat-adviser relationship. Questions such as how the powerful could recognize good advice and good advisers, how advisers could help decision-makers see the limits of political action, and the possibilities for and obstacles to frank speaking under conditions of risk were not taken to be regime-specific. The ancient Greek theory of political counsel was a strikingly portable one, traveling across political boundaries in surprising and enlightening ways. It stands to reason, then, that reading Greek reflections on autocracy and democracy alongside one another can enrich our understanding of accountability and advice in both types of regime.

Or so, at least, I hope to convince you.

II. Against "Democratic Exceptionalism"

One of the central aims of this book is to argue that democratic and autocratic politics in ancient Greece shared structural features that contemporary scholarship overlooks. In particular, in fifth- and fourth-century Greek thought, decision-making and advice-giving in autocracies and democracies were understood to be, in key respects, closely related, and this has important implications for our understanding of Athenian politics. Standing in the way of accepting such a thesis are a number of views we could group under the banner of *democratic exceptionalism*. Such views have in common a conviction that there is something about democracy that makes comparisons to autocracy inapt or misguided. I want to begin, therefore, with a discussion of some prominent views that might seem to preclude the thought that ancient Greeks recognized important similarities between autocratic and democratic politics (and, indeed, that these similarities really existed in any meaningful way). I will not deal decisively with these views here—I develop my response more fully in the chapters to come. I will, however, offer a few preliminary reasons for thinking that they can be answered convincingly. In the process, I introduce some of the main themes and ideas to be explored in the coming chapters.

DELIBERATION AND ADVICE

In 330 BCE, the Athenian orator Demosthenes found himself under attack from his political opponent Aeschines.[6] In defending his career in Athenian politics before an Athenian popular jury, Demosthenes cites one episode in particular. In 339 BCE, Philip of Macedon was threatening the city. Demosthenes claims that he was in a unique position to help the Athenians at that point in time, for he had been following Philip's activities closely. As he puts it,

> Someone who did not know these things and had not studied the situation for a long time, even if he was devoted and even if he was wealthy, would not be better informed about what had to be done or be able to advise you [*sumbouleuein*]. The one who emerged as the right man on that day was I. I stepped forward and addressed you. . . . I alone of the speakers and politicians did not abandon my post of civic concern at the moment of danger but rather proved to be the one who in the very midst of the horrors both advised and proposed the necessary measures for your sake.[7]

At this climactic moment of the speech (*On the Crown*), Demosthenes identifies his distinctive role as "advising" (*sumbouleuein*) the demos. As Harvey Yunis has noted in an incisive analysis of the speech, Demosthenes identifies himself throughout as Athens' foremost *sumboulos*. *Sumboulos* is sometimes translated as "statesman," perhaps in an effort to capture both the importance of such figures to the democracy and the generally positive valence of the word.[8] Yet such a translation obscures more than it reveals, as it offers no sense of the actual activity such "statesmen" engaged in: the giving of advice. *Sumboulos* is best translated, then, as "adviser" or "counselor." Demosthenes was not alone in describing his political activity in these terms. Both *sumboulos* and the verb form, *sumbouleuein*, are frequently used by Attic orators to describe the speaker's role and activity in the assembly (and less frequently the courts).[9] The words are also used by historians and philosophers to denote the activity of speaking before the demos.[10] The verb is straightforwardly translated as "to counsel" or "to advise." We also see the *sumboul*-root used by Aristotle to denote one of the three kinds of rhetoric: *sumbouleutikē rhētorikē*, often translated—potentially misleadingly, as we shall see—as "deliberative rhetoric."

Scholars have long called attention to the role orators played as advisers in the democratic city. Moses Finley and Shalom Perlman, in influential articles from the 1960s on Athenian "demagogues" and "politicians," both emphasized the advisory function of speakers in the assembly. Neither, however, explored in any detail the vocabulary used by orators and others to denote the advising function.[11] M. H. Hansen later called attention to the explicit uses of the term *sumbouloi*, alongside terms such as *rhētores*, *dēmagōgoi*, and *politeuomenoi*, to refer to that "small group of citizens who regularly addressed the ecclesia, proposed laws and decrees, and frequented the courts as prosecutors or *syn-egoroi* [advocates]."[12] As Yunis argues in his reading of *On the Crown*, the term could be used by an orator "to suggest a higher moral purpose and intellectual status than a mere speaker might enjoy: the wise, experienced, loyal adviser to whom one turns for guidance, especially in difficult circumstances."[13] The orator's assumption of the mantle of the adviser is no mere metaphor or loose talk, as some scholars have suggested.[14] Rather, this characterization of the orator's activity follows from his position in the political structure of Athens. Decision-making power belonged to the demos in the assembly. If the orator wished to influence the demos' decisions and policies, he had to step up to the speaker's platform and advise the assembled citizens with respect to what they should do.

Yet in addition to recognizing Athenian orators as advisers, contemporary scholars are also partial to an alternative (and, in my view, incompatible) model of the orator-audience relationship in democratic Athens. This alternative model takes as its starting point a particularly influential way of thinking about the Athenian assembly: as an organ of deliberative democracy. If Athenian orators can be taken as advisers to the demos, they are also frequently depicted as something potentially different: as codeliberators with their fellow citizens.

Alongside interest in the theory of deliberative democracy has come an interest in its history, and many contemporary theorists see in Athens a potential pedigree—and perhaps even a model case—for their favored views. As one theorist boldly and succinctly states the matter, "The idea of deliberative democracy and its practical implementation are as old as democracy itself. Both came into being in Athens in the fifth century B.C."[15] Athens as a deliberative democracy is an attractive image that has the further merit of having some basis in Athenian practice. Meetings of the assembly were open to all Athenian male citizens over the age of twenty; were held frequently, upward of forty times a year; and as best we can tell from the evidence, were well attended by a diverse cross section of the Athenian citizenry.[16] All citizens in attendance had the right to vote on the issues facing the assembly, including elections for key magistrates, decisions of war and peace, questions of citizenship, and more.[17] Crucially for the image of Athens as a *deliberative* democracy, anyone who wished could stand up and address his fellow citizens. As the Athenians turned their attention to a new item on the assembly's agenda, the herald would call out, "Who wishes to speak?" This was the institutional embodiment of a key principle of Athenian democracy: *isēgoria*, or equality of public speech.[18] Scholars invested in this portrait of Athenian democracy will approach my argument with doubts. After all, to view the Athenian assembly, an experiment in self-government and collective deliberation, as importantly analogous to the closed councils of a king or tyrant might seem strange, to say the least.

Bernard Yack's account of democratic deliberation, which he seeks to reconstruct from a reading of Aristotle, is exemplary in this regard. Yack's goal is to offer what he calls an "Aristotelian" account of political deliberation, which he defines as follows: "Political deliberation is a social practice in which citizens communicate with each other about how they should direct the actions of their political communities. As such, it has two basic elements: some form of public reasoning, in which citizens exchange their views about matters of common interest; and an opportunity to consider together this exchange of opinion and argument in reaching decisions about which collective action to support."[19] Yack's primary concern is to differentiate his "Aristotelian" account of political deliberation from contemporary deliberative theories.[20] Yet Yack's definition of political deliberation also points to a set of assumptions that he *shares* with contemporary deliberative democrats. Both understand deliberation as a "first person plural" activity. It is something that the citizens of a community undertake together and with a common aim— their collective good—in mind: "citizens communicate with each other" to decide on how to "direct the actions of their political communities," they "exchange their views about matters of common interest," and they "consider together this exchange" to decide on "collective" actions. Such deliberation "informs and prepares" the "collective decision" that follows through a separate decision procedure "such as majority rule or consensus."[21] Yack therefore treats deliberation as separable from, but always preparatory to, a certain kind of collective decision-making in which all the citizens' "individual choices" are taken into account and turned into a "collective choice" by means of some (democratic) decision procedure.

This framing misses something fundamental about the Greek conception of deliberation (*bouleusis*) and its relation to advice (*sumboulia*). On the Greek view, the *sumboulos* is *not* necessarily "deliberating" with his audience. Rather, deliberation and advice are generally thought of as separate (if related) activities.[22] This comes out clearly in Aristotle's account of deliberation in book 3 of the *Nicomachean Ethics*. Aristotle limits the sphere of deliberation to things that can "be brought about by our own efforts"; "we deliberate about things that are in our power and can be done."[23] This is why, for instance, "no Spartan deliberates about the best constitution for the Scythians."[24] A Lacedaemonian with a view about the political affairs of Scythians could not easily deliberate with the latter, given the great distance between them. Yet even were our Spartan to journey to Scythia, he still could not deliberate with them insofar as they and not he would be in control of Scythian political affairs. But imagine that our Spartan had a reputation for great wisdom, and the Scythians invited him into their councils, to serve as a *sumboulos* and offer them advice. Would the Lacedaemonian now be deliberating with the Scythians? When a *sumboulos* speaks, is he deliberating with his audience?

We can come to an Aristotelian answer to this question by looking at some of the uses of *sumboulia* in the *Politics*. In that text, Aristotle reflects on the "advice of Periander to Thrasybulus" (*tēn Periandrou Thrasuboulōi sumboulian*): "The story is that Periander, when the herald was sent to ask counsel of him, said nothing, but only cut off the tallest ears of corn till he had brought the field to a level. The herald did not know the meaning of the action, but came and reported what he had seen to Thrasybulus, who understood that he was to cut off the principal men in the state."[25] In an Aristotelian framework, it is clear that Periander, the tyrant of Corinth, is not deliberating with Thrasybulus, the tyrant of Miletus, in giving him advice. As Aristotle makes clear, humans deliberate only about what is in their power, since deliberation is preparatory to choice. For Periander and Thrasybulus to deliberate together, they would have to consider jointly what is in their joint power, with the aim of choosing a course of action together. Yet in this scenario, the choice remains solely in the hands of Thrasybulus. Insofar as Periander has any control over the outcome, *it is only by virtue of speaking.* Periander's effect works through Thrasybulus' choice; they are not choosing together. *Sum-boulia* is thus an activity that goes along "with" deliberation; it is not "*deliberating-with.*" Periander may deliberate about the appropriate means to persuade Thrasybulus,[26] but he is not deliberating *with* Thrasybulus. Rather, he is serving as Thrasybulus' adviser—as Aristotle's references to *sumboulia* with regard to this example make clear.[27]

Consider Aristotle's formulation in the *Nicomachean Ethics*: "We make use of advisers [*sumbouloi*] on issues of great import, not trusting in our own selves as adequate to discern."[28] The language here is forthrightly instrumental and preserves the difference between the *sumboulos* and the deliberator. It captures the role of an adviser: to clarify what is confused, to identify key issues and help weigh them, to offer a considered view about the best course of action—and all this in a context where the power to decide is not itself in the adviser's hands.

Let us return to Demosthenes' claim, in *On the Crown*, to be Athens' preeminent *sumboulos*. Demosthenes, we might say, comes into the assembly with two hats. On the one hand, insofar as Demosthenes is considering with his fellow citizens what course of action they should jointly decide on, he can straightforwardly be described as deliberating with his fellow citizens—he is a voting member of the polis.[29] But when Demosthenes refers to himself as a *sumboulos*, he is making a claim to have a different relationship to the democratic decision-making process. A *sumboulos*, in a political context, advises a party with decision-making power—the deliberator (whether a single person or a collective agent).[30] It is true that a *sumboulos* in a democracy is typically also a member of the deliberating body. But does that shared membership entirely transform the act of giving advice?

To speak before the assembly was not to take part, on an equal footing, in the common deliberations of a participatory democracy. Rather, it was to attempt to offer counsel to a sovereign, nearly all-powerful demos. As I will demonstrate in the coming chapters, how Greeks talked and wrote about advisers and advising (*sumbouloi* and *sumbouleuein*) does not support efforts to cordon off the democratic *sumboulos* from his autocratic counterpart. To think that the democratic *sumboulos* is "deliberating" with his audience while the autocratic *sumboulos* is merely advising his ruler and to read much into the distinction is to import our own assumptions about what the differences between democracy and autocracy *must have been* into our analysis of Greek concepts.

For as we shall see, the *sumboulos* appears across regime types. *Sumbouleuein* does not denote an essentially democratic activity, and the word *sumboulos* has no democratic connotations. If we wish to understand Greek reflections on the theory and practice of political advice, we cannot limit ourselves to the democratic context. Take as an example the following famous passage in the Platonic *Seventh Letter*:

> So too with a city, *whether its* kurios *[sovereign or ruler] is one or the masses,* if the regime marches on a straight path according to custom, if it seeks advice [*sumbouleuoito*] about what would be suitable, the one with intelligence should advise such people. But those stepping altogether away from the right constitution, and in no way wanting to go to the [right] path, ordering the *sumboulos* to abide by the regime and not to change it, saying that he will be killed if he changes it—if they order him to serve them with respect to their purposes and desires and to advise them how to do so in the easiest and quickest manner—the one remaining as such an adviser is cowardly, and the one who does not stay is the real man.[31]

Let us leave aside the letter writer's argument here. What I want to stress is the claim that the *sumboulos* can be expected to play a similar role in different regimes. There is no assumption here that he has one kind of relationship to an autocrat and a radically different one to a demos. There is no suggestion that *sumbouloi* in a democracy are "deliberating" with their audience,

while *sumbouloi* in a monarchy are "advising" their king. Rather, both regimes have *sumbouloi*, whose activity is to advise (*sumbouleuein*). The suggestion here is that the role of the adviser is, at least in certain respects, not
regime-dependent. And as I hope to make clear in the following chapters,
this is not a quirk of Platonic political theory but rather central to Greek
reflections on political discourse across genre (philosophy, history, rhetoric,
drama) and time (fifth- and fourth-century texts).

THE DEMOS AND THE TYRANT

Even granting that the democratic orator and the autocratic counselor are
both, in the Greek conceptual world, *sumbouloi*, we might think that there are
fundamental differences between a collective decision-maker—the demos—
and an individual decision-maker—a king or a tyrant. Of course, Greek literature, from history to philosophy and drama, frequently *analogized* the
demos to a tyrant.[32] But such texts, we might think, are operating at the level
of metaphor and, in any event, are mostly deployed with polemical intent.
They may tell us something about an author's view of democracy and ideological commitments or biases, but they give us (and gave the Greeks!) little
analytical purchase on either democratic or autocratic politics.

In what follows, I take the demos-tyrant analogy seriously, arguing that
it captures something essential about Greek reflections on the relationship
between accountability and advice. This involves treating it as more than
mere polemic. As William Clare Roberts has argued recently with respect to
a very different set of texts and political contexts:

> When socialists and communists, including Marx, call capital a vampire, they
> do so because the metaphor seems to them to be an apt one. And the aptitude
> of the metaphor can be discussed and articulated in a language that is not
> itself merely an elaboration of the metaphor. The sense that capital is parasiti-
> cal upon something—labor—that is both more primary to human existence
> and more natural and lively than is capital can be spelled out . . . the judgment
> against capital implied by the vampire metaphor can, by this process, come
> to be considered independently of the metaphor itself, and can be assessed as
> more or less cogent.[33]

The demos-tyrant metaphor, too, can be reconstructed and analyzed using
language and concepts that transcend the metaphor itself. Without ignor-
ing the polemical valence of the metaphor, it is possible to do the work of
reconstruction and analysis in a way that illuminates fundamental questions
concerning political accountability and political counsel.

In doing so, I do not deny the differences between democratic and autocratic politics in Greek political theory and practice. Athenian democracy was highly participatory, and the Athenian demos was composed of a (relatively) inclusive body of citizens. If we can think of the demos as an actor, it is as a collective agent whose membership was constantly shifting. Each year, new citizens came of age and were enrolled, and old citizens died. Even on a day-to-day basis, the citizens comprising the demos might change as different individuals attended assembly meetings or sat on juries for important political trials. The tyrant, by contrast, was an individual exercising autocratic power in the community. The difference between counseling collectives versus individual actors, and the vicissitudes of collective versus individual decision-making, will play a role in the analysis to come.[34]

Still, it is striking that the demos-tyrant analogy is frequently deployed precisely with respect to questions of accountability and advice. Consider Aristotle's description of the demos' political role in demagogic forms of democracy: "The people becomes a monarch, one composed of many, and the many are sovereign—not as individuals, but all together." The demos as monarch attracts demagogic politicians, who have their precise analog among the counselors of tyrants: "Each is very powerful in their respective cases, flatterers among tyrants, demagogues in democracies of this kind."[35] Here Aristotle claims that the dynamics of a certain kind of democratic politics are best understood by positing for the demos a kind of supraindividual personality, and one that makes comparisons to the tyrant particularly apt. Aristophanes, in the *Knights*, also personifies the demos to portray its relationship with the city's advisers, imagining the demos as a master and advisers like Cleon as slaves.

Democratic ideology and political practice also employed the image of the demos as a supraindividual sovereign actor. For example, a 337/6 BCE decree enacted against tyranny includes on its inscribed column a relief of the goddess Dēmokratia crowning the demos, personified as a dignified older man (see figure 2). As Greg Anderson has argued, this points to an "established Athenian propensity for visualizing [the Athenian state] precisely as a single persona, a perpetual corporate self in which the 'power' that underwrote *dēmokratia* was believed to reside."[36] This "perpetual corporate self" found expression and embodiment in the central popular institutions of the Athenian democracy: the assembly (*ekklēsia*), the popular courts (*dikastēria*), and the council (*boulē*). Whatever unity, coherence, and power to act that the demos possessed were a function of those institutions. Exploring the contours of the demos-tyrant analogy need not involve erasing the real differences between ancient democracies and autocracies. Instead, it involves careful

FIGURE 2. "Demos personified and crowned by the goddess *Dēmokratia*"

consideration of the institutional mechanisms and dynamics that both make the analogy good to think with and also help us see its limits.

Again, varieties of democratic exceptionalism threaten to stand in the way of this pursuit. In the view of a number of scholars, it is just with respect to questions of accountability that Athenian democracy and ancient Greek conceptions of tyranny are most opposed. As I show in chapters 1 and 2, a number of political theorists are invested in a view of Athenian accountability politics as diffuse and reciprocal—the very antithesis of the Greek understanding of tyranny as unaccountable rule. Here again, I argue for important continuities between autocratic and democratic forms of power. Institutions of accountability in Athens were asymmetrical. Ordinary citizens, acting collectively through the assembly and the popular courts, were the final decision-makers in Athenian accountability politics—but were themselves unaccountable. The demos-tyrant metaphor, far from being merely polemical, helps raise questions about the role of unaccountable decision-makers—whether tyrant or demos—in a regime's accountability politics.

As I go on to argue in the later chapters of the book, Greek thinkers made accountability central to their analyses of the politics of advice in both democracies and autocracies. The underlying continuity in their analyses, however, has been obscured by views that advising a collective decision-maker, such as the demos, differs fundamentally from advising a king or tyrant. For example, one might think that the demos is sorely in need of good advice, but advice-giving might be all but impossible in the democratic context for structural reasons that do not have obvious autocratic analogs. This is an influential claim in the history of political thought, with a long pedigree.

Such a claim probably stands behind Hobbes' depiction of democratic decision-making in the Thucydidean frontispiece with which we began. Quentin Skinner has linked the frontispiece with a critique of democratic deliberation: "Under democracies, as Hobbes was later to explain in *The Elements of Law*, 'there is no means any ways to deliberate and give counsel what to do.'"[37] Skinner ends his quotation from *Elements of Law* at that point, but the effect is somewhat misleading. Consider the whole quotation:

> In all democracies, though the right of sovereignty be in the assembly, which is virtually the whole body; yet the use thereof is always in one, or a few particular men. For in such great assemblies as those must be, whereinto every man may enter at his pleasure, there is no means any ways to deliberate and give counsel what to do, but by long and set orations; whereby to every man there is more or less hope given, to incline and sway the assembly to their own ends. In a multitude of speakers therefore, where always, either one is eminent alone, or a few being equal amongst themselves, are eminent above the rest, that one or few must of necessity sway the whole; insomuch, that a democracy, in effect, is no more than an aristocracy of orators, interrupted sometimes with the temporary monarchy of one orator.[38]

Hobbes' claim is not that deliberation and counsel are *impossible, per se*, in a democratic assembly but rather that they are constrained to follow a certain form, "long and set orations." There is an unspoken contrast here with other regimes, such as monarchy, in which the decision-maker at least has the opportunity to challenge, question, and converse with his advisers. The end result, in Hobbes' view, is that democracy collapses into either monarchy ("either one [orator] is eminent alone") or "an aristocracy of orators" (in which "a few being equal among themselves, are eminent above the rest"). The collective decision-maker, unable to interact effectively with its putative advisers, ends up ceding all control to them. In a democracy, Hobbes argues, the problem of counsel collapses into the problem of manipulation.

There is also a strain in Greek thought that holds that the demos, by virtue of its status as a collective agent, is particularly liable to be fooled or deceived. Aristophanes has the Sausage-Seller of the *Knights* speak to the incompetence of assemblymen, at least when they gather together:

> SAUSAGE-SELLER: *(aside)* Oh blast my luck, I'm finished. When he's at home the old fellow's the shrewdest of men, but when he's sitting on that rock [the Pnyx, the location of assembly meetings] he gapes like a chewer of dried figs.[39]

The problem is not the character of individual democratic citizens but the qualities of the collective actor they comprise. The Sausage-Seller does not complain that each Athenian citizen is a simpleton; however, joined together in the assembly, the shrewd Athenians somehow become less than the sum of their parts. Similarly, Herodotus takes Aristagoras of Miletus' success in requesting aid from the Athenians, coupled with his failure in Sparta, as demonstrating the truth that it is "easier to deceive and impose upon a whole throng of people than to do so to just one individual, since he had failed with Kleomenes of Lacedaemon, who was alone, but then succeeded with 30,000 Athenians."[40]

If the many are easier to deceive than a single ruler, it might also be true that it is easier to persuade a single individual to do the right thing without resorting to crude deceit and manipulation. This, at least, is part of Plato's defense of his decision to leave Athens for Sicily, as set out in the *Seventh Letter*:[41] "I weighed the question and was uncertain whether or not to yield to his [Dion's] urging and undertake the journey. What tipped the scales eventually was the thought that if anyone ever was to attempt to realize these principles of law and government, now was the time to try, *since it was only necessary to win over a single man and I should have accomplished all the good I dreamed of.*"[42] A similar thought can be found in Leo Strauss' reading of Xenophon's *Hiero*. In *On Tyranny*, Strauss reads Xenophon's Socrates as claiming that "the rule of a tyrant who . . . listens to the suggestions of reasonable men, is essentially more legitimate than the rule of elected magistrates who refuse to listen to such suggestions, i.e., than the rule of elected magistrates as such."[43]

First, let me say something briefly about Hobbes' worry that assembly democracies are less counseled than usurped by their orators. The Greeks anticipated this Hobbesian line of argument. Yet they also recognized that the facts could be taken to support precisely the opposite conclusion: that in a democracy, orators were little more than the servants of the demos. I consider the implications of these conflicting interpretations of the power struggle between orator and demos in chapter 6.

More generally, I do not wish to deny the extensive record of complaints found in our elite sources about the quality of democratic discourse, the difficulty of offering the demos sound advice, and the unwillingness of the demos to accept that advice in any case. In part, such complaints may reflect an ideological bias against democratic politics, well explored in the scholarly literature.[44] Yet it is worth stressing that just as the *sumboulos* is a figure who appears in multiple regime types, complaints about the difficulties of political advice are by no means limited to the democratic context. As I will argue below, many of the problems diagnosed in democracies have their autocratic counterparts. For example, tyrants are, in the Greek imagination, willful, perverse, and seemingly impervious to wise counsel (see chapters 2 and 3 for evidence from Herodotus). What both discourses reflect—over and above ideological critiques of either democracy or tyranny—is the Greek view that political counsel is *difficult*. But neither democracy nor autocracy was thought to have a monopoly on either good or bad counsel. Greek texts that dramatize or otherwise reflect on instances of failed counsel should not be read simply as offering critiques of democratic (or, for that matter, autocratic) politics. They are also attempting to work out a theory of counsel, explicate central problems, and assess existing practices. The Greek discourse I reconstruct and analyze in this book characteristically treats such problems by considering them within their political and institutional contexts—including accountability politics.

A similar obstacle to the comparative approach I take here arises from the connection between rhetoric and mass audiences. In mounting the speaker's platform, the democratic orator's chief aim (let us suppose) is to persuade the assembled audience. The art of doing so, we might say, is rhetoric. It is this thought that leads us to the final objection that I want to consider here. Recall Hobbes' depiction of decision-making among hoi polloi; perhaps it is not incidental to understanding the orator's activity that he is addressing a crowd. On such a view, rhetoric is not the art of persuasive speech so much as the art of persuasive speech before a *mass audience*. If so, then there might be no interesting connections to draw between speaking persuasively before a mass audience and speaking persuasively before an individual. Perhaps the Greeks just thought of these as fundamentally different activities.[45]

That, at any rate, seems to be a common claim. Gorgias offers a version of it in Plato's eponymous dialogue: "[Rhetoric makes you] able to persuade by speeches judges in the law court, councillors in the council, assemblymen in the assembly, and in every other gathering whatsoever [*en allōi sullogōi panti*], when there is a political gathering."[46] Gorgias seems to be claiming here that the orator's powers of persuasion can only be put to use before large audiences. Aristotle also stresses the relationship between rhetoric and large audiences in the *Rhetoric*,[47] leading some scholars to assume a tight relationship between rhetoric and mass persuasion on his view: "Aristotle's vision of rhetoric is that it be a practical discourse; an important counterpart to philosophical dialectic in a real-world setting where a speaker is seeking the best available means of persuasion in the face of mass audiences."[48]

Yet does the evidence really bear this out? Both the *Gorgias* and the *Rhetoric* contain passages that point in another direction. While Gorgias promises his audience that they will be able to persuade Athens' mass political gatherings with the help of rhetoric, he gives as an example of his own abilities a case where he used rhetoric to persuade a single man: "On many occasions now I have gone in with my brother and with other doctors to one of the sick who was unwilling either to drink a drug or to submit himself to the doctor for surgery or cautery; the doctor being unable to persuade him, I persuaded him, by no other art than rhetoric."[49] Gorgias thus acknowledges the utility of rhetoric outside of democratic institutions—and indeed, outside of any political context. Aristotle, too, points to rhetoric's use across contexts. His characterization of the aim of deliberative rhetoric is broad and inclusive: "Deliberative advice is either protreptic ['exhortation'] or apotreptic ['dissuasion']; for both those advising in private and those speaking in public always do one or the other of these."[50] The *Rhetoric to Alexander*, written (probably) by Anaximenes around the same time that Aristotle's *Rhetoric* was composed, also points to the uses of rhetoric outside of democratic politics: "persuasion and dissuasion" (Aristotle's sumbouleutic rhetoric) are used "most of all in private conversations and in public harangues."[51]

Discussions of rhetoric frequently place themselves within democratic contexts while simultaneously pointing beyond them. What should we make of this puzzle? On the one hand, the rise of rhetoric as a discipline is closely associated with democracy.[52] It was in Athens that rhetoric rose to prominence as a self-conscious discipline and an object of study and inquiry. Even the mythological founders of rhetoric, Corax and Tisias of Syracuse, were said to have worked out the discipline in the wake of the fall of Syracuse's tyrants, when speaking before mass audiences became newly important.[53] Yet if rhetoric found its beginnings in democracy, it was also self-consciously universalist in aspiration, at least in the formulations of fourth-century philosophers such as Plato and Aristotle. As Harvey Yunis has aptly put it, "The art of rhetoric concerns the manipulation of linguistic resources and the use of the art of rhetoric emerges whenever it matters that some message, regardless of its truth, beauty, or advantage, be presented to a particular audience as forcefully as possible. Thus neither the art nor the use is peculiar to democracy or any other political system; and politics in general, though it offers a highly charged setting, does not begin to exhaust the occasions for which rhetoric is appropriate."[54] Of course, we cannot impute the same universalist aspirations that we see at work in Plato's and Aristotle's reflections on persuasion and counsel to earlier authors such as Herodotus, Aristophanes, and Thucydides or to practicing orators such as Demosthenes. Nonetheless, as I will argue throughout, such authors were more comparative in their sensibilities and aspirations than we might think. All were alive to the differences between autocracy and democracy, of course, but they were also alive to the ways in which the logics of the regimes could converge. They were interested not only in theorizing democratic discourse but in thinking through its problems in light of the autocratic case—and, in the case of a figure such as Isocrates, in thinking through the problems of advising autocrats in light of the democratic case.[55]

Rather than fixating on the connection between rhetoric and democracy, between the art of persuasion and the art of managing mass audiences, I focus in what follows on the rhetorical situation faced by orators in democracies and by counselors in autocracies. As I will argue, that situation in both regime types was shaped by accountability politics.

III. Evidence, Assumptions, and Starting Points

Before turning to a more detailed overview of the argument, I wish to say a few words about my approach to Greek political thought. Let me begin with my approach to Athenian democracy. My analysis is by and large synchronic (although I do offer analyses of some specific historical events, such as the trial of the Arginusae generals). That is to say, I do not place much emphasis on the institutional or ideological differences between fifth- and fourth-century democracy. Much ink has been spilled by proponents and opponents of the view that in the wake of the Peloponnesian War and the oligarchic revolutions of 411 and 403, the Athenians replaced their "radical" democracy with a more "moderate" regime.[56] In particular, the argument goes, the fourth-century democracy was structured around the rule of law, as opposed to the unchecked rule of the demos.[57] On the whole, I am inclined to side with those who downplay the differences between the fifth- and fourth-century democracy, stressing instead the central importance of massed groups of citizens—in the *boulē*, the *ekklēsia*, and *dikastēria*—in both the fifth and fourth centuries.[58]

However, I do not think my arguments hinge much on taking a strong position on such questions (i.e., about the evolution of the rule of law or the relative moderation of the fourth-century democracy). This follows from my relatively narrow focus on institutions of accountability. It is true that there was some change in these institutions over the course of fifth- and fourth-century Athenian history. For example, by the end of the fifth century, ostracism ceased to be practiced. Also (and perhaps not coincidentally), at some point in the late fifth century (perhaps the year 416), the *graphē paranomōn*—a charge of initiating an unlawful proposal, a key institution for holding orators accountable—was introduced. Yet regardless of the development of specific institutions, the basic contours of the institutional architecture, and the terms of debate concerning its strengths, weaknesses, and effects, are discernible from at least the post-Periclean period on. The association of the Athenian democracy with a robust system of accountability can be traced as far back as Aeschylus and Herodotus. The observation that the demos—in contrast with other political actors, including orators—is conspicuously *unaccountable* can be traced at least as far back as the 420s.[59] Nor is there a material change in these facts in the fourth century, even if there are perhaps new ways of thinking about them (see chapters 1 and 2). The issues I am most concerned with thus traverse the fifth and fourth centuries regardless of what other claims we might want to make about the similarities or differences in democratic institutions, ideology, and practice in the two time periods.

Set against the backdrop of the Athenian democracy—which I treat somewhat statically but I hope not misleadingly—I explore a series of debates and arguments about the nature, function, and problems of political accountability and advice. I take a broad view of what "counts" as a contribution to political theory. I read historians, dramatists, philosophers, and rhetoricians alongside one another, and I treat them as responding to not only the realities of Athenian democracy but also each other. Where the evidence allows for it, I make arguments for the direct influence of one thinker on another. But more generally, I am interested in showing the development of ideas about a series of questions and problems, centering on issues of accountability and advice, across time and across political contexts. From this perspective, the precise influence of author A on author B matters less than the development of an overall narrative in which these thinkers build on, and respond to, a common set of ideas and arguments. In this way, I read all of these genres and texts as contributing to the Athenian "public sphere," reflecting on central political questions and practices and producing work that might influence political practice in turn.[60]

The speeches of orators such as Demosthenes and Aeschines play a particularly important role in the project. I use the extant sumbouleutic and forensic speeches from the fifth and fourth centuries to establish certain claims about what Athenians thought—the tenets of democratic ideology, common views, accepted wisdom, and the like. Using the rhetorical corpus in this way requires caution and judgment. But as Josiah Ober has influentially argued, insofar as these speeches depict what orators said in the assembly and the courts, they are a record of ideas and arguments that ordinary Athenian citizens would have found convincing.[61] Moreover, given the lack of alternatives—scholars since A. H. M. Jones have noted and lamented the absence of texts that give extended coherent statements of Athenian democratic theory and ideology—the rhetorical corpus, carefully interpreted, is one of the best sources we have for such views.[62]

I also portray orators such as Demosthenes and Aeschines as active participants in the larger intellectual and theoretical debates about accountability and advice that I trace throughout this work. Their speeches have a special role, since unlike Herodotus and Aristotle (non-Athenians both) or Plato and Isocrates (not actively involved in democratic politics), Demosthenes (for example) was himself an adviser accountable to the Athenian demos. As direct participants in Athenian politics, their speeches give us particular insight into how Greek theories of counsel were transformed and adapted as they were put into practice.[63]

Finally, I should say a brief word about my approach to tyranny and autocracy. My focus is primarily on representations of these rather than "the real thing." My analysis of advisers in the courts of tyrants and kings relies primarily on evidence from literary sources—chiefly Athenian sources and Herodotus. My treatment of democracy and autocracy is thus by necessity somewhat imbalanced. We lack a record of speeches made before tyrants and kings comparable to the rhetorical corpus we have from Athens.[64] Yet even if we take the view that we cannot learn anything about "real existing autocracies" from Herodotus and Athenian texts, the main thrust of my argument—that accountability and advice were theorized across political contexts—remains valid. Moreover, as I will show in chapter 5, Isocrates's actual letters to autocrats reflect his engagement with this tradition. Thus even if the depictions and analyses of advice in autocracies in many of the fifth- and fourth-century sources are only loosely based on fact, they come, at the end of the period under analysis, to be applied by Isocrates to the real world of autocratic politics.

IV. Chapter Outline

In the first part of the book (chapters 1 and 2), I analyze the politics of accountability that structured the relationship between *sumboulos* and decision-maker in both democratic and autocratic regimes. Chapter 1 explores accountability and unaccountability in Athenian democracy. One hallmark of Athenian democracy was a system of institutions to hold to account all citizens prominently participating in politics. I begin with an analysis of those institutions, arguing that the system was popular, discretionary, and asymmetrical. Large groups of ordinary citizens, voting (but not speaking) in the assembly or serving as jurors in the popular courts, were given wide latitude in holding political elites accountable but could not themselves be held to account for their judgments. I explore a number of possible justifications for popular unaccountability, including feasibility constraints, the "wisdom of the masses," and the question of collective versus individual responsibility for the decisions of the demos. I analyze one prominent justification in particular, which relied on the equation of the juror and assemblyman with the figure of the powerless, amateur, and therefore deservedly unaccountable *idiōtēs* (private citizen). However, that identification was always a tenuous one, given the Greek association of unaccountability with tyrannical rule.

In chapter 2, I pursue the link between tyranny and unaccountability in Greek thought. Authors such as Aeschines, Herodotus, and Plato argue for a close relationship between unaccountability and the excesses of the tyrannical life. Through a reading of Aristophanes' *Wasps* and Xenophon's account of the trial of the Arginusae generals, I show how images of the demos as an unaccountable tyrant could work to undermine the identification of jurors and assemblymen as justifiably unaccountable *idiōtai*. I argue that the demos-tyrant analogy not only provided a useful framework for criticizing the character of democratic rule but could also be used to analyze the nature of other political relationships in the democratic polis. In particular, it helped conceptualize the asymmetric relationship between an unaccountable collective decision-maker (the demos in the assembly and jurors in the courts) and the accountable advisers who attempted to persuade it.

Building on those arguments, I proceed in the following four chapters to look at a series of Greek texts reflecting on the politics of advice across political contexts. Each places the relationship between accountability and

advice at the center of its exploration of counsel. Chapter 3 turns to Herodotus' *Histories*, one of the first texts to make extensive use of the *sumboul-*
family of words and the first extended treatment of the figure of the "accountable adviser." Through a reading of Herodotus' depictions of counsel,
primarily in the courts of the Persian kings, I argue that Herodotus is less
interested in providing a schematic account of the differences between free/
Greek and unfree/Persian political discourse than in exploring the dynamics of political decision-making and advice under conditions of power asymmetries. Herodotus treats giving and receiving advice as an intricate process
that can misfire at multiple stages. He offers models for how political actors
and advisers can navigate their difficult relationships and raises foundational
questions about how the powerful can recognize good advice and good advisers and how advisers can help rulers understand the limits of their own
power. While Herodotus builds his theory of counsel primarily through the
depiction of non-Greek kings interacting with their advisers, he also suggests
that similar political dynamics and problems can obtain in Greek contexts—
including democratic Athens.

Chapter 4 takes up Thucydides' depiction of the Athenian assembly's
debate over the fate of Mytilene, a rebellious ally during the Peloponnesian
War. I read the debate as a clash over the place of assessments of responsibility
(*aitia*) in both domestic and international politics. Cleon urges the Athenians
to identify and punish those responsible for Mytilene's revolt—including the
Mytilenean demos. His critique of Athenian deliberative practices likewise
focuses on identifying responsibility for the problems he identifies. I argue
that Cleon's politics of responsibility is powerfully attractive but ultimately illusory, premised as it is on the thought that assessments of *aitia* can be simple
and transparent. Diodotus, by contrast, offers a more chastened view, acknowledging the limits on our ability to assess and act on *aitia* in politics. Yet
Diodotus also notes that a move away from a politics of responsibility might
also entail challenging the Athenian commitment to accountability politics.
As Thucydides' narrative ultimately shows, it is far from clear that Athens is
in a position to learn from Diodotus' advice, even if his motion prevailed in
the debate over Mytilene.

Chapter 5 turns from history to rhetoric. Building on the similarities
between the politics of accountability in autocratic and democratic regimes, I
analyze the dynamics of advice in both. I focus primarily on a single issue: the
problem of *parrhēsia* (frank speech) and flattery. *Parrhēsia* is usually understood as a practice intimately connected to Athenian democracy. I begin the
chapter with an analysis of *parrhēsia* in nondemocratic regimes. I show that

parrhēsia could arise in two ways in the courts of autocrats. First, the ruler could try to elicit it from his advisers by signaling that frankness would be welcome. Second, even without such encouragement, an adviser could accept the risks of being punished and speak frankly. I argue that the dynamics of *parrhēsia* in democratic Athens took similar forms and that much of the discourse of *parrhēsia* in Athens assumed, implicitly or explicitly, similarities between the demos and an unaccountable tyrant. In both democracies and autocracies, advisers willing to practice *parrhēsia* could offer a counterweight to flattering rhetoric. But a *sumboulos' parrhēsia* in both regime types was a remedial virtue, necessitated by the asymmetries of accountability that the regime types shared. Athenian rhetoricians faced with the question of how to serve as advisers to an empowered, unaccountable demos, were thus conscious participants in a longer tradition of Greek reflections on the possibilities and limits of political advice. Isocrates, in his letters to kings and tyrants as well as in his writings for an Athenian democratic audience, attempts to persuade the powerful in both regime types of their need for good advice. Demosthenes, in portraying himself as Athens' most trustworthy *sumboulos*, remained indebted to and continued to build on earlier Greek reflections on the role of the accountable adviser across regimes.

Chapter 6 begins by contrasting two seemingly contradictory ancient views of demagoguery as both enabling the demos' rule and usurping the demos' power. Both of these conflicting evaluations of the balance of power between the demos and its advisers can be traced to Plato's *Gorgias*. The dialogue famously offers competing visions of the power of rhetoric, ranging from Gorgias' claims that orators can enslave their audiences to Socrates' warning that orators only gain power in democratic cities by effectively enslaving themselves to the demos. Far from endorsing either view, I argue that Plato subverts both. In the dialogue, Socrates develops a philosophical account of power linked to knowledge of the good. This argument radically undermines almost all claims to exercise political power, whether made by the orator, the demos, or an individual tyrant. Yet this argument is politically inert. I argue, then, that Plato also gives to Socrates a second series of arguments that address orators and partisans of popular power on their own terms. This second line of argument attempts to show that neither orators nor ordinary citizens will get what they think they want from the practice of democratic politics. The inability of Socrates to convince his interlocutors in the *Gorgias* of the value of philosophy makes the dialogue appear fundamentally pessimistic, underscored by the way it foreshadows Socrates' own failures to persuade politically at his trial. But the second line of argument leaves open the possibility, at least, of a persuasive mode of Platonic advice that could work in real politics.

In the conclusion, I offer an overview of the book's central arguments and consider the relevance of the Greek theoretical tradition I reconstruct for contemporary democratic politics.

1

Accountability and Unaccountability in Athenian Democracy

Introduction

In his prosecution of Ctesiphon in 330 BCE, Aeschines offers the assembled jurors the following reflections on the fundamental differences between political regimes: "You know well, men of Athens, that there are three types of regime among all mankind—tyranny, oligarchy, and democracy. While tyrannies and oligarchies are administered according to the will and pleasure of their leaders, cities with democratic constitutions are administered according to established laws."[1] Democratic Athens could be so governed only because, in contrast to tyrannies and oligarchies, "there [was] nothing in the city that [was] exempt from audit, investigation, and examination."[2] As Aeschines elaborates, "In this city, so ancient and so great, no one is unaccountable [*oudeis estin anupeuthunos*] who in some way has applied himself to public affairs."[3] The essential difference between democratic and tyrannical or oligarchic regimes comes to light as one of accountability. While the tyrant administers the polis by his own lights and for his own good, political actors at Athens are held accountable and limited by law.[4]

Aeschines' portrait of Athens neatly captures the centrality of accountability to Athenian politics. By accountability, I do not mean anything particularly foreign to our own understanding of the concept. As Peter Euben has noted, "In many respects the Greek idea of accountability has the same range, breadth and ambiguity as our own. To render an account is to provide a story or description of events or situations as well as to explain oneself (often to a superior). To give an account is to give reasons . . . to call to account is to hold someone responsible or blame them."[5] Yet there are also important differences between ancient Greek and modern democratic accountability practices. Contemporary democratic theory often cashes out accountability in terms of representativeness and elections: "Governments are 'accountable' if citizens can discern representative from unrepresentative governments and can sanction them appropriately, retaining in office those incumbents who perform well and ousting from office those who do not."[6] Electoral accountability, it is hoped, will produce a government responsive to the beliefs, preferences, and interests of the voting populace. By contrast, election as an accountability (as opposed to a selection) mechanism in Athens played at most a peripheral role. Instead, for Aeschines and his fellow citizens, holding political office—whether elected or chosen by lot—meant submitting oneself to multiple accountability procedures before, during, and after one's service to the polis. Active participants in politics were called upon to give an account of their actions and could be punished by their fellow citizens should their accounts be deemed unsatisfactory. As Aeschines' boasts suggest, Athenian accountability procedures were remarkable in scope and the intensity of their practice. Contemporary scholarship affirms this view, stressing the thoroughness of accountability procedures, their wide applicability, and the potential severity of punishment.[7]

Yet Aeschines' account might also mislead in two ways. First, in spite of his insistence on democratic exceptionalism, measures to hold political officials responsible for their actions in office were not uniquely democratic. As P. J. Rhodes puts it, "Accounting procedures were widespread under regimes of various kinds."[8] What, then, differentiates ancient Greek *democratic* accountability politics from practices in other regime types? Second, there were exceptions to Aeschines' confident assertion that nothing and no one escaped the purview of Athens' accountability mechanisms. And understanding the exceptions to Aeschines' rule of political accountability will in turn help us answer the first question posed. For there were two important modes of political participation that stood outside of—or better yet, above—the dense network of accountability institutions. Citizens voting (but not speaking) in the assembly (*ekklēsia*) and serving as jurors in the large popular courts (*dikastēria*) could not be formally called on to explain or justify their votes before their fellow citizens, nor could they be punished for how they voted. At the same time, the unaccountable citizens participating in these institutions played central roles in holding other officials to account. This fundamental asymmetry is the central fact of Athenian accountability procedures: at Athens, accountability was *to the people*—and the people, in their capacity as assemblymen and jurors, were unaccountable.

Scholars have primarily taken two approaches to the exceptional status of jurors and assemblymen within the system of accountability. The dominant strategy is to note it briefly in passing and then to leave it virtually unexplored.[9] For example, Jan Elster observes that "the system of checks and balances through mutual accountability had an 'unmoved mover' or unchecked checker, in the Athenian people meeting in the Assembly or serving as jurors." He takes this to be a "lacuna" in the system but does not subject it to further investigation.[10] Jennifer Tolbert Roberts has little to say about the unaccountability of jurors and assemblymen in her otherwise thorough *Accountability in Athenian Government* other than to report that "there were two overlapping groups at Athens who remained unaccountable. These were the private citizens in their capacity as voters in the Assembly and in the Popular Courts (*dikastēria*). These men nobody could hold to account. A man could be impeached for giving bad advice, but not for taking it."[11] She recognizes that this was fertile ground for those critical of the democracy but leaves her analysis at that.

The second approach, not incompatible with the first, seeks to minimize the degree to which the treatment of assemblymen and jurors really was an exception in Athenian politics. Peter Euben, for example, has argued influentially that Athenian democracy was characterized by a "culture of accountability," which consisted in "the people being accountable to each other and to themselves." He does not consider whether this claim for generalized accountability is undermined by his recognition that "for better or for worse, members of the juries and nonspeakers in the Athenian Assembly . . . were not subject to the same intense scrutiny [as other participants in political life]."[12] Other scholars have followed his lead. Elizabeth Markovits has tried to demonstrate the ways in which "the average Athenian (even those who chose a relatively apolitical life) remained tied to [Athens'] overall culture of accountability," instantiated in such practices as drama, the taking of oaths, and gossip and rumor.[13] Moreover, political participation at Athens was extremely widespread. The proliferation of offices and the role of ordinary citizens in holding magistrates to account meant that many citizens would, at different times, both exercise accountability over others and find themselves held to account for their own actions. In this way, as one scholar has argued, the Aristotelian principle of "ruling and being ruled in turn" had a democratic corollary at Athens "in the expectation that rulers and ruled [would] hold and be held to account in turn."[14] These scholars are invested in a view of Athenian accountability as a rich network of mutual and reciprocal ties; the unaccountability of jurors and assemblymen fades into unimportance against the backdrop of a generalized accountability culture.[15]

Neither of these approaches is wholly satisfactory. Popular unaccountability[16] was a central fact of Athenian democracy and deserves more sustained reflection than it typically receives. Attempts to treat it as an unimportant exception to a generalized culture of reciprocal accountability distort our understanding of Athenian democracy and gloss over a fundamental tension in its politics. As I will argue throughout this book, the basic asymmetries in Athenian accountability practices structured Athens' politics in far-reaching ways and are central to understanding the discourse on counsel developed in our fifth- and fourth-century literary sources. In this chapter and the next, I analyze how and why jurors and assemblymen were treated differently from other political actors. I show how Athenian democrats attempted to justify this differential treatment and how critics of democracy exploited it.

I begin with an analysis of Athens' extensive system of political accountability, comparing Athenian institutions and practices with their counterparts in other democratic and in oligarchic regimes. Athenian accountability institutions were popular, discretionary, and asymmetrical: masses of citizens gathered in the assembly and popular courts were given wide latitude in holding political actors to account but could not themselves be held to account for their judgments. Next, I consider institutional and cultural factors that might have served to mitigate popular unaccountability. I argue that practices such as review of assembly decisions, the jurors' oath, and public pressure on juries and assemblymen all plausibly served in various ways to structure and channel popular decision-making. Nonetheless, these factors were different in kind, not just in degree, from the accountability mechanisms all other political actors faced. Finally, I consider how Athenians might have justified to themselves their system of accountability and the role of popular institutions within it. I canvass a number of possible justifications, including feasibility constraints on holding masses of citizens accountable, the Athenian belief in the "wisdom of the masses," and the relationship between unaccountability and a conception of the demos as sovereign. I argue that one promising avenue of justification centered on identifying jurors and assemblymen with the figure of the powerless, amateur *idiōtēs*, or "private citizen." Yet as I show, that identification was always a tenuous one. The tension between the relative powerlessness of individual Athenians and the power of the collective demos was not easily resolved.

I. Athenian Accountability in Comparative Perspective

As A. H. M. Jones aptly notes, while Athenian democrats believed that "all citizens could be trusted to take their part in the government of the city . . . on one point the Athenians were distrustful of human nature, on its ability to resist the temptations of irresponsible power."[17] This distrust of "irresponsible power" manifested itself above all in the complex machinery of democratic accountability that arose in the fifth century alongside the democracy itself.[18] In this section I outline the major institutions of accountability in democratic Athens, comparing them with institutions from other ancient Greek poleis. I stress the central role played by assemblymen and jurors—ordinary members of the demos—in the accountability politics of Athens and other democratic regimes in contrast with their role in oligarchic poleis. I consider the procedures all Athenian magistrates routinely faced at the beginning and end of their tenures: the *dokimasia* and *euthunai*. I also take up two major Athenian institutions used on a discretionary basis to hold magistrates and other politically active citizens to account, including the demos' advisers: the *eisangelia* and *graphē paranomōn*.

In offering this overview, I highlight three salient features common to Athenian institutions of accountability. First, the institutions were *popular*. The final arbiters in accountability procedures were large groups of citizens, serving as either voters in the assembly or jurors. Second, the institutions were *discretionary*. While the laws typically set out specific crimes and acts of malfeasance for which a political actor could be punished, Athenian institutions of accountability characteristically allowed considerable room for judgment on the part of the citizens trying the cases. Third, the institutions were *asymmetrical*. Members of juries and voters in the assembly could not be called to account for their actions, even while holding others to account. Taken together, these features set Athenian accountability institutions apart from their oligarchic counterparts and explain what was distinctively democratic about Athens' accountability politics.

ORDINARY PROCEDURES: *DOKIMASIA* AND *EUTHUNAI* FOR MAGISTRATES

In fifth- and fourth-century Athens, the day-to-day administration of the democratic polis lay in the hands of perhaps seven hundred magistrates (including the five hundred members of the *boulē*), most of them selected by lot.[19] All magistrates underwent accountability procedures at the beginning and end of their terms of office. The *dokimasia tōn archōn*, held before a popular jury, screened potential magistrates selected by election or sortition before they assumed office. At his *dokimasia*, a putative magistrate could be rejected for failure to meet citizenship or age requirements or if he had been previously found guilty of a crime punishable with *atimia* (loss of citizenship rights). In addition, any citizen could come forward at an official's *dokimasia* and require the prospective magistrate to explain and defend his past actions and way of life. For example, in the wake of the oligarchic revolution of 404/3, some citizens were rejected at their *dokimasia* for harboring oligarchic sym-pathies.[20] One Mantitheus, suspected years later of complicity with the Thirty Tyrants, used his *dokimasia* to offer a wide-ranging defense of his character and role in Athens: "In the case of *dokimasiai*, it is just to give an account of one's entire life."[21] Candidates rejected at their *dokimasia* could not serve in office but received no further penalty.

Upon completion of their duties, all magistrates were audited through the *euthunai*. The first phase consisted in a financial audit, with magistrates ac-counting for their disbursement of public funds during their time in office. This phase was overseen by the ten *logistai* and ten *sunēgoroi*—the inspec-tors of Athenian public accounts and their assistants. Accusations of financial misconduct were tried before a popular court. A second phase looked beyond financial matters, with magistrates "made to answer for any other offences they might have committed in the exercise of their duties."[22] Both citizens and metics (resident aliens) could present written accusations to the board of *euthunoi* (public examiners) against the outgoing magistrate, charging him with "any conceivable offense."[23] Again, serious accusations were adjudicated before a popular court.

Dokimasia and *euthunai* procedures applied to all magistrates, whether selected by lot or elected. Accountability procedures and the selection of mag-istrates were thus discrete (if related) processes. The Athenians believed both that magistrates selected by lot still required scrutiny and accountability *and* that elections alone were not sufficient for holding political actors to account. We might speculate that this was so in part because elections lacked the dis-cursive element common to both the *dokimasia* and the *euthunai*. The sanc-tion of declining to reelect, the main tool modern electorates have to hold their leaders to account, may also have been deemed insufficient to the task.[24] The independence of elections from the *euthunai* and other accountability procedures is nicely illustrated by a detail in Thucydides' history: in 430, the Athenians punished Pericles with a fine, but this did not stop them from re-electing him as general a short time later.[25]

Athens was by no means the only polis to institutionalize regular *euthu-nai* or other accountability mechanisms. Eric Robinson has compiled evi-dence for *euthunai* in fifth- and fourth-century democracies across the Greek world, including Mantinea, Argos, Arcadia, and Croton.[26] Aristotle takes as a central institutional feature of democratic politics that questions concerning audits (*euthunōn*) be judged by all citizens or by a subset selected from all.[27] Even in democratic cities where regular *euthunai* are not directly attested, Robinson has argued that "an abiding concern for keeping officials in line can be detected in other ways," ranging from imprecation decrees to high-profile trials of generals and other leading politicians.[28] Regularized institutions of accountability are also attested in nondemocratic regimes. The early predemocratic (pre-Solonian) Areopagus council played a role in supervising officials and holding them to account.[29] In Sparta, the ephors, annually elected officials who were themselves unaccountable, were instrumental in holding other Spartan officials to account.[30] Important political trials in Sparta were held before a court consisting of ephors, the council of elders, and the kings.[31]

Rhodes and other scholars who argue for the ubiquity of accountability institutions in Greek poleis are thus correct: the accountability of magistrates was not a uniquely democratic commitment. What set democracy apart was the commitment to accountability *to the* demos. As Aristotle argues in the *Politics*, control of the *euthunai* was one of the most important powers in the city.[32] How such power is distributed and exercised can therefore tell us much about the identity and nature of a regime. In keeping with this view, Aristotle in both the *Politics* and the *Constitution of Athens* emphasizes the post-Solonic assumption of control over *euthunai* by the demos as a pivotal institutional shift toward democratization.

By contrast, oligarchic regimes did not place the exercise of accountability functions in the hands of ordinary citizens: to do so would undermine oligarchic control of the regime. A rare case of ordinary members of the demos participating in accountability politics under a narrow oligarchic regime in fifth-century Megara serves as an exception that proves the rule. Thucydides recounts that the Megaran oligarchs conducted an "inspection of arms" (*exetasin hoplōn*) in which they "forced the people to hold an open vote" against the oligarchs' enemies; after this show trial, the enemies of the oligarchic faction so convicted were executed. Here the demos participated in a political trial, but a highly manipulated one and only under compulsion.[33]

Democratic accountability thus differed from oligarchic accountability precisely insofar as, in a democratic city, the magistrates were accountable *to the people* and the people could exercise considerable discretion in how to judge those who came before them. In Athens, through the *dokimasia* and the *euthunai*, all magistrates, as a matter of routine, faced the people at the beginning and end of their tenures. These institutions of accountability tested whether magistrates met formal requirements to serve office and whether they had committed specific crimes. Yet they also allowed large panels of citizens to exercise considerable latitude of judgment in deciding whether selected magistrates were "fit" for office and whether they had abused their powers and the public trust during their tenure. So far as the evidence allows us to judge, magistrates were rarely rejected at their *dokimasia*, and trials resulting from accusations brought out during the *euthunai* were also relatively rare.[34] Nonetheless, the ubiquity and regularity of *dokimasia* and *euthunai* stand as both testament of and contribution to the popular control of magistrates in democratic Athens.

In addition to the *dokimasia* and *euthunai*, magistrates were also subject to popular recall and punishment during their tenures through impeachment procedures such as the *eisangelia*. At the *ekklēsia kuria* each prytany,[35] *eisangelia* charges could be leveled against any citizen, potentially leading to trials held before either popular courts or the assembly itself. Our best source of evidence for the *eisangelia* law is Hyperides' speech *On Behalf of Euxenippus*: "So what crimes do you think the impeachment procedure [*tas eisangelias*] should cover? You have already written down each one in the law so that no one could be in doubt. It says, 'If someone seeks to overthrow the Athenian people' . . . 'or,' it continues, 'if he meets anywhere for the purpose of subverting the democracy, or forms a political club, or if someone betrays a city, or ships, or a land or naval force, or if a politician (*rhētōr*) does not give the best advice to the Athenian people because he has been bribed.'"[36] Hyperides' quotation of the law is thought to be incomplete, but we can see that *eisangelia* was intended to prosecute serious breaches of public trust, such as treason, sedition, and corruption. Given their prominence and power, it is no surprise that Athenian *stratēgoi* (generals) in particular were frequent subjects of *eisangelia* procedures. Indeed, Mogens Herman Hansen has calculated that from 432 to 355 BCE, perhaps 20 percent of all generals (on average two members from each yearly board of ten) faced *eisangelia* charges.[37] As with the *dokimasia* and the *euthunai*, the law as written seems to offer considerable discretion for citizens in trying an *eisangelia* case.

Importantly, unlike the *dokimasia* and the *euthunai*, *eisangelia* procedures were not restricted solely to magistrates. After all, one did not have to hold office to be guilty of "conspiring to overthrow the Athenian people," and there are a number of cases on record of nonmagistrates subjected to *eisangelia*, most notably in the wake of the mutilation of the Herms in 415 BCE.

The last clause in Hyperides' recounting of the *eisangelia* law also points to another category of nonmagistrates potentially liable to *eisangelia*: orators in the assembly. Orators suspected of taking bribes to influence the demos could find themselves charged under the *eisangelia* law. Holding speakers in the assembly to account for their advice was a central feature of Athenian politics in both the fifth and fourth centuries, and *eisangelia* was by no means the only avenue for doing so.[38] Fourth-century orators in particular often held no official public office and hence were not subject to either the *dokimasia* or *euthunai*, but other institutions filled this potential accountability gap. Some scholars have argued that the *thorubos*, the clamorous response of the demos that could drive a speaker from the rostrum, served as a kind of informal accountability mechanism for orators.[39] More significantly, orators were liable to the *graphē paranomōn*, probably from the beginning of the Peloponnesian War on.[40] The name of the latter charge suggests it was used against speakers initiating unlawful or unconstitutional proposals. A *graphē paranomōn* could be used in cases of procedural abuse, to prosecute, for example, someone illegally initiating a proposal in the assembly without a *probouleuma* (recommendation from the council). Yet its use also extended to cases where the proposal had been found to be unwise, harmful, or merely undesirable—thus again leaving a considerable amount of discretionary judgment to those deciding the case.[41] Tried before a popular court, a successful *graphē paranomōn* resulted in both the annulment of the decree and a fine for its proposer, which could range from the merely nominal to the crushingly heavy.

Thus men who spoke before the assembled demos in the capacity of adviser were potentially accountable for the advice they gave. They could be called on to defend their advice and could be punished if they were unable to do so to the satisfaction of a popular jury. Those orators who made proposals could be held accountable whether the proposal was accepted or not by means of the *graphē paranomōn*. Even those who merely spoke on an issue without moving a formal proposal themselves could still be held accountable for their advice under the *eisangelia* law.

Accountability for advice was a fundamental feature of Athenian democratic politics and is central to the discourse comparing the demos to a tyrant that I explore further in later chapters. Here, however, a brief comparison with *oligarchic* accountability practices will be instructive. Oligarchies, like democracies, made use of corporate bodies that arrived at decisions after listening to advice. Such bodies might even include assemblies open to all citizens. In such cases, the assembly's powers would be circumscribed in various ways (as we've already seen in the case of the assembly, recounted by Thucydides, that was convened and manipulated by oligarchs in fifth-century Megara). The practices of the Spartan assembly are illustrative in this regard. Some decisions, such as whether to go to war, were taken by an assembly open to all Spartan citizens. Yet in general, the decisions of the Spartan *damos* were not final: they could be overturned by the gerousia and kings. In addition, access to speech was strictly controlled. The Athenian principle of *isēgoria*, which in principle allowed any citizen who wished to speak in the assembly to do so, had no counterpart in Sparta. Rather, it seems, only the gerousia, ephors, and kings had the power to make proposals and speak before the assembled *damos*. Control of the assembly of citizens through the regulation of speech, the manipulation of the agenda, and the exercise of a veto all appear in Aristotle's *Politics* as regular tactics deployed by oligarchic regimes.[42]

Oligarchic regimes also made decisions in narrower councils, open only to those with the requisite property qualification or to councilors elected from the enfranchised oligarchs. Yet we should not be led astray by the Hobbesian idealized depiction of oligarchic deliberation from the frontispiece (see fig. 1) to overstate the differences between oligarchy and democracy on this score either.[43] As Margaret Cook has argued, voting in the Boeotian oligarchic councils was not always predetermined by factional allegiances and politics. Rather, persuasion and decision-making often involved "a large group of unaffiliated voters listening to appeals to pride, fear, nationalism, greed, inertia, and so on," a description that could aptly apply to decision-making in the Athenian assembly.[44] The author of the *Rhetoric to Alexander* takes as a given that counsel has a home in both democratic assemblies and oligarchic *bouleutēria* and provides his readers with guiding principles for speaking persuasively about legislation in oligarchic regimes.[45] Likewise, Aristotle in the *Rhetoric* implicitly assumes that rhetorical appeals will be part of ordinary oligarchic politics. He advises students of rhetoric that "we should be acquainted with the kinds of character distinctive of each form of constitution; for the character distinctive of each is necessarily most persuasive to each."[46] Nonetheless, evidence that oligarchies routinely held their advisers accountable in the way that democracies did is hard to come by. Two cases from fourth-century Theban politics will help illustrate the point.

DANGEROUS COUNSEL IN FOURTH-CENTURY BOEOTIA

The fourth-century *Hellenica Oxyrhynchia* is one of our best sources for the Boeotian oligarchic constitution and Boeotian and Theban politics. In that text, we learn of a split among the Theban oligarchs in the 390s between pro- and anti-Spartan factions in the city. The anti-Spartan faction—led by Ismenias, Antitheus, and Androcleidas—favored open war against Sparta, calculating that the Athenians, Corinthians, and Argives would enter the war on their side. Yet Ismenias and his followers also realized that maneuvering Thebes and Boeotia into war would not be easy: they recognized that "neither the Thebans nor the Boeotians would ever be persuaded to make war on the Spartans, who were supreme in Greece."[47] They therefore devised a stratagem: they persuaded the Phocians to invade the western Locrians, and when the Locrians sent ambassadors to the Boeotian *koinon* for aid, Ismenias and Androcleidas persuaded the Boeotians to intervene on their side. When Sparta tried to broker peace and warned against retaliatory attacks on the Phocians, Ismenias and his followers seized the moment to create further conflict between the Boeotians and Spartans: "With the people who had set up the whole deceitful business urging them on [*paroxunontōn autous*], the Boeotians sent away the envoys of the Spartans with nothing achieved, then themselves took up arms and marched against the Phocians."[48] The Oxyrhynchus historian deploys the same word for persuasive speakers galvanizing action—*paroxunontōn*—that he earlier uses to describe successful counsel in the Athenian assembly.[49] This is a case of a few leading citizens persuading—even manipulating—the main decision-making bodies of the Boeotians into a confrontation with Sparta.

This proves a risky course of action: when the pro-Spartan faction within the city ultimately gains the upper hand in 382 BCE, Ismenias and Androcleidas find themselves the objects of Spartan anger and reprisal. Androcleidas is assassinated in Athens by Spartan agents, and Xenophon relates that Ismenias is tried and executed by a court of Sparta and her allies. Notably, one of the charges was that "he and Androcleidas were the most responsible [*aitiōtatoi*] for all of the disorder throughout Greece."[50] Here the adviser of a course of action in an oligarchic regime is held responsible, and punished, for his advice. But it is not the Theban oligarchs or the Boeotians who are holding Ismenias to account; it is the Spartans. It is not clear that any oligarchic regime had a regularized constitutional mechanism for holding citizen advisers accountable for their advice.

The treatment of Ismenias nicely contrasts with a later trial in Theban history, this time under a democratic regime.[51] In 369 BCE, Epameinondas and Pelopidas continued a campaign against the Spartans past the final month of their term as Boeotarchs. Upon returning to Thebes, they were tried and, according to Plutarch, acquitted. In recounting the trial, Plutarch also tells the story of Menecleidas, a political opponent of the two generals who attempted to turn the Thebans against them. Menecleidas proposes a motion to have the politician Charon honored as part of an attempt to "dim the reputation of Pelopidas and Epameinondas."[52] Pelopidas responds with a singularly democratic move: he indicts Menecleidas using a *graphē paranomōn*, claiming that Theban tradition required the fatherland to be honored rather than a single individual.[53] The Theban demos punishes Menecleidas with a crushing fine he is unable to pay.

It is worth reflecting on the different fates of Ismenias and Menecleidas, separated by only thirteen years but active in Theban politics under very different political regimes. Persuading bodies of citizens is a crucial political tactic in both regime types. But it does not appear there was any regular oligarchic institution to hold Ismenias accountable for the advice that led directly to the clash with Sparta; it is only once Sparta is in control of Thebes that he is held accountable. By contrast, under a democratic regime, barely more than a decade later, Menecleidas' attempts to manipulate the Thebans are checked by the deployment of an accountability mechanism familiar to us from the Athenian democratic context: the *graphē paranomōn*. Robinson cautions against attributing such practices to "specific borrowing from Athens";[54] nonetheless, it is striking to see similar mechanisms and political dynamics playing out in another democratic setting.

The presence of the *graphē paranomōn* in democratic Thebes and its absence in the former oligarchic regime calls for some explanation. Why is such an institution compatible with democratic but not oligarchic politics? We can rule out one explanation quickly: it is not because oligarchs were not concerned with the possibility of manipulation or bad advice that could subvert their control of the polis. To the contrary, it is clear that oligarchies recognized these threats and took their own steps to deal with them (as I argue below). But there are good reasons to think that oligarchies could not confront these problems using the institutional tools of democracy. First and foremost is the problem of oligarchic unity. As Matthew Simonton has recently argued, oligarchies in the fifth and fourth centuries faced a serious problem: they were unpopular regimes that could only survive if oligarchs maintained a united front and quelled dissension in the ranks, relying on "specialized social and political institutions that kept the elite united."[55] To that end, it was "absolutely crucial that power be equalized as much as possible and that this arrangement be scrupulously maintained."[56] Drastic swings in power and influence among oligarchs might easily prompt the losers in the game of status and power to undermine the regime. Indeed, the context of Ismenias' attempt at manipulating the Boeotians into war with Sparta was just such a destabilizing competition between oligarchic elites: both Xenophon and the Oxyrhynchus historian describe the competition between Ismenias' faction and the pro-Spartan side as a period of *stasis*.

The *graphē paranomōn* as a tool of accountability and legal review was fundamentally adversarial and divisive and could be taken up by politicians to further their own disputes. Democracies could tolerate and even make good use of—intraelite competition and conflict, for which the *graphē paranomōn* proved a popular outlet. By contrast, oligarchic fears of disorder and concern with the potential threats posed by disunity rendered an institution like the *graphē paranomōn* unsuitable for such a regime.

Plutarch takes the failure of Menecleidas' attempt to strike at Pelopidas and Epameinondas, and his subsequent destruction at the hands of the demos, as an instance of a general pattern in democratic politics, which he casts in a moral light:

> For attacking, through motives of envy, a good man who, on account of his virtue, is leader of the state, as Pericles was attacked by Simmias, Themistocles by Alcmeon, Pompey by Clodius, and Epameinondas by Menecleides the orator, is neither conducive to a good reputation nor advantageous in any other way; for when the people have committed a wrong against a good man and then (which happens quickly) repent of their anger, they think the easiest way to excuse themselves for this offence is the most just, namely, to destroy the man who was the author of it and persuaded them to commit it.[57]

Here Plutarch blames both Menecleidas and the demos for implicating themselves in what he takes to be a basic pattern of democratic politics. Robinson makes a related point (while avoiding Plutarch's moralizing tone) when he writes that "one also can sometimes detect a hesitation in oligarchies to mete out the kinds of severe penalties that our accounts show angry democratic assemblies eagerly embraced when its leaders were suspected of misbehavior."[58] Yet there is no reason to assume that oligarchs were ethically above such political maneuvers—rather, the politics of regime stability dictated that they did not pursue them.

Oligarchic regimes did have institutional mechanisms for limiting the destructive potential of bad advice. But rather than holding advisers directly accountable for the advice they gave, oligarchic regimes sought to limit the damage an adviser could do through restrictions on rights of speech and address, limitations on the ability to make proposals, and the exercise of veto power. The exercise of such checking powers broadly fell under the rubric of *nomophulakia*—guardianship of the laws. *Nomophulakia* is attested at Athens during the postdemocratic regime of Demetrius of Phaleron, in which the *nomophulakes* sat in the council and the assembly and prevented them from doing anything "inexpedient to the city." As Mirko Canevaro has argued, the invocation of inexpediency recalls democratic procedures such as the *graphē paranomōn*. Of course, "rather than a democratic control performed on a voluntary basis in the popular lawcourts, they [the *nomophulakes*] seem to perform a pre-emptive control on whether something can be discussed or not in the Assembly."[59]

Democratic accountability, then, unlike accountability in oligarchic regimes, consisted in accountability *to the people*. Magistrates were accountable to citizens in the assembly and the popular courts through such procedures as the *euthunai* and the *eisangelia*. Those who sought to advise the demos were accountable for their advice. Even the individuals who brought accountability cases to trial were themselves accountable. The Athenian legal system did not, as a rule, make use of public prosecutors. In most cases, it relied instead on individual citizens to bring charges before the court, including in cases of *eisangelia* and the *graphē paranomōn*.[60] Such citizen-prosecutors, too, faced accountability mechanisms—primarily aimed, it seems, at limiting frivolous and malicious lawsuits.[61] In many cases, charges, once laid, could not be withdrawn without facing severe penalties. This would have deterred those unsure of whether they wanted to go through with a prosecution and helped address Athenian worries about the prospect of *sukophantai*—that is, volunteer prosecutors who might bring charges against others as a mode of blackmail or otherwise to enrich themselves.[62] If prosecutors failed to secure one fifth of the jury's vote at trial, they would be punished with a large fine and barred from prosecuting further cases (a penalty known as "partial *atimia*"). To bring a high-profile charge before the people was not only to subject the accused to a trial; it was to submit oneself to the judgment of the people.

II. Jurors and Assemblymen as Exceptions

The truth of Aeschines' claim that no one in Athens who applied themselves to public affairs was unaccountable might seem borne out by the previous discussion. Nonetheless, there were two important exceptions: ordinary citizens voting in the *ekklēsia* and those serving as jurors. Each year, six thousand citizens were selected by lot to serve as jurors (*dikastai*). This marked jury duty off from participation in the assembly, which was essentially an ad hoc function—any adult male citizen in good standing could attend an assembly meeting and vote with his fellow citizens on the issues of the day. There were also stricter age restrictions on jury service as compared to assembly attendance: whereas citizens could attend the assembly from the age of twenty, serving as a *dikastēs* was restricted to citizens more than thirty years of age.[63] Despite these differences, jurors and assemblymen shared a privileged position in the Athenian system of accountability. They faced neither *dokimasia* nor *euthunai*. Jurors' votes were protected from scrutiny by the secret ballot. Voting in the assembly was by an open show of hands, but voters were not accountable for their decisions. Insofar as anyone could be held accountable for a decree of the assembly, it was the orator who made the proposal, not the assembled citizens who voted for it, who was held to account, as through the *graphē paranomōn*. Jurors and assemblymen played central roles in Athenian politics—not least, as we saw, in holding other political actors to account. They themselves, however, were unaccountable.

Jeremy Waldron's distinction between "agent" and "forensic" accountability can help clarify the role of ordinary citizens in Athens' accountability practices. Two features in particular are relevant. First, "agent accountability involves accountability *to* someone: it indicates the privileged position of someone to whom another person is accountable."[64] In democratic Athens, ordinary citizens acting within the assembly and the courts occupied this privileged position. Second, while in cases of forensic accountability "the basis of assessment is given, . . . in agent accountability, the principal herself decides the basis on which she will assess the actions of her agent."[65] This distinction captures the wide discretion ordinary citizens wielded in accountability procedures, from *dokimasia* to the *graphē paranomōn*.

Yet as I noted above, there is considerable resistance to accepting this portrait of Athenian accountability in the scholarly literature. Scholars have analyzed a number of mechanisms, institutions, and practices in an attempt to undermine one or both of the features of the agent-accountability model as it applies to Athens: the claims that ordinary citizens occupied a privileged position in an asymmetrical accountability relationship and that they wielded wide discretionary power. In the following sections, I respond to some of these arguments, focusing on oaths and divine accountability, responses to the possibility of bribery, informal scrutiny of jurors and assemblymen, and the review of assembly decisions. Taken together, these practices provide evidence for Athens' "culture of accountability" and lend support to the thought that Athenians were concerned with how jurors and assemblymen exercised their (considerable) power individually and collectively. Nonetheless, both jurors and assemblymen faced a markedly lower level of scrutiny, control, and liability to sanction than others participating in politics.

THE HELIASTIC OATH AND JUROR DISCRETION

In an effort to show that Athenian jurors, at least, were not unaccountable political agents, some scholars have placed great weight on the Heliastic Oath, sworn by all jurors upon their selection for jury duty each year. On this view, the oath performed two crucial functions. First, it instantiated the Athenian commitment to the rule of law. While jurors may not have been accountable to other political agents, they were nonetheless subordinate—and perhaps in some sense accountable—to the real sovereign power at Athens, the laws themselves.[66] Second, the oath, along with other rituals such as curses, pro-

vided another agent to whom Athenian jurors were ultimately accountable—
the gods. To assess these claims we can begin by turning to the oath itself.

While we have no reliable single source that gives the oath in its entirety,
the following reconstruction is thought to capture its core clauses: "[i] I will
cast my vote in accordance with the laws and decrees passed by the Assembly
and by the Council, but, [ii] if there is no law, in consonance with my sense
of what is most just, without favour or enmity. [iii] I will vote only on the
matters raised in the charge, and [iv] I will listen impartially to accusers and
defenders alike."[67] The clauses of the oath, taken together, give us some sense
of how the Athenians thought the rule of law served to delimit the capacities
and responsibilities of jurors. Clauses (i) and (iii) seem to limit juror discretion by offering a standard for their decision and limiting the range of
relevant considerations. Jurors are to vote in accordance with the law and
consider only matters relevant to the charges. Clauses (ii) and (iv) warn jurors against partiality. They are not to be swayed by their personal feelings for
either the prosecutor or the defense but are to give each side a fair hearing.
Even where the law is silent, and hence where some degree of juror discretion
would be inevitable, jurors are admonished to vote in accordance with their
sense of justice rather than out of "favour or enmity."

That the Athenians took jurors to be bound by the Heliastic Oath could
undermine the picture of Athenian agent accountability and the claim that
jurors were unaccountable. First, if we read the clauses of the oath as highly
restrictive, requiring jurors to apply the law narrowly, juror discretion might
appear to collapse: Athenian accountability in the courts would look more
like an exercise of forensic accountability, where the standards for decision
are externally given. On this reading, jurors would be highly constrained by
and accountable to the rule of law. Second, the threat of divine punishment
suggests a sense in which jurors, after all, were accountable to some agent. If
they failed to hold themselves accountable to the standards given by the oath,
divine sanction would fill the accountability gap.

The existence of the oath suggests that the Athenians wanted jurors to take
their role seriously. Yet does this imply that jurors felt themselves highly constrained by, and accountable to, the rule of law, ultimately enforced by fear of
divine punishment? There are reasons to doubt this highly constrained interpretation of jurors' competence. The oath may not have significantly limited
jurors' discretionary power, and the extent to which we should take the oath
and its attendant curse as a formidable check on juror behavior is unclear.

To assess the scope of juror discretion, we must read the clauses of the
oath against the backdrop of Athenian legal practices and norms. We need to
know how much room for interpretation and discretion the laws themselves

left the jurors. Was clause (i) of the Heliastic Oath highly restrictive or relatively permissive? With respect to clause (iii), we might ask what standards
of relevancy obtained in Athenian popular courts. How narrowly was the requirement to vote only on matters raised in the charge construed? There is no
scholarly consensus on these issues.[68] Without attempting to resolve intrac-
table debates, I want to offer some reasons to think that even a juror following
his oath in good faith would necessarily exercise considerable discretion in
rendering judgment.

The first point to emphasize is that Athenian laws characteristically left
crimes underdefined. A favorite example is the Athenian law against hubris:
"If someone commits hubris against someone, either a child or woman or
man, whether free or slave, or if someone does something against the law
[*paranomon ti*] to one of these people, any Athenian who wishes may bring a
public indictment before the *thesmothetai*."[69] The crime of hubris is here left
conspicuously vague, to say nothing of the further indictable offense of doing
"something against the law" to any man, woman or child in the city, and the
question of what exactly *hubris* consisted in is still debated.[70] It is likely that
unwritten communal norms and expectations would place limits on what
could or could not realistically be considered an instance of a given crime.[71]
Nonetheless, the evidence from existing forensic speeches suggests considerable latitude, including in accountability trials.

Hyperides' speech *On Behalf of Euxenippus* offers a striking example of
how ambiguities in the definitions of crimes left room for considerable juror discretion in *eisangelia* trials. Euxenippus has been charged under the
eisangelia procedures for a report he gave to the assembly. It seems there was
some controversy over whether land allotted to two tribes, Hippothoöntis
and Acamantis, actually belonged to the temple of the god Amphiaraus. In
the wake of this uncertainty, Euxenippus and three others were ordered by
the demos to sleep in the temple in an effort to ascertain, through dreams,
whether Amphiaraus had a claim to the land.[72] Euxenippus reported back to
the assembly with a dream favorable to the interests of the two tribes. One
Polyeuctus charged him with taking bribes from those who stood to gain
from the ruling and reporting the dream falsely.

The central issue that Hyperides raises in Euxenippus' defense is less
substantive than definitional: Who really counts as a rhetor? The *eisangelia*
statute he cites includes a section authorizing charges against those who, taking bribes, speak against the interests of the people (see the excerpt from
the speech above, page 32). Yet in Hyperides' view, the law ordains that "*eisangelia* be used against rhetors themselves when they speak against the best
interests of the people, but not against all Athenians."[73] Euxenippus may

have spoken to the assembly in reporting on his dream, but this action in itself, Hyperides' argument presumes, does not establish him as a rhetor and hence as legally liable to an *eisangelia* prosecution. The category of rhetors instead delimits only that small subset of citizens who frequently make speeches and proposals in the assembly—the expert political speakers. There is some debate over the precise legal meaning of the term *rhētōr* in fourth-century Athenian law and over whether Polyeuctes' prosecution of Euxenippus constituted a flagrant misuse of the statute.[74] I find the actual details of the law less important than what Hyperides' defense suggests about the power of jurors to interpret ambiguous laws and crimes. The intense debate over Euxenippus' status—was he a rhetor or merely someone who once made a report to the assembly?—reflects the workings of a judicial system in which jurors wielded considerable discretionary power in interpreting laws.

Juror discretion was also bolstered by the wide standards of relevancy that were adhered to in Athenian trials. Again, while there is scholarly dispute over the precise contours of the Athenian approach to relevancy in the popular courts, there is considerable agreement that the standards were much looser than they are today.[75] Nor do we see any obvious tightening of standards with respect to the accountability procedures that are our focus. Harvey Yunis, in an analysis of the extant forensic speeches from *graphē paranomōn* trials, has argued that prosecutors typically followed a two-pronged strategy in their quest for a guilty verdict. Prosecutors would offer a legal plea showing the ways in which the defendant's decree conflicted with existing statute. They would also offer a political plea showing the ways in which the decree was inexpedient and arguing that overturning it would benefit the Athenian people. Where the decree under indictment granted honors or citizenship, the prosecutor would also usually claim that the honored person was unworthy.[76] Yunis argues that both the legal and political pleas were necessary to secure a conviction and hence that the "*graphē paranomōn* was legal and political review at once."[77] Adriaan Lanni, in her study of the *dikastēria*, has argued convincingly that the proliferation of types of pleas worked to increase juror discretion: "the relative importance of legal and contextual evidence in any individual case was open to dispute," and hence it was up to jurors to decide how to weight the competing claims.[78]

The above analysis underscores the ways in which the Athenian understanding of the rule of law nonetheless left considerable room for juror discretion. Jurors were ultimately responsible for interpreting broad laws and vaguely defined crimes, assessing competing legal and political claims, and balancing and weighing those claims according to their own lights. The Heliastic Oath cannot therefore be taken as evidence that jurors were ultimately exercising forensic rather than agent accountability in judging important political trials.

So much for the question of whether the oath severely limited juror discretion. What of the question of divine accountability? Did the oath represent a kind of off-loading of accountability, at least for jurors, to the gods? It would be rash to dismiss the effect of the oath altogether. According to M. H. Hansen, "The oath was sworn in the names of Zeus, Apollo and Demeter, and ended with the juror uttering a curse against himself if he should break his oath."[79] The general importance of oaths in Athenian society is captured in the orator Lycurgus' claim that "what preserves our democracy is the oath."[80] Hansen rightly cautions against viewing the oath as "an empty formality" even though no juror could be called to account for violating it. Yet I do not agree, as Hansen concludes, that ultimately "our evaluation of the oath must depend on our evaluation of religion in the Greek city-state."[81] We do not need a complete understanding of Greek religion to see that the Heliastic Oath could not have been taken by the Athenians as a functional equivalent to the complex system of accountability that magistrates and other politically active citizens faced.

Divine and political accountability were not functionally equivalent substitutes for each other. We can see this from the multiple instances where the Athenians combined the use of oaths and curses with the regular machinery of political accountability. For example, meetings of both the assembly and the council—and possibly meetings of the popular courts as well—began with a curse against those who would mislead the people.[82] Orators before the assembly, then, were also divinely accountable for the advice they gave. Yet this measure ensuring divine accountability did not lead the Athenians to excuse these figures from the system of political accountability. This is strong evidence that Athenians did not consider divine accountability and political accountability to be functionally equivalent.

THE THREAT OF BRIBERY

The Heliastic Oath is not the only evidence of Athenian concern for the ways in which jurors might choose to exercise their considerable power. The system of randomized juror panels was instituted, at the latest, in the 370s, and Aristotle offers a lengthy description of the elaborate procedure in the *Constitution of Athens*. On a typical court day, more jurors would present themselves for service than were needed for the day's judicial business. The day's jurors were selected randomly from the pool of those who showed up and were then randomly impaneled among the day's courts so that the juror would "go to the court which he [had] drawn by lot, not the one he wishe[d] to sit in, and it [would] not be possible for anyone to arrange to have the jury he wishe[d]." At each trial, five jurors were given the important roles of keeping time and counting votes, and these jobs, too, were randomly assigned. Again, Aristotle stresses that the randomization of these roles was to prevent any possible tampering.[83] As some scholars have argued, it is likely that these procedures were introduced in the wake of actual bribery scandals.[84]

There is no doubt, then, that Athenians were concerned with the possibility that juries could be bribed, and they eventually took concrete steps, beyond the administration of the oath, to combat the possibility. Persons convicted of bribing members of juries and assemblymen, as well as persons found guilty of accepting such bribes, faced the death penalty.[85] Yet even if, according to the letter of the law, jurors could be punished for accepting bribes, I have found no evidence that any juror was ever actually so tried. There are a number of cases of bribery attested to in the literary record, but they all refer to prosecutions of citizens who offered bribes rather than of voters who received them.[86] Even at the limit case of selling one's vote, then, it seems that jurors were rarely, if ever, held accountable. The system of juror randomization made it difficult for jurors to sell their votes, and the bribery laws made it (at least theoretically) risky to do so, yet none of this amounts to a system of accountability comparable to the strictures placed on other forms of political activity.

AN INFORMAL *EUTHUNA*?

There is one final factor to consider. Adriaan Lanni has argued that the *corona*, the crowd of spectators who were drawn to the courts each day and observed the judicial proceedings, "helped to rectify one of the perceived institutional weaknesses of the Athenian democracy, the immunity of its mass juries from formal accountability."[87] Lanni explores in some detail the composition of this observing crowd (foreigners, jurors who failed to secure a spot on a panel for one of the day's trials, those too young to serve on juries, other interested citizens, and probably some elite politicians) and offers persuasive arguments that it both served an educative function for its members and exerted an influence on the judicial proceedings themselves. She points out the way in which litigants spoke directly to the members of the *corona* and argues that their presence could have "inhibited the litigants by giving them reason to avoid wild exaggerations and lies." She also claims that "the spectators' reactions most likely influenced the jury as well" and could thus be considered a kind of "informal *euthyna*," with the spectators exerting a "sort of informal social control, a compensation for the legal unaccountability of the jurors."[88] Lanni's argument has been picked up by scholars such as Elizabeth Markovits, who marshals it as further evidence for a generalized culture of accountability in Athens.[89]

Lanni's arguments are thought-provoking, but the evidence she adduces in support of her claims is subject to multiple interpretations. Consider two examples she offers. Lanni correctly notes that "speakers sometimes ask the jury how they will defend their verdict when questioned by the *corona* as they leave the courtroom" and cites a passage from Demosthenes' speech *Against Aristogeiton* as a prominent example: "You will soon leave the court, and the spectators, both foreigners and citizens, will be watching, and looking at each man as he passes to detect by their look which ones have voted to acquit. What will you say, gentlemen of the jury, if you walk out having betrayed the laws? With what expression will you face them?"[90] She also cites a passage from Aeschines, noting that even absent "spectators" might "exert an influence on the jury"; Aeschines admonishes the jurors to "vote in this way, not only as judges but as men being watched, anticipating the judgement of citizens, who though not now being present, will ask you what verdict you have given."[91] Lanni takes such passages as evidence for the influence the *corona* could and likely did have on the jurors; while they might not have been formally accountable, the eyes of the spectators and their insistent questioning after the trial helped fill the gap.

In contrast with Lanni, I read these passages less as a description of a compensatory informal institution replacing the *euthunai* than as an *attempt* to get jurors to act *as if* they were accountable, even though they manifestly were not.[92] Two details support my interpretation. First, it is striking that the spectators in Aeschines' example are hypothetical: jurors are asked to conjure up an audience and think about what its members would ask them. Second, the method Demosthenes offers for picking out those who voted to acquit and those who voted to convict is telling: the spectators, he claims, will be able to detect which jurors voted to acquit by peering into their (presumably abashed) faces. This method of sussing out votes through shame detection is necessitated, of course, by the jurors' use of the secret ballot, which stands as ultimate guarantor of their unaccountability even in the face of prying spectators. I thus read appeals to the judgment of spectators as acknowledging jurors' unaccountability and offering a hortatory response in the face of it. Lysias' plea to the jurors in his prosecution of Eratosthenes can be read in a similar light. In that speech, Lysias attempts to convince the jurors that voting to acquit Eratosthenes, a member of the Thirty, is an implicit vote in favor of tyrannical oligarchy. As he warns them, "I counsel you not to condemn yourselves by acquitting them. Nor should you suppose that your voting is in secret, for you will make your judgment manifest to the city."[93]

Of course, for each individual juror, the vote *was* secret. Only the collective judgment is made clear. How to respond to this disconnect was a tricky matter for litigants. In some speeches, Demosthenes, like Lysias, draws a strong link between individual jurors and the collective judgment of the court. In his speech against Leptines, Demosthenes tells the jurors, "Each of you will individually share in the reputation of judgments made collectively."[94] Yet it is not clear what would follow from this claim if true. Taken seriously, it might actually imply the opposite of what Demosthenes is arguing for: that is, it might imply that each juror should simply vote however he wishes, since other citizens will assume he voted with the majority regardless. It is also clearly in tension with Demosthenes' claim in *Against Aristogeiton* that spectators will have sophisticated vote-detection abilities and will be able to differentiate between those who voted for and against acquittal. That Demosthenes was happy to try both strategies—sometimes arguing that individual responsibility is preserved, sometimes that all jurors will be lumped together—is strong evidence that the spectators here and elsewhere are a rhetorical device, a carrot or stick for Demosthenes to wield, rather than an independent check on juror behavior. The Heliastic Oath could be exploited rhetorically in a similar fashion by skilled orators. As Aeschines reminded the jurors in his prosecution of Ctesiphon, the votes they cast are secret, and so it is useless to try to vote to please another. Rather than appealing to a conjured-up audience or the spectators watching the trial proceedings, Aeschines instead offers the oath personified: "the oath which the juror has sworn in judging will follow him and harm him" if he votes to acquit Ctesiphon.[95]

A litigator concerned that the jury might not vote in his favor might find it advantageous to frame the jurors' decision in terms of accountability to communal norms, a sense of justice, social pressure, or whatever else. Such appeals are premised on the unaccountability of the jurors and their discretionary power: they are pleas, not instructions that might serve to limit juror discretion and the unaccountable exercise of their own best judgment. Spectators, real or imagined, could be invoked by prosecutors and defendants, but the secret ballot and lack of formal accountability remained to mitigate the effectiveness of such invocations.

REVIEW OF ASSEMBLY DECISIONS

Thus far, I have primarily focused on jurors rather than assemblymen. Let me turn briefly to the latter group. In some respects we might think of assemblymen as operating under less scrutiny than jurors. It is true that voting was by show of hands and thus one's vote was public (unlike the juror's vote). But assemblymen did not swear an oath and might therefore be seen as freer to vote as they pleased. Moreover, as noted above, participating in an assembly was an ad hoc activity open to all male citizens in good standing over the age of twenty. If we think of the Heliastic Oath and the age restriction on jury duty as manifestations of Athenian concern for how jurors might exercise their power, we might be tempted to conclude that assemblymen were even less constrained than their judicial counterparts.

These considerations in turn must be balanced by the limitations on the assembly's powers in the restored fourth-century democracy. Most importantly, the assembly was (for the most part) limited to passing "decrees" rather than "laws," and those decrees were subject to appeal through the *graphē paranomōn*.[96] Even the assembly's power to elect the major magistrates was subject to review by the courts through *dokimasia* (although, as discussed above, magistrates were rarely rejected at this phase).

It might therefore be tempting to view the assembly as subordinate to the courts in the fourth-century democracy. This claim is often coupled with a thesis about the moderation of fourth-century democracy in comparison with the more radical fifth-century regime. Yet even if we accede to the view that the assembly was subordinate to the courts, it does not follow that the limitations on the assembly's competence in the fourth century should be taken as institutions that held assemblymen *accountable*. There was still no possibility for calling them to account for their votes. While decisions of the assembly were subject to review and could be overturned, those who voted for a given decree were never called on to explain their votes, nor were they ever punished for having so voted.

III. Justifying Unaccountability

I have been arguing that the institutions and practices many scholars adduce as evidence of a pervasive culture of mutual accountability at Athens— including the review of assembly decisions, the deployment of informal social sanctions, and the threat of divine punishment—should not distract us from the fundamental fact of accountability politics in Athens. Jurors and assemblymen played a privileged role, serving as unaccountable political agents able to hold other political actors to account. In this section, I consider a number of ways to understand the significance of that privileged status. They all take their bearings from the same starting point: the assembly and the courts were the two central popular institutions of the Athenian democracy. The unaccountability of assemblymen and jurors is best understood in light of the identification of these institutions with the demos and popular rule. At Athens, only the demos was unaccountable.

I begin by examining feasibility constraints on implementing accountability procedures in the face of mass political participation. This poses a sharp question: Does the unaccountability necessitated by mass participation count as a consideration against it? I then look to views stressing that the unaccountability of the demos could be understood and justified as a sign and guarantor of its power in the city. I conclude by considering the opposite possibility: Athenians may have considered members of the demos justifiably unaccountable not in recognition of their power in the city but rather on account of their powerlessness and weakness.

FEASIBILITY CONSTRAINTS

We might think that unaccountability is simply the price to be paid for opening an institution to mass collective participation. It would have been difficult to hold individual assemblymen to account, given the nature of their political role. Participation was ad hoc, and voting was done by a show of hands, so there was no record either of attendance or of individual votes. And the secret ballot would have impeded efforts to hold individual jurors even informally accountable for their votes. If individual accountability was out of reach, it is also unclear how the assembly or a popular court could be held collectively accountable. To sanction hundreds or thousands of citizens for poor voting decisions would have been impractical, not to say absurd. Mass popular decision-making and mass political unaccountability may go hand in hand.

Plato's proposed system of accountability in the *Laws* provides an instructive counterpoint. In that dialogue, the Athenian Stranger constructs a system of mutual accountability for the city of Magnesia, but only at the cost of direct popular control over the workings of the system.[97] Like the Athenians, the founders of Magnesia recognize the importance of accountability politics. When the Athenian Stranger turns the conversation to the subject of *euthunoi*, he notes that "it is not at all easy to discover a ruler of rulers, surpassing in virtue; all the same, it is necessary to try to find divine examiners [*euthuntas*]."[98] The differences between Magnesian theory and Athenian practice, however, are crucial. First, unlike the Athenian *euthunoi*, Plato's officers undertake the audits of the magistrates themselves rather than bringing the charges before the people in the *dikastēria*. In Magnesia, the role of massed groups of ordinary citizens—the demos—is limited to the selection of the *euthunoi*, who then hold office until the age of seventy-five. These differences—

sortition in Athens versus election in Magnesia, one-year terms versus long tenure in office—presumably reflect Plato's emphasis on the need for men "surpassing in virtue" to serve as *euthunoi* and his understanding of what that criterion would require. They also stand as an implicit critique of the Athenian principle of accountability to the demos, even if Athens itself is not mentioned in these sections of the dialogue. While ordinary citizens may be trusted with choosing officials through election, their role in supervising and sanctioning those officials is strictly curtailed.

Yet this does not imply that the officials do not require supervision and control: Plato does not rely solely on the "virtue" of the chosen *euthunoi*. Unlike Athenian *dikastai*, the *euthunoi* of Magnesia are themselves accountable. The Athenian Stranger provides multiple avenues for holding those selected to be *euthunoi* to account. First, magistrates who believe they have been judged unjustly can bring the *euthunoi* before a court of "select judges," consisting of former magistrates. The select judges can overrule the *euthunoi*'s decisions, and, if acquitted, the magistrate can prosecute the *euthunoi* in turn.[99] Second, citizens can bring charges against any of the *euthunoi* who, "trusting in his having been chosen displays his human nature by becoming bad after his selection"—that is, anyone who does not live up to the "divine" demands and honors of the office.[100] These cases are tried before a court consisting of the other *euthunoi* joined by the Guardians of the Law and a panel of select judges. *Euthunoi* so convicted are stripped of their office and its attendant honors.[101]

Having displaced the demos from their privileged position in Athenian accountability politics, there is no need for an unaccountable agent at the center of Plato's Magnesian system. It is true that at one place in the dialogue, the Athenian Stranger asserts that "no judge or magistrate should rule or render judgments without being subject to an audit, except those who, like kings, make final decisions."[102] This statement might seem to license something like the unaccountability of Athenian jurors, citing the need for *someone* to make a final decision. Yet this would be a misreading of the dialogue. The Stranger accepts that some decisions must be final and hence not subject to appeal. But no judge or magistrate has a monopoly on making such decisions, and more important, every official in Magnesia faces scrutiny and can be called to account. The *euthunoi* can be called to account before the Guardians of the Law and the select judges. In turn, these high officials are under scrutiny from the *euthunoi*, and from each other. The end result is a system in which "each of these bodies [serves as] a check upon the activity of the others."[103]

Plato's system of mutual accountability is only achieved by reducing the importance of mass political participation in the system. Indeed, insofar as Magnesia leaves a role for mass groups of ordinary citizens in its system of accountability—in electing the *euthunoi* and in serving as *dikastai* in public trials[104]—they remain unaccountable. Electors who choose bad *euthunoi* never face scrutiny or punishment for their choices, nor are ordinary *dikastai* ever scrutinized and punished. But the role of these unaccountable popular actors in Magnesia is drastically reduced.[105] The "unchecked checker" central to the Athenian democratic politics of accountability has been relegated to the sidelines.

Plato's Magnesia cannot be taken as illustrative of oligarchic accountability practices in general (as a comparison of his scheme with the oligarchic practices discussed in section I above should make abundantly clear). Nonetheless, regimes already inclined to limit the role of mass decision-making in their politics could, if they so desired, more easily adopt a system of mutual accountability akin to the one outlined in Plato's *Laws*. On the other hand, political regimes, such as democracies, that wished to place power directly in the hands of massed groups of ordinary citizens faced a more recalcitrant problem. The Athenian system, like Plato's in the *Laws* and indeed our own, can be seen as facing a stark choice: to either limit mass political participation in decision-making or grant considerable power to unaccountable agents (i.e., ordinary citizens acting together collectively in large numbers) in key political processes. Athenian democracy opted consistently for the latter.

UNACCOUNTABILITY AS A MARKER OF SOVEREIGNTY

One way to understand the Athenian decision to accept the central role of unaccountable decision-makers in their politics is through the lens of popular sovereignty. There is a long-standing debate in political theory over the applicability of the language of sovereignty to the ancient Greek world. On one side, we have those who claim that sovereignty is essentially an early modern concept, unavailable to Greek thinkers and inapplicable to the world of the polis. More recently, political theorists, including Kinch Hoekstra and Melissa Lane, have looked to the use of Greek and Roman politics made by early modern theorists such as Jean Bodin to explicate their theories of sovereignty as an impetus to reconsider whether the concept may have premodern roots.[106]

On this line of thought, in classical Athens, the demos was sovereign (here translating the Greek word *kurios*), and the assembly and courts were the twin institutional loci of that popular sovereignty. Popular unaccountability follows straightforwardly from the shared status of the assembly and courts as the institutions through which the demos truly ruled. Jurors and assemblymen are not to be scrutinized or questioned in the exercise of their power, let alone punished for its misuse. To hold them accountable would be to misunderstand the nature of their power in the city. This view might seem to find some support in the customary opening of Athenian assembly decrees: *edoxen tōi dēmōi* (it seemed best to the demos). The formula could be read as implying that the mere fact that the people willed something is justification enough for its enactment—no further scrutiny or argument is required. Unaccountability is not only a *privilege* of sovereignty but also a condition of its exercise. The demos' power to make decisions without being called to account could be taken as a necessary condition for the free exercise of its political will. We could call this the *sovereign* view of popular unaccountability. Of course, decisions of the demos were not final. Future assemblies could overturn the decisions of previous ones. But this is compatible with sovereignty, which can also be understood as entailing the power to change one's mind. Moreover, as we have seen, at least in the fourth century, assembly decisions were also subject to review by panels of jurors. Yet this does not pose a challenge in itself to the sovereign view, provided that both institutions—assembly and popular courts—remain firmly identified with the people.

The demos-as-sovereign view coheres well with the framework of agent accountability used above to analyze the role ordinary citizens played in accountability politics. But it is worth emphasizing how uneasily it coheres with the Athenian emphasis on the need for power to be exercised accountably. Defended in such stark terms—that unaccountability is the privilege and enabler of the sovereign demos and needs no further justification—popular unaccountability is clearly in tension with Aeschines' elaboration of democratic ideology with which I began this chapter. The confident distinction he made between accountable democracy and unaccountable tyranny and oligarchy becomes difficult to sustain.

Perhaps in light of this tension, we also see efforts to argue that members of the demos are particularly deserving of the privilege of unaccountability. One such argument adverts to what many scholars take to be a central tenet of democratic ideology—the epistemic superiority of the judging demos.[107] As Hansen puts it in a discussion of the *graphē paranomōn*, "There seems something absurd about punishing a political leader for a proposal that the people had accepted, possibly unanimously. The philosophy behind the penalty was, however, that the people are never wrong, and will indubitably reach the right decision if a matter is properly put to them, but they can be misled by cunning and corrupt orators and make erroneous decisions against their better judgement."[108] Hansen's view is compatible with the demos-as-sovereign account insofar as both imply a displacement of scrutiny and blame away from the collective demos. But Hansen offers, in addition, an epistemic argument. Popular unaccountability is justified by the Athenian faith in the "wisdom of the masses." Why hold jurors and assemblymen accountable when, if given the right information, they cannot help but judge well and thus perform their duties admirably? We could call the view that Hansen claims to reconstruct the *infallibilist argument* for popular unaccountability.

Yet is Hansen's reconstruction plausible? It is true that plenty of evidence attests to Athenian confidence in the ability of regular citizens, assembled together in the *ekklēsia* and *dikastēria*, to judge matters correctly and wisely. This confidence in collective decision-making was buttressed by a general belief in the rectitude of mass opinion, nicely captured by Demosthenes' comment that he only felt willing to speak on a particular issue when he knew that the citizen body was divided on it; if all but he were in agreement, he would stay silent, since, as he remarks, "I, being one, would be more likely to be mistaken than all of you."[109] Nor was this strain of democratic thinking mere ideological cant. Aristotle, at least, took it seriously enough to offer a qualified endorsement in the *Politics*. In considering the claims of ordinary citizens to some share in the governing of the polis, he takes note of the argument that groups of people might be as good as or better than even wise individuals at judging at least some matters.[110]

Yet Hansen's infallibilist argument for popular unaccountability goes too far. In his view, Athenians justified popular unaccountability on the grounds that poor collective decision-making could *only* be the result of oratorical interference, manipulation, and deception. Consider the passage that Hansen cites in support of this view, from Demosthenes' *Against Aristocrates*: "[i] If [a juror] fails to understand something explained to him, he should not be punished for his misunderstanding. [ii] But the man who knowingly betrays and deceives the jury, he is the one liable to the curse. That is why, at each meeting of the assembly, the herald calls down curses not on those who are deceived, but on he who deceives in speaking to the council, the assembly, or the court."[111] In my view, Demosthenes has two different scenarios in mind in this passage, which I have marked above as (i) and (ii). We will do well to keep them distinct, although Hansen runs them together.

In the first scenario, the failure of understanding is not caused by a sly orator's efforts to mislead and deceive his audience. Rather, it simply represents cases where jurors fail to understand what they are being told. Far from bolstering the claim that collective decision-making is infallible absent oratorical abuses, the passage is striking for the seemingly casual way that Demosthenes *denies* that ordinary citizens are immune to errors of judgment. Of course, Demosthenes is also keen to highlight a second scenario, in which orators do actively mislead and deceive jurors. In this latter case, it is no surprise that he thinks it is the orators who should be held responsible. What is perhaps more surprising is that even where the fault seems to lie with the juror (as in case [i]), Demosthenes assumes that it would be inappropriate to hold him responsible (or at least, to punish him). The passage is less an endorsement of the infallible wisdom of the masses than a claim about *whose* mistakes in the polis rise to the level of culpability. In Demosthenes' view, jurors unable to follow arguments should be given a pass, while malevolent rhetors, whose attempts to deceive their audience represent a much graver crime against the state, are justly the objects of punishment. Demosthenes' division of responsibility may be perfectly reasonable, but it is clear that the passage makes it difficult to ascribe to him anything like the infallibilist argument for popular unaccountability. If Demosthenes recognizes that he lives in a world of mistake-prone jurors, he could not accept something like Hansen's reconstructed argument, which denies that such jurors exist. Athenians could not have rejected accountability for jurors and assemblymen on the grounds of their infallibility insofar as it was recognized that groups of citizens were both vulnerable to manipulation and (most importantly) had their own limitations.

UNACCOUNTABILITY AS A MARKER OF WEAKNESS: THE UNACCOUNTABLE *IDIŌTĒS*

Demosthenes' awareness of mistake-prone jurors points to a family of justifications for popular unaccountability rather distant from those we have just examined. Athenians seeking to justify popular unaccountability could turn their attention away from the power of the sovereign demos and toward the powerlessness of the individual ordinary citizen. Underlying this justification of popular unaccountability was an analysis of the varying levels of responsibility that properly accrue to different modes of participation in politics. Assemblymen and jurors on this view could be justifiably unaccountable less because they were above the law than because their characteristic political activities were almost beneath the law's notice.

To understand popular unaccountability in this light, we must turn to the figure of the *idiōtēs*. The word *idiōtēs* comes from the Greek adjective *idios*, meaning "private" or "personal." Its antonyms are *koinos* and *dēmosios*, what is "common," "public," or belonging to the people. *Idiōtēs* is therefore often translated as private citizen, as opposed to a magistrate or a citizen more actively involved in political life. At the limit, to be an *idiōtēs* was to play no role in politics at all. Such a figure, totally withdrawn from public life, was anathema to the Athenian participatory ideal and is met with scorn in such texts as Pericles' Funeral Oration: "We alone regard the person who fails to participate in public affairs not just as harmless but as positively useless."[112] Yet to be an *idiōtēs* did not primarily connote a retreat from all politics. *Idiōtai* also denoted the class of amateur but actively participating citizens whose level of participation nonetheless did not surpass some (ill-defined, as we shall see) threshold.

Who exactly counted as an *idiōtēs* in this sense was a matter of some debate. In some contexts, everyone not currently serving as a magistrate might be considered an *idiōtēs*. For example, a law cited by Demosthenes refers to "*idiōtai* and archons" as an exhaustive division of the citizen body, and in some speeches, former officers are referred to as *idiōtai* to differentiate them from those currently serving office.[113] Yet in other contexts, the status of *idiōtēs* encompasses all unskilled or amateur participants in politics, even those holding offices. Demosthenes differentiates between those members of the council who speak frequently and those who do not, identifying the latter group as *idiōtai*.[114] Similarly, he refers to the typical holder of a small-time magistracy—a market overseer or city regulator or deme judge—as "a poor man, and an amateur [*idiōtēs*], without much experience and selected by lot."[115] The contrast here is between those who devote much of their time and energy to politics and those who do not rather than between officeholders and others. In keeping with this understanding of the *idiōtēs*, Athenian rhetoric is filled with contrasts between *idiōtai* on the one hand and *politeuomenoi* (those citizens very active in politics) or *rhētores* (orators) on the other.[116] Given that there was no single stable definition of *idiōtēs*, it is unsurprising that the line separating these two classes of citizens was difficult to draw, a fact underscored by Aeschines' claim in his speech *On the Embassy* to be an *idiōtēs* himself, despite being one of Athens' leading political figures at the time.[117]

Scholars usually take *idiōtēs* to have a negative political valence, assimilating the term to Pericles' critique of the *apragmōn*. Yet to be an *idiōtēs*, in the sense of an amateur participant in politics, was, at least in some respects and contexts, a good thing. Aeschines' efforts to portray himself as one attest to that fact, as does, for example, Demosthenes' preference in *Against Androtion* for the *boulē* to be dominated by *idiōtai* rather than "talkers."[118] The preference for *idiōtai* can be read as a democratic version of Plato's thought in the *Republic* that those who wield political power should not be lovers of political rule.[119] Just as Socrates voices suspicion that those who desire to rule will invariably rule poorly, Athenian democrats may have been suspicious of those who were too eager to play an active role in politics as compared with the less ambitious *idiōtai*. Accompanying this preference for amateurs was broad agreement that *idiōtai* and *politeuomenoi* should be treated differently in politics and public life. In particular, Athenians generally thought that *idiōtai* should not be held to the same strict standards of accountability as the more politically active members of the polis.

Judicial rhetoric abounds with claims that defendants who are *idiōtai* should be treated leniently. Defendants often represented themselves as mere private citizens, unfamiliar with the court system and its rhetoric, in an effort to garner sympathy from the jury.[120] For example, in a *graphē nomon mē epitēdeion theinai*, Demosthenes allows that his target, Timocrates, could potentially be excused had he been a mere *idiōtēs* and not a frequent (and potentially corrupt) proposer of laws: "I wonder what he will dare to say [in his defense]. For he will not be able to show that his law does not contradict the others. Nor will he be able to show that he, being an inexperienced amateur [*apeirian idiōtēn*], did not know what he was doing; for some time, he has been seen composing and introducing laws for pay."[121] Similarly, in his speech *On the False Embassy*, Demosthenes accepts that a speaker's status as an *idiōtēs* acts as a kind of excusing condition, affecting his culpability and even his liability to accountability procedures: "If Aeschines were an *idiōtēs*, talking foolishly and blundering about, you wouldn't be excessively critical; you would let it go, and forbear judgment."[122] The set of *idiōtai* might be loosely defined, but counting as one before a jury was clearly advantageous: to view a defendant as an *idiōtēs* was to hold him to a lower standard of culpability, if not to excuse his misdeeds altogether.[123]

We can also see the special status of *idiōtai* in the frequency and ferocity of the rhetorical assaults on those who would prosecute them improperly.[124] As Demosthenes put it in his prosecution of Aristogeiton, famous for bringing *graphai paranomōn* before the people,

> What then is this man [Aristogeiton]? "The guard dog of the democracy!" they say. Yes, but what sort? One that does not bite those he censures as wolves but instead devours the cattle he says he guards. *Which of the orators has he harmed to the degree that he has harmed those regular citizens [tous idiōtas], against whom he has been convicted of moving decrees?* What orator has he accused since he again started speaking in public? Not a single one—but many regular citizens [*idiōtas pollous*]. But they say that dogs given a taste of cattle must be cut to pieces—and the sooner he is destroyed, the better.[125]

Demosthenes' denunciation of Aristogeiton might be rhetorically spectacular, but its message was commonplace: to direct the full force of Athens' legal machinery—including the institutions of accountability—against *idiōtai* was seen as a gross abuse.

As Aeschines neatly sums up the matter, when it comes to holding citizens accountable in Athens, "the law closely scrutinizes those who are active in public life [*tous politeuomenous*], not regular citizens [*tous idiōteuontas*]."[126] This was a bedrock assumption of Athenian politics. As Demosthenes told an opponent, "No one is ignorant" of the fact that "the life of regular citizens [*ton men tōn idiōtōn bion*] involves no danger and is secure and free of strife, while the life of those actively involved in politics [*tōn politeuomenōn*] is perilous, liable to censure, and each day filled with trials and evils."[127] In another speech, Demosthenes justifies this bifurcation of responsibility with a metaphor: "Consider mistakes made on naval voyages. Just as, when it is a common sailor who errs, the harm produced is small, but when the pilot goes astray he produces a common disaster for all embarked on the voyage, so too the mistakes of private citizens [*ta men tōn idiōtōn hamartēmata*] bring harm to themselves but not to the mass of citizens, while the mistakes of the archons and those actively engaged in politics reach everyone."[128] Most members of the polis, on this view, are akin to ordinary sailors. They are not immune from making errors, but when they do, the damage done to the ship of state is small. It is those men who participate more intensively in politics, akin to the captains and pilots of ships, who have the potential to cause real harm to the state. Hence, Demosthenes concludes, it is right that the laws of Athens place a premium on prosecuting, speedily and surely, the crimes of magistrates and orators while taking a more lenient approach to prosecuting the misdeeds of regular citizens.[129]

Popular unaccountability can be understood in light of the above analysis. Perhaps all that is needed to justify it is an understanding of jurors and assemblymen as fundamentally *idiōtai*, not professional politicians. As such, they were not the proper objects of Athens' legal machinery and accountability mechanisms, and these institutions correctly did not focus on them. One need not advert to the infallibility of group decision-making to defend the unaccountability of assemblymen and jurors. Rather, one must only consider them as ordinary citizens—fallible, perhaps, but not deserving of censure and punishment in the same way that other, more active citizens, might be. Hyperides' speech *On Behalf of Euxenippus* makes this understanding of jurors explicit: "Ever since you decided to participate actively in politics—and by Zeus, you certainly are able—you should not have brought regular citizens [*tous idiōtas*] to judgment nor treated them with your youthful insolence. Instead, if some orator does an injustice, prosecute him—or if some general does wrong, impeach him! The power to do harm to the city belongs to these men, whichever of them who choose to do it, but not to Euxenippus or to any of the jurors."[130] Hyperides is attacking Euxenippus' prosecutor with a move analogous to Demosthenes' rhetorical assault on Aristogeiton. Yet here, the speaker also assimilates the defendant *and the jury* to the category of rightfully unaccountable private citizen. The familiar rebuke for prosecuting *idiōtai* is present, as is the claim that it is orators and generals rather than *idiōtai* who "have power to harm the city." In addition we see the explicit identification of the jurors with the class of blameless, harmless *idiōtai*.

If, in the Athenian political consciousness, jurors and assemblymen were fundamentally *idiōtai*, popular unaccountability might seem to follow naturally. Moreover, this justification of popular unaccountability fits neatly with the Athenian emphasis on the accountable exercise of power. All that is required is a new gloss on it: accountability is for the *politeuomenos*; the *idiōtēs* is justifiably unaccountable because he is weak, an amateur, and does not have the power to harm the city.

Nonetheless, I want to close this chapter by calling attention to the way in which the identification of jurors with *idiōtai* was, if understandable, also problematic. After all, even if jurors were not formally magistrates, serving as a juror was an intensive form of political activity, involving full-day commitments on perhaps as many as two hundred days of the year.[131] There is evidence that the precise status of jurors in the city struck contemporaries as something of a puzzle. The orator Lycurgus, for example, divided the *politeia* into three parts—archons, jurors, and *idiōtai*—suggesting a desire to keep *idiōtai* and jurors conceptually distinct (although just what distinction Lycurgus is trying to make here is a matter of debate).[132] Aristotle, too, had trouble figuring out where to place jurors and assemblymen in a schema of the city: "Perhaps someone would say that such persons are not magistrates at all and that sharing in these activities does not constitute holding office, but it is laughable to withhold the title of official from those who are most powerful."[133]

Aristotle's claim that there is something absurd in denying that jurors are magistrates raises a further consideration: if jurors were *idiōtai*, they were nonetheless *idiōtai* who wielded great power, if only collectively. This aspect of their status is brought out nicely in Aeschines' speech *Against Ctesiphon*, in which he reflects on the proper role of the jurors:

> In the same courts, do you disenfranchise those convicted of taking bribes and then yourselves honor with a crown a man whom you know to be a politician-for-hire? If the judges at the Dionysian Festival do not judge the cyclical choruses justly, you punish them, but will you yourselves, established as judges not of cyclical choruses but of laws and political excellence, give rewards, not in accordance with the laws and to the few and deserving, but to a successful schemer?
>
> Furthermore, such a judge will leave the courts having made himself weaker and the orator stronger. *For in a democratic city the private citizen rules*

as king through the law and his vote, but when he hands these over to another, he has dissolved the basis of his own power.[134]

In this passage, Aeschines accepts that jurors are unaccountable. The judges of choruses can be punished if they do not judge correctly. No such possibility exists for the jurors, those judges of the "laws and political excellence"; in pleading with them to judge in accordance with the laws, Aeschines acknowledges that no power in the city can compel them to do so. Aeschines makes the familiar move of identifying the jurors as *idiōtai*—but *idiōtai* dignified with a political epithet: "In a democratic city, the private citizen rules as king." Given the association of the figure of the *idiōtēs* with powerlessness, Aeschines' formulation has the whiff of paradox. Yet if the formulation is borderline contradictory, it is because it represents an attempt at bringing together two very different ways of understanding the demos' unaccountability, neatly capturing an important tension in the status of jurors and assemblymen in the democratic city: they are ordinary citizens, but they wield an almost royal power.

We might try to resolve the tension by claiming that sovereignty and powerlessness operate on different levels. That is, individually, each juror and each assemblyman is an *idiōtēs* and does not wield enough power to be held accountable for his actions; it is only collectively, as the demos, that they do. There are two problems with this formulation. First, it calls for a strict distinction between individual and collective power, which the sources do not bear out; after all, Aeschines encourages each juror to think of his power as his own individual possession, with each *idiōtēs* ruling as a king. More important, ascribing unaccountable power only to the collective agent—the demos—merely shifts the problem up a level: we are still faced with the tension between an Athenian ideology of accountable power and an undeniably *unaccountable*, powerful, collective actor. That is, even if jurors and assemblymen are individually *idiōtai*, is the collective demos an *idiōtēs*?

Rather than trying to resolve these tensions, we should acknowledge them as expressive of Athenian ambivalence about the power of the demos. The ideology of the unaccountable *idiōtēs*, applied to jurors and assemblymen, reflects uneasiness with unaccountable power. It is an attempt to find a justification for the unaccountability of jurors and assemblymen that fits neatly with the general Athenian emphasis on accountability. The need for such a justification is perfectly understandable, for unaccountability, as we saw at the beginning of the chapter, is linked closely in the minds of Athenians to tyrannical power. The unaccountability of the demos thus opens the way to comparisons with the unaccountable tyrant, as I show in the following chapter.

The Tyrant: Unaccountability's Second Face

Introduction

I left off the previous chapter with the figure of the unaccountable *idiōtēs*. There, I considered efforts to assimilate unaccountable jurors and assemblymen into a benign category, that of private citizens (*idiōtai*) rightfully excused from examination, interrogation, and punishment. Yet I also noted the tension between the jurors' status as *idiōtai* and the real power that they wielded in the city.

In this chapter, I focus on another archetypically unaccountable figure in Greek thought, the tyrant. The Greek association of unaccountability with tyranny is strong and consistent; to a large extent, our sources develop their accounts of the badness and dangers of political unaccountability through reflecting on—and engaging with—the figure of the tyrant. Attempts to associate the unaccountability of the demos with tyranny could therefore work to undermine the identification of the juror or the assemblyman with the figure of the *idiōtēs*. I show this logic at work through an analysis of Aristophanes' *Wasps* and Xenophon's account of the trial of the generals in the aftermath of the battle of Arginusae. I link the discussion of accountability in Athens directly to the problem of political counsel by focusing on how the unaccountability of the demos and the tyrant structured political relationships, including the relationship between decision-maker and adviser, in both regime types.

I. Holding Tyrants to Account

I want to begin with three Greek stories in which tyrants are held to account—almost.

Peisistratus, tyrant of Athens in the mid-sixth century BCE, was famous in antiquity for the mildness of his rule. In offering his own reasons for concurring in this judgment, Plutarch recounts the following story:

> [Peisistratus] preserved most of Solon's laws, abiding by them himself and compelling his friends to do so. Once, while tyrant, he was called before the Areopagus on a charge of murder. He appeared before the court, ready to offer a moderate defense, but the accuser dropped the charges.[1]

On Plutarch's account, Peisistratus submitted himself to the judgment of the court, and the accuser, perhaps impressed with his willing submission to the rule of law, declined to prosecute.

A version of this story can also be found in Aristotle's *Constitution of Athens*. Aristotle, too, tells the story in the context of emphasizing the moderation of Peisistratus' reign; the language in the two accounts is close enough to warrant a guess that Aristotle was Plutarch's source. However, Aristotle includes one extra detail that changes the complexion of the story (which is why, perhaps, Plutarch saw fit to omit it[2]):

> And the greatest of all the things said of [Peisistratus] was that he was popular and benevolent in his character. For he was willing to administer all things in all other ways according to the laws, giving himself no advantage. Once he was called before the Areopagus on a charge of murder. He himself appeared to make his defense, *but the man who summoned him to court was frightened and left.*[3]

Aristotle does not elaborate on why the accuser "was frightened," but it is not hard to imagine the reason. Behind the mildness of Peisistratus' rule must have been a willingness to use force if the situation required it. Peisistratus was noted for making use of a bodyguard of club bearers rather than spear carriers, but blunt-force trauma is still trauma.[4] Perhaps Peisistratus could come before the Areopagus prepared to offer a "moderate defense" precisely because he knew he would not actually be required to do so. In showing up in person, he called the summoner's bluff.

The second story takes us to Syracuse, to the court of the fifth-century tyrant Gelon. Like Peisistratus, Gelon had a reputation for fair dealing; according to Diodorus Siculus, this was so "mostly because this was just his way, but not least because he was eager to have all men as his own by goodwill."[5] As an example of Gelon's good rule, Diodorus recounts a momentous assembly in 479 BCE. The tyrant was preparing his men and navy to set sail in aid of the Greeks in their struggle against the Persians. As he was preparing to sail off, word arrived from Corinth that Xerxes had been defeated at Salamis and was now in retreat. As Diodorus continues, Gelon

> called [the demos] to assembly, ordering all of them to come fully armed. But he himself came to the assembly not only without his arms but without even a tunic, wearing only a cloak. Coming forward he offered an account of his whole life and of the things he had done for the Syracusans. And when the mob signified its approval at each of the things he said, marveling particularly that he had surrendered himself unarmed to whoever might wish to destroy him, so far from being punished as a tyrant, in one voice all declared him benefactor, savior, and king.[6]

In offering a vigorous defense of his conduct, Gelon gives a kind of speech familiar to any Athenian who had watched or participated in a *euthuna*.[7] In Gelon's case, however, his carefully stage-managed "accountability trial" before the demos became his coronation.[8]

The final story can be found in Herodotus. Upon the death of Polycrates, tyrant of Samos (522 BCE), the tyranny devolved to Maiandrius, his former secretary. Unlike Gelon and Peisistratus (and presumably Polycrates as well), Maiandrius did not want to be a tyrant. So upon Polycrates' death, he dedicated a temple to Zeus Eleutherius (Zeus the Liberator) and called an assembly. There he castigated the former tyrant—"I was not pleased to see Polykrates lording it over his equals, nor would I like anyone else to behave in that manner"—and proposed a new form of government for the city: "I am placing the government in the hands of the public, and I proclaim that equality under the law [*isonomia*] is now yours."[9] All Maiandrius asked in return for the Samians' freedom was a portion of Polycrates' estate and the priesthood of Zeus Eleutherius at the temple he had dedicated.

Maiandrius' proposal did not fall on receptive ears. A prominent Samian replied with invective—"You are a scoundrel!"—and a counteroffer: "Instead of what you propose, you must render an account [*logon dōseis*] of the money you have already under your control."[10] In rejecting Maiandrius' proposal, the Samian can also be seen as pushing it to its logical conclusion. We are already familiar with the central role of accountability institutions in Athenian democracy, of which Herodotus was also well aware: he has Otanes claim in the constitutional debate that under regimes that rule in accordance with the principle of *isonomia*, officials are accountable to an audit.[11] In trying to hold Maiandrius to account, then, the Samians were merely acting in accordance with the principles he himself promulgated.

Unfortunately for the Samians, Maiandrius did not quite see it that way.

Fearing that "someone else would soon make himself tyrant," Maiandrius "decided not to give up power but instead withdrew to the acropolis, from which he then sent for the citizens one by one, on the pretext of rendering to them an account of the money, but really in order to have them arrested and imprisoned."[12] The Samians' enthusiastic, if naïve, attempt to hold Maiandrius accountable in the ways of a well-ordered polis thus ended in failure.[13]

The three stories offer vivid illustrations of a fundamental tenet of the Greek understanding of tyranny: there would be something incongruous, even contradictory, about an accountable tyrant. This holds true for the seemingly most benevolent of tyrants, such as Peisistratus and Gelon, as well as for those who do not even want to be tyrants, such as Maiandrius. The stories offer different perspectives on the nature and etiology of tyrannical unaccountability—highlighting by turn the role of fear, popularity, and cunning—but are united in depicting tyrants who avoid being held to account. As stories of near misses, they might lead their readers to reflect on what might have been. Perhaps Peisistratus' accuser could have stood his ground, perhaps Gelon's carefully orchestrated show trial could have ended in accountability and not acclamation, and perhaps the Samians could have figured out a better way to hold Maiandrius to account than visiting him on the acropolis one by one. Yet insofar as these counterfactuals remain just that, each story reinforces rather than undermines a basic thought: tyrants can be exiled—or even killed—but they are never held to account by the normal standards and in the normal ways of the polis. Nino Luraghi, in a rich analysis of the deaths of tyrants in ancient Greek sources, finds only two cases of "Greeks who were tried for tyranny," and significantly, neither is tried in the cities over which he exercised tyrannical rule.[14] In these stories, tyrants are tortured and assassinated, killed alone or with their families, even slain at altars. But "normal judicial procedures"—and, I would add, normal political processes of accountability—are conspicuously absent.[15]

Luraghi attempts to discover the "themes that recur most frequently in Greek representations of tyranny in order to try and define the rules that govern such representations," to glean from stories and discourses about tyrants "elements for a definition of tyranny and for the set of representations it was associated" with.[16] In a similar spirit, I offer in the following sections an investigation of the theme of tyrannical unaccountability, arguing for its centrality to Greek representations of tyrannical politics. I show how the Greeks used the figure of the tyrant as the basis for reflecting on the nature of unaccountable, arbitrary power—whether that power was exercised in an autocracy or a democracy, by an individual ruler or by the collective demos.

TYRANNICAL UNACCOUNTABILITY IN AESCHYLEAN
TRAGEDY AND HERODOTUS' *HISTORIES*

The tragedies of Aeschylus are some of the earliest Greek sources for the trope of tyrannical unaccountability. In plays such as the *Persians* and *Prometheus Bound*, Aeschylus' characters discuss the ways in which unaccountability benefits the autocrat while posing a potential threat to his subjects.[17] In the opening scene of the *Persians*, Xerxes' mother, Atossa, reports to the chorus of Persian elders a dream she had that seemed to prophesize her son's defeat at the hands of the Greeks. She takes comfort, however, in the fact that even if he were defeated, he could not be held to account for his mistakes: "These things are terrifying to me as witness, and to you as audience. For you are well aware that if my son were to succeed he would be a man to excite great admiration, but that if he fails—he is not accountable to the community [*ouch hupeuthunos polei*]. Provided that he has survived he is still sovereign of this land."[18] Atossa thus emphasizes the way in which unaccountability insulates the autocrat from the consequences of his actions and thereby maintains his rule.

While unaccountability is a boon to the autocrat, his subjects (at least some of them) are bound to view it differently. Throughout *Prometheus Bound*, the other gods remark on the harshness of Zeus' tyranny. Prometheus is punished so that he might "be taught to be content with the tyranny of Zeus," and Oceanus advises Prometheus to rein in his behavior as "a savage monarch now rules who is in no way accountable [*oud' hupeuthunos*]."[19] The critique of unaccountable tyranny from the subjects' perspective is also at work in the *Persians*. Xerxes' unaccountability is implicitly contrasted with the Athenian system of *euthunai*, which "shields the common citizens from the abuse of the men in power and liberates them from the fear of being at the mercy of a master with unrestrained authority, who is beyond punishment."[20]

We can read the constitutional debate in Herodotus' *Histories* as echoing this Aeschylean association of autocracy with unaccountability while also amplifying it considerably.[21] There, Otanes criticizes monarchy as the form of government where "it is possible for the ruler to do what he pleases without having to render an account [*tēi exesti aneuthunōi poieein ta bouletai*]."[22] Whereas in Aeschylus the contrast between democratic accountability and tyrannical unaccountability is only implicit, Otanes makes it a central part of his argument. He identifies the accountability of magistrates as one of the three hallmarks of "rule by the majority," along with selection of magistrates by lot and referral of all proposals to the public. In contrast, he posits a close connection between unaccountability and the character of tyrannical rule.

As his initial critique of monarchy emphasizes, the ruler's power to do what he pleases depends on his unaccountability—if there were an authority over the autocrat, his freedom of action would be compromised. This freedom from restraint affects what the autocrat chooses to do. Unaccountable rule, Otanes claims, would render any man a bad ruler: "Even the best of men, if placed in this position of power, would lose his normal mental balance."[23] As Otanes elaborates, a tyrant "overturns ancestral customs; he uses brute force on women and he kills men without trial."[24] In addition, then, to a descriptive and institutional claim—the autocrat's rule is characterized by his ability to do whatever he desires with impunity and without having to justify those actions—Otanes explicitly links unaccountability to stereotypical "tyrannical" behavior. In referencing the atrocities that the tyrant's unaccountable power sets in motion, Otanes offers the beginnings of a theory of how unaccountability has a tendency to ramify throughout the autocrat's life—with distorting and even perverting effects on the ruler's actions and desires.

As Victoria Wohl has argued, in the Greek imaginary, the tyrant is a "supremely erotic being." Characters in Herodotus voice their desire for tyrannical power in no uncertain terms: "Deioces is in love with tyranny and woos rule. . . . Pausanias likewise 'harbors a passion for becoming tyrant of Greece.' . . . Tyranny has many lovers."[25] The focus of Herodotus' discourse might seem to be on the tyrant and would-be tyrant as psychological character types: "Excessive and insatiable in his desire, indiscriminate as to his objects, the tyrant is eros as pure drive."[26] The constitutional debate complements this picture by providing an institutional structure to support and explain the tyrannical psyche: the violent, hubristic, and unrestrained desires and actions of tyrants on display throughout the *Histories* arise as a result of or are exacerbated by the tyrant's unaccountability.[27]

The mutually sustaining relationship between unaccountability and unlimited desire is perhaps best exemplified in Herodotus' recounting of Cambyses' attempt to marry his sister. Cambyses, Herodotus tells us, had fallen in love with his sister and wanted to marry her but recognized that to do so would be "unconventional." He therefore summoned the royal judges, interpreters of "ancestral ordinances and institutions," to inquire whether "there was any law that would sanction a man's marrying his own sister." The response of the judges, Herodotus notes, was both "just and safe: they said they had discovered no law that would sanction marriage between a man and his sister, but they had found another law stating that the king of the Persians was permitted to do whatever he wanted." Cambyses thereupon "married the sister he had fallen in love with, but a little while later, he married his other sister, too."[28] Cambyses' actions illustrate the dynamic relationship between unaccountability and stereotypical tyrannical behavior. In coming before the royal judges in the first place, Cambyses engaged in an attempt to negotiate the extent of his desires and see what limits, if any, could be placed on them. The judges' decision reinforced his unaccountability and underlined their inability to place any limits on his sphere of action. The result was that Cambyses felt free to marry not one sister but two, illustrating the way in which his unaccountability was implicated in a process of ever-expanding desires.[29]

Over time, the relationship between unaccountability and the metastasizing of desire characteristic of the tyrant would become both a commonplace and an object of further inquiry and elaboration, as we can see in Plato's treatment of tyranny and tyrannical desires in his dialogues.

GYGES' RING, SOCRATES' DAGGER: IMPUNITY AND THE TYRANT'S LIFE IN PLATONIC DIALOGUE

The centrality of unaccountability to Plato's depiction of the tyrant and the (false) attractions of the tyrannical life is brought out most clearly in the obsession of various Socratic interlocutors with the idea of doing injustice *with impunity*. This, of course, is the basic idea behind Glaucon's presentation of the story of Gyges, in Book II of the *Republic*.[30] Glaucon asks Socrates to respond to the claim that the best life involves doing "injustice without paying the penalty [*mē didōi dikēn*]."[31] Gyges' ring, which renders its wearer invisible, serves as the central element of a thought experiment Glaucon proposes in support of his claim.[32] The ring simulates a condition where one cannot be punished for one's actions—that is, unaccountability. The development of accountability as a theme is reinforced by a detail in the story that Glaucon tells: Gyges discovers the ring's power when he, along with the other shepherds, comes before the king to make his monthly report on the status of the flock. It is while taking part in an exercise of accountability, then, that Gyges discovers the ring's power to liberate him from such constraints.[33] In Glaucon's view, the unaccountability that the ring provides would lead any man, whether just or unjust, to give free rein to his desires: "He could take whatever he wanted from the marketplace with impunity, go into people's houses and have sex with anyone he wished, kill or release from prison anyone he wished, and do all the other things that would make him like a god among humans."[34] As other scholars have noted, Glaucon's ring wearer closely parallels the stereotypical tyrant in his misbehaviors and misdeeds.[35]

The relationship between impunity and the excesses of the tyrannical life is also on display in an exchange between Polus and Socrates in the *Gorgias*. Here the would-be tyrant's accoutrement consists in a dagger, not a ring, and one that lacks any special power. As Socrates puts it to Polus, "Imagine me in a crowded marketplace, with a dagger up my sleeve, saying to you, 'Polus, I've just got myself some marvelous tyrannical power. So, if I see fit to have any one of these people you see here put to death right on the spot, to death he'll be put. And if I see fit to have one of them have his head bashed in, bashed in it will be, right away. If I see fit to have his coat ripped apart, ripped it will be. That's how great my power in this city is!'"[36] Socrates continues by noting that upon seeing (in implicit contrast with Gyges' ring) his dagger, no one would believe that he truly had the great power he claimed. As Socrates pushes Polus to admit, this is because "the person who acts in this way is necessarily punished."[37] Even (and perhaps especially) from the perspective of the would-be tyrant, then, it is not enough simply to do "what one sees fit," Socrates tells Polus. Rather, as Otanes stressed and Polus is made to see, one must be able to do it with impunity.[38]

Taken together, Plato's stories of Gyges' ring and Socrates' dagger suggest a theory of unaccountability as an enabling condition for unjust behavior. Insofar as desires to act unjustly exist, they are (usually) held in check by fear of the law and punishment. It is unaccountability that gives these desires free rein. However, it is less clear that unaccountability itself contributes much to those desires' genesis and growth. Both Glaucon's presentation of the ring of Gyges story and Socrates' discussion with Polus suggest that tyrannical desires in a soul can and do arise in the absence of unaccountable power.

Plato's analysis of the evolution of the tyrant in book 9 of the *Republic* affirms the view that the corruption of the tyrant's soul may precede his achieving power in the city. There Socrates claims that tyrannical desires are common but also commonly suppressed: certain "lawless" desires "are probably present in everyone, but they are held in check by the laws and by the better desires in alliance with reason." Such desires appear when sleeping, and that "savage" part of the soul "doesn't shrink from trying to have sex with a mother, as it supposes, or with anyone else at all, whether man, god, or beast. It will commit any foul murder, and there is no food it refuses to eat. In a word, it omits no act of folly or shamelessness."[39] Here, two of Otanes' stereotypical tyrannical desires—murder and sexual excess—are ascribed to people in general: such desires do not arise only or primarily in a tyrant, spurred on by his unaccountability. As Socrates continues, in a well-ordered soul these desires remain repressed, but in a tyrannical soul, they come to dominate. As Socrates claims, "A man becomes tyrannical in the precise sense of the term when either his nature or his way of life or both of them together make him drunk, filled with erotic desire, and mad." As he continues, "Don't many terrible desires grow up day and night beside the tyrannical one, needing many things to satisfy them?"[40] Plato thus depicts the metastasis of tyrannical desire in great detail. Strikingly, however, none of this analysis is predicated on the "tyrannical man" having achieved the status of tyrant in his city or the unaccountability that comes with it.

It would therefore be a mistake to assimilate Plato's theory of tyrannical desire entirely to Herodotus' analysis in the *Histories*. Yet it would also be a mistake, I think, to push the two accounts too far apart and to argue that "while Herodotus depicted the tyrant as transgressor of norms without accountability (3.80), Plato focuses on the soul of the tyrant."[41] It is arguably true that Plato offers a richer portrait of the tyrant's soul than anything we find in Herodotus.[42] Even so, it is not the case that Herodotus is concerned only with institutions and Plato only with the soul and growth of "tyrannical" desires. Rather, both writers are concerned with the relationship between the two.[43] We have already seen the psychological dimension of Herodotus' account: the narrative links tyranny and *erōs* throughout, and Otanes warns of the effect of unaccountability on the tyrant's thoughts and desires. Similarly, Plato's attention to the importance of unaccountability or impunity in the tyrannical life is clear from the stories of the ring and dagger.

Should any more reinforcement of this point be required, we can find it straightforwardly expressed in the *Laws*, where the Athenian Stranger makes clear the connection between unaccountability and rule in accordance with one's own desires. When the Athenian Stranger turns to the question of whether a single ruler, even one who has acquired the necessary political knowledge, should be put in charge of a state, he answers in the negative, citing exactly the now-familiar concern that unaccountability is dangerous: "The second difficulty is that even if a man did get an adequate theoretical grasp of the truth of all this, he might then attain a position of absolute control over a state, with no one to call him to account. In these circumstances he would never have the courage of his convictions; he would never devote his life to promoting the welfare of the community as his first concern, making his private interests take second place to the public good."[44] In both Herodotus' *Histories* and Plato's discussions of tyranny, then, we see the recognition that it is the *conjunct* of destructive desires and unaccountability that is particularly worrisome. Where the authors differ, perhaps, is in their analysis of what the precise relationship between those two things might be. The Herodotean view, to recapitulate, is that unaccountability *ramifies* throughout the tyrant's life, perverting and expanding his desires in proportion to his sphere of action. It is the familiar idea, to offer the anachronistic cliché, that "absolute power corrupts absolutely."[45] Plato nowhere directly contradicts this idea, and passages such as the one just quoted from the *Laws* may even offer it some support.

Nonetheless, Plato also focuses on the relative independence of the growth of tyrannical desires from any particular institutional framework. In doing so, he offers a different, if compatible, vision of an already corrupted soul seeking out absolute power in a (vain) attempt to satisfy its limitless desires.

UNACCOUNTABILITY AND TYRANNY POST-PLATO

The association of tyranny with unaccountability continued throughout the fourth century and beyond.[46] In the *Politics*, Aristotle identifies tyranny in its most realized form as consisting in the tyrant exercising "unaccountable" (*anupeuthunos*) rule "in accordance with his own advantage, but not in the advantage of the ruled."[47] Aristotle refers to the tyrant as the "counterpart" (*antistrophos*) to absolute monarchy (*pambasilea*), in which "the king rules over everything according to his own will."[48] As the distinction suggests, the Greeks could imagine an unaccountable ruler exercising his power benevolently and for the common good. But this was by no means the expected outcome of autocratic rule. The good king remained a utopian figure whose image "was created by simply turning as many of the vices of the *turannos* as one could think of into their opposites."[49] The close association of unaccountability and tyrannical rule may also have made the development of a positive theory of monarchy more difficult. As Luraghi concludes, even in Hellenistic texts, "the ideology of monarchy kept concentrating almost exclusively on the personality of the ruler. How exactly monarchy was supposed to function as a political institution remained largely undiscussed."[50] Eventually the language of unaccountability, like the language of rule in accordance with one's own desires, came to be deployed as a shorthand for tyranny itself. Plutarch describes the rewards Lysander gave out to his friends and allies as "unaccountable oligarchies" (*anupeuthunoi dunasteiai*) and "unexamined tyrannies" (*turannides anexetastoi*). Plutarch needs only to cite the *structure* of these regimes to evoke an image of harsh misrule.[51]

The critique of the tyrant as an irresponsible, unaccountable ruler represented a crucial point of agreement between critics of the Athenian democracy and exponents of its ideology.[52] I began the previous chapter with Aeschines' views concerning the difference between democracy and tyranny: "While tyrannies and oligarchies are administered according to the will and pleasure of their leaders, cities with democratic constitutions are administered according to established laws."[53] In Athens, in contrast with tyrannies, "there is nothing in the city that is exempt from audit, investigation, and examination."[54] We can now appreciate the way these Aeschinean observations fit into a tradition of associating unaccountability with misrule.

At this point in the analysis, we have come a long way from the unaccountable *idiōtēs* with whom we ended the previous chapter. Unaccountability now has its second (and more familiar) face. Whereas the *idiōtēs* is politically benign in his unaccountability (indeed, is unaccountable just *because* he is benign), the tyrant's unaccountability is inextricably bound up with the free exercise of power and proves to be an enabling condition for the most destructive forms of social and political behavior. Herodotus, Plato, and others take the link between unaccountability and misrule to be a general political problem, whether because those with overweening desires seek out unaccountability to better pursue them or because the status of being unaccountable itself engenders such desires.

The family of views that takes the tyrant as the archetypal unaccountable agent is animated by this basic question: how does unaccountability interact with the exercise of power? Characterizing jurors and assemblymen as *idiōtai* implicitly insulates them from such critical investigations. Yet as I suggested in the last chapter, insofar as jurors are identified not simply as *idiōtai* but as *idiōtai* with royal power, that insulation could never be complete. The association of the *idiōtēs* with powerlessness fit uncomfortably with the power that jurors and assemblymen wielded in the city. To the degree that this was recognized, arguments for popular unaccountability that hinged on the jurors' status as *idiōtai* threatened to dissolve into circularity.[55] The image of the juror as *idiōtēs* was potentially unstable and vulnerable to deconstruction.

In the following two sections, I look at a pair of attempts to scrutinize the unaccountability of Athenian jurors and assemblymen. As we will see, in their depictions of jurors and the assembly, both Aristophanes and Xenophon play with the stock image of the unaccountable tyrant acting in accordance with his desires. In deploying tyrannical images and language to describe, satirize, and critique Athenian politics, they also raise questions about the nature of the demos' power and its relation to its advisers.

II. The Unaccountable Juror in Aristophanes' *Wasps*

Aristophanes deployed the demos-tyrant analogy most explicitly in the *Knights*, where the demos, personified as an old man, is explicitly compared to a tyrant: "Demos, you have a fine rule [*kalēn archēn*], since all mankind fears you like a man with tyrannical power."[56] Yet it is in the *Wasps*, produced two years later in 422 BCE, where Aristophanes elaborates most fully on the theme of the demos' exercise of tyrant-like unaccountable power in the city.[57] The *Wasps* is, among other things, an exaggerated but trenchant critique of the Athenian jury system. Aristophanes' portrayal of Philokleon serves to undermine the idea that jurors fit the "amateur ideal" of Athenian politics. In Philokleon, Aristophanes offers in the place of the juror as unaccountable *idiōtēs* an opposing image, that of the juror as unaccountable tyrant. While Aristophanes is unsparing in his identification of the unaccountability of the juror and of the problems this engenders, he also, I argue, points to the limits of the demos-tyrant analogy.

The *Wasps* opens on a scene of two slaves, Xanthias and Sosias, keeping watch on their master's father, Philokleon. The reason, Xanthias explains to the audience, is that the old master suffers from a strange sickness. The problem is that "he's a jury-addict [*phileliastēs*] like no other man; he's in love with judging, and he groans if he cannot sit on the front bench."[58] Philokleon's love of judging, Xanthias explains, has taken over the old man's life. Night and day, his world revolves around the courts: he dreams of the water clock and scrawls graffiti rhapsodizing the alluring beauty of the voting urn's funnel. Each morning he wakes up with three fingers pressed together, as though he were holding a voting pebble. Shortly after dinner (presumably after spending the day in court, happily judging away), "he calls for his shoes and then goes down there and sleeps in front of the court, hours early, clinging to the pillar like a limpet."[59]

Xanthias links Philokleon's love of judging with his anger and desire to punish, observing that the old man always chooses the harsher punishment during the penalty phase of the trials he judges.[60] The anger and ferocity of the jurors is, of course, a major theme of the play and the basis for its central image, the swarm of juror-wasps ready to sting whoever angers them.[61] The conversation among the chorus of jurors often revolves around whom they have punished and whom they will have the opportunity to punish next.[62] Yet even among that tribe of angry old men, Philokleon stands out. He prides himself on never voting to acquit, explaining, "Once I consulted the oracle at Delphi and the god prophesied to me that when I let anyone get off I'd just shrivel up then and there."[63] His fellow jurors agree with the characterization of Philokleon as a particularly unsympathetic juror: "Truly he was far the fiercest of those in our place, the only one who couldn't be talked round; when anyone begged for mercy he'd lower his head, like this, and say 'You're trying to cook a stone.'"[64]

The relation between the two dominant features of Philokleon's character— his love of judging and his anger or ferocity—is worth reflecting upon. It is tempting to assume that Philokleon simply finds pleasure in feeling angry and punishing others. When his fellow jurors arrive at his house looking for him, Philokleon calls out, "What I've been wanting to do for a long time is to go with you to the voting urns and do some harm to someone!"[65] Yet Philokleon is not—or not merely—mean-spirited; his addiction to judging is not simply an addiction to the pleasures of cruelty. Rather, his anger and ferocity are instrumental in achieving what Philokleon takes to be the central good of jury service—a sense of empowerment. This comes out most clearly in the debate staged between Philokleon and his son, Bdelykleon. Bdelykleon offers the view that Philokleon, in devoting his energy to serving as a juror, is nothing more than a powerless fool: "You don't understand that you're being made a fool of by men whom you all but worship. You're a slave, and you're not aware of it." Philokleon responds that he is "lord of all."[66] It is in defending this claim that he makes clear both the source of his addiction to judging and how his ferocity benefits him.

Philokleon begins his defense of the jury-lover's way of life with the following claims: "Yes, right from the start I'm going to prove as far as our power is concerned that it's equal to that of any king. What creature is there today more happy and enviable, or more pampered, or more to be feared, than a juror, and that though he's an old man?"[67] As Philokleon elaborates on these claims, it becomes clear that the fear that others feel for him is central to his vision of the superiority of his way of life. For example, it is fear of the juror's power that makes young, strong men bow down before Philokleon and beg him for mercy.[68] As Philokleon continues to elaborate on the lengths that even the rich and powerful will go to in their efforts to assuage his anger, the connection between their fear and his feeling of empowerment is reinforced, as is the suspicion that, in his mind at least, this is the chief benefit of serving as a juror.[69] Philokleon concludes,

PHILOKLEON: Do I not wield great power, in no way inferior to that of Zeus—seeing that the same things are said of Zeus and of me? For example, if we get noisy, every passerby says, "What a thunder's coming from the court! Lord Zeus!" and if I make lightning, the rich and the very grand all cluck and shit in their clothes for fear of me. And you yourself are terribly afraid of me—by Demeter, you are—but I'll be damned if I'm afraid of you![70]

Philokleon's anger and ferocity generate fear in those who come before the court, and that fear is central to his feeling of empowerment.

As Philokleon elaborates on the power he has as a juror, a second theme comes to prominence: he is able to exercise his power unaccountably. After accepting the supplications of those outside the courthouse, Philokleon does not let their pleas affect him: "Then when I've been supplicated and had my anger wiped away and gone into court, once I'm inside, I take no account of

all the promises I've made."[71] He brags that the jurors do not have to follow
the law: "If a father leaves a daughter as heiress and gives her to someone on
his deathbed, then we tell the will it can go and boil its head, and the same
to the shell that's lying very grandly over the seals, and we give the girl to
anyone whose entreaties persuade us."[72] All that the jurors do, in Philokleon's
view, they do with impunity, a point he takes care to emphasize: "And doing
all these things we cannot be called to account—a power not given to anyone
else" (*Kai taut' anupeuthunoi drōmen, tōn d' allōn oudemi' archē*).[73]

Philokleon here evokes the unaccountability of the tyrant, not the *idiōtēs*.
Philokleon takes his unaccountability as the guarantor of his power, not the
marker of his powerlessness. Philokleon's character and actions undermine
the idea of juror as *idiōtēs* at every turn. While the amateur ideal dictates
occasional political participation for the benefit of the polis, Philokleon par-
ticipates every day that he is able and does so explicitly for the benefits he
gains. If the amateur ideal is predicated on a suspicion of those who wield
too much power or who love "serving the city" too much and on a dislike
of ambition and distrust of the ambitious, then Philokleon repudiates that
ideal even while seeming to serve it. He couples distrust and disrespect for
career politicians with his own love of jury service. If the amateur ideal is in
part predicated on an Athenian version of Plato's dictum that only those who
do not wish to rule are suitable rulers, then Philokleon has missed the mark.
Philokleon's open exultation in the power of the juror and in his unaccountability underscores the tension between the image of the juror as *idiōtēs* and
the actual role the juror played in the polis.

With the juror as supposed *idiōtēs* unmasked, Aristophanes happily goes
about dressing Philokleon in the robes of a tyrant (quite literally at 1130–50,
where Bdelykleon has him exchange his homespun cloak for Persian garb).[74]
Philokleon's defense of jury service is a masterful satire on the tyrannical life,
even though the word *tyrant* is never uttered.[75] We have already seen the way
in which Philokleon stresses the unaccountable nature of the juror's power.
His self-identification with the tyrant is also underscored by his invocations
of Zeus and claim to be "lord of all."[76] Jeffrey Henderson has noted the way
in which "the hallmarks of the Classical tyrant" feature prominently in Aristophanes' portrayal of demagogues usurping the power of the demos: "Cleon
uses public and imperial funds for his own pleasures, especially sexual excess,
gluttony, and heavy drinking; violently suppresses opposition; lords it over the
people's administrative and military officers and over the allies; intrigues with
enemy states; harasses the elite classes, including homosexuals."[77] Philokleon
lays claim to a remarkable number of these tyrannical vices in his speech. He
clearly takes great delight in "lording it over" the city's archons, who must

face him at their *euthunai*, and in harassing "the elite classes." Moreover, after expounding at length on the joys of domination, Philokleon paints a scene of domestic pleasure that serves as a send-up of the tyrannical pleasures of "sexual excess, gluttony, and heavy drinking." Food, sex, and drink feature prominently in Philokleon's description of the juror's home life. Its eroticized account of his daughter's attempts to get a share of his jury pay even reenacts the tyrant's infamous flouting of sexual boundaries and norms:

> But what's the most delightful of all of them, which I'd forgotten, is when I come home with my pay. . . . First of all, my daughter washes me and anoints my feet and bends down to kiss me and keeps calling me "daddy dear" while really trying to fish my three obols out of me with her tongue. And the little wife fawns on me, bringing me a puff pastry and then sitting down beside me and forcing me to have it—"eat this, take a nibble of this." . . . If you don't pour wine for me to drink, I bring in this "donkey" full of wine and then tip it up and pour myself some.[78]

In Philokleon, then, Aristophanes seems to have offered his audience a member of the demos who, at least in his own self-image, bears more than a passing resemblance to a tyrant. We might be tempted to conclude that just as Otanes predicted in the case of the autocrat, Philokleon's unaccountability has ramified throughout his life, leading to stereotypically tyrannical behavior.

Yet we should not draw too hasty conclusions about what, precisely, Aristophanes is up to in having Philokleon portray himself in these ways. First, Aristophanes offers up this vision of the tyrant-juror enjoying his pleasures with a wink and a nod at his audience. Philokleon's pleasures are relatively austere compared to the luxuries of the tyrant (after all, his pay is only three obols a day), which should make us wary of the comparison, as should the obvious comic exaggeration at play. Most important, Philokleon's attempts at self-aggrandizement cannot be read in isolation because they are not the only allusions to tyranny in the text. Indeed, the main accusations of tyranny in the *Wasps* are leveled not against Philokleon but against his son. Bdelykleon's attempts to prevent Philokleon from leaving the house to judge are met with anger and suspicion by the other jurors: "Is this not terrible and open tyranny?"[79] As Philokleon continues to resist, the jurors' verbal assault grows:

> CHORUS: It is not now patent / to the poor, how tyranny has stealthily / crept up and tried to seize me, / when you, you villainous villain, you long-haired Amynias, / seek to shut us off from the laws the city has made / without offering any justification / or any quick-witted argument, / but like a sole autocrat?[80]

Bdelykleon responds to the jurors' accusations that he is aiming at tyranny with telling mockery:

BDELYKLEON: How you make everything into "tyranny" and "conspirators," if anyone makes a criticism of anything big or little! I hadn't ever heard the word for fifty years back, but now it's a good deal cheaper than salted fish, so much so that its name is actually bandied about in the marketplace. If someone buys perch and doesn't want sprats, straightaway the man selling sprats nearby says, "This man seems to buying fish like a man after tyranny."[81]

Bdelykleon's response is frequently read as an important commentary on the state of political discourse in Athens in the 420s, and the role therein of the image of the tyrant. Henderson's interpretation is typical: "The picture painted by Aristophanes in *Knights* and *Wasps* shows that populist charges of tyrannical conspiracies were a novelty. They were also leveled so frequently, were so broadly construed, and directed at such unlikely targets as to be arguably absurd, as in this passage from *Wasps*."[82]

Attuned to the importance of Bdelykleon's remark as a statement about political discourse at large, commentators miss its relevance to Aristophanes' own portrayal of (in this case) Philokleon as a tyrant-like figure. We might think that the contrast between the explicit way that the discourse of tyranny is (mis)applied to Bdelykleon and its more covert (and more accurate?) application to Philokleon sharpens Aristophanes' criticism of the demos: he is lampooning Athenian accusations of tyranny directed against demagogues while dramatizing what he takes to be the real similarities between demos and tyrant. Yet we can also read the two passages together in a different way. In having Bdelykleon call attention to the vacuity of many accusations of tyranny, Aristophanes may implicitly invite his audience to apply the same standard to his own exaggerated critique of the jurors. Aristophanes has at least left it open to readers and audience members to see him as in effect undercutting his own critique: if he faithfully reproduces every aspect of tyrannical behavior in his portrait of the juror, he may do so at least in part to mock the idea of jurors as tyrants.[83]

The ambiguity of Aristophanes' use of the demos-tyrant analogy in the *Wasps* finds a parallel in the *Knights*. Much of that play consists in a competition between two slaves, Paphlagon (a stand-in for Cleon) and the Sausage-Seller, for who can best curry favor with and please their master, Demos. At the end of the play, the Sausage-Seller emerges victorious, in part through engineering a transformation of Demos, boiling him down from "ugly" to "beautiful."[84] When the boiled-down Demos reappears on stage, he is toasted by Paphlagon as "the monarch of Greece and of this land."[85] Yet as Victoria Wohl and others have argued, the rejuvenated Demos may have sacrificed more than he has gained in the transformation.[86] Ominously, the Sausage-Seller heralds Demos' return by calling for an end to judicial activity: "Keep your language pure, everyone; close your mouths, call no more witnesses, shut up the lawcourts that this city's so fond of [*kai ta dikastēria sugklēiein, hois hē polis hēde gegēthen*], and on the occasion of our revolutionary good luck, let the audience sing a paeon!"[87] Read alongside the *Wasps*, where jury service is depicted as an essential element of popular power in the city, the Sausage-Seller's celebratory announcement is disquieting. The depoliticization of this kingly Demos is seemingly confirmed when the Sausage-Seller declares that Demos now smells of peace accords rather than the mussel shells ordinarily used by jurors as voting markers.[88]

Indeed, whether Demos was truly in need of the Sausage-Seller's transformative treatment is far from clear. Earlier in the play, the chorus acknowledges Demos' power as akin to tyranny but complains, "You're easily led astray: / you enjoy being flattered / and thoroughly deceived, / and every speechmaker / has you gaping. You've a mind, / but it's out to lunch."[89] If the chorus' rebuke seems aptly to describe the part Demos has played thus far in the play—a pliant subject to Paphlagon's and the Sausage-Seller's ministrations and manipulations—then Demos' response comes as a surprise:

DEMOS: There's no mind under your long hair, / since you consider me stupid; / but there's purpose / in this foolishness of mine. / I relish / my daily pap, / and I pick one thieving / political leader to fatten; / I raise him up, and when he's full, / I swat him down.[90]

Here Demos assures the chorus (and, by extension, the audience, which has witnessed his—which is to say, their—abasement throughout the play) that he is firmly in control. Yet it is precisely the means to this control—the ability to raise a "political leader" (*prostatēs*) up and then knock him down using the city's machinery of accountability, including the courts—that the rejuvenated Demos, for all his trappings of power, abjures at the end of the play.[91] Like the *Wasps*, then, the *Knights* offers a complex account of the demos' power, simultaneously building up and undermining the image of the demos as monarch or tyrant.[92]

None of this implies that Aristophanes rejects the demos-tyrant analogy altogether but only that it has its limits. What remains of Philokleon's portrait of the juror as tyrant is the problem posed by unaccountability, which manifests itself in interactions between jurors and those who come before them to be judged. Importantly, the claim that jurors enjoy unaccountable power is never refuted in the play. When Bdelykleon responds to his father's paean to jury duty, he accepts the characterization of jurors as unaccountable as the only good point Philokleon has made.[93] His rebuttal of Philokleon focuses instead on the jurors' poverty: jury service does not secure them great material goods, even though Athens is a rich empire. Lisa Kallet has read Bdelykleon's response as an effective refutation of Philokleon's view: "Like a tyrant in his city, the demos is all-powerful and without checks on that power. Its power was perceived as being connected to its wealth. Thus when Loathecleon [Bdelykleon] pokes holes in what he sees as an illusion of power, his argument is that Lovecleon [Philokleon]—and the demos by extension—is not as wealthy and therefore not as powerful as he thinks; and by implication, he is not a tyrant."[94] In contrast, I read Bdelykleon's response as something of a non sequitur. In focusing solely on the jurors' relative poverty, he does not address the real issue, which is their central institutional role in the city.[95]

Aristophanes, then, offers a portrait of the juror as tyrant that shares in many of the classical tyrannical topoi discussed above. Even if some of the sting of his portrayal is weakened when considered as comic exaggeration rather than serious critique, the claim that jurors were unaccountable rings true and is never refuted. The jurors have been given their own ring of Gyges. Even if their unaccountability does not lead them immediately to embark on a campaign of terror, the play leaves open how we should understand its potential political effects. I will return to these questions in the conclusion of this chapter. First, I want to turn to one other case where the unaccountability of the demos licenses comparison to a tyrant.

III. Arginusae and the *Graphē Paranomōn* in Xenophon's *Hellenica*

Xenophon's account of the aftermath of the battle of Arginusae (406 BCE) also trades on the unaccountable demos-tyrant analogy. At a critical moment in the Peloponnesian War, the Athenians sent a large naval force to assist the general Conon, whose ships were under blockade by the Spartans at Mytilene.[96] The importance that the Athenians ascribed to this naval mission may be gleaned from the participation of higher-status citizens as rowers in the relief expedition, from evidence suggesting that slave-rowers who performed well would be given their freedom, and from the supervision of the expedition by eight of the ten Athenian generals.[97] The Spartans and the Athenians met near the islands of Arginusae, and the Athenian forces were victorious. Faced with two imperatives—following up on their victory by chasing down the crippled enemy ships and rescuing their own sailors whose ships had been destroyed—the generals chose to split their forces to accomplish both, assigning the rescue mission to a pair of trierarchs. However, a fierce storm after the battle rendered both plans of action moot, and many Athenian sailors drowned when help failed to arrive.

In the wake of the battle, six generals were tried collectively, found guilty, and executed for their failure to rescue the Athenian sailors whose triremes had been destroyed. The trial is perhaps best known to political theorists as the occasion for one of Socrates' few overt political actions, as recounted in Plato's *Apology*. Socrates was a member of the *boulē* that year and happened to be serving as prytanis at the assembly meeting in which the generals were tried; he protested against the plan to try to punish the generals collectively, considering such a trial to be illegal.[98] Yet quite aside from Socrates' involvement, the trial offers an important look at the politics of accountability in action. Procedures for discovering who or what was at fault for the loss of life began soon after the battle. The generals were recalled to Athens, with six answering the summons and two going into exile. They were quickly imprisoned on the proposal of one Timocrates. In the next assembly meeting, Theramenes, one of the trierarchs assigned to rescue the sailors and thus not an uninterested participant, demanded that the generals "give some explanation as to why they did not rescue the shipwrecked men."[99] The generals refused to blame the trierarchs, maintaining that the storm was at fault. At this point, their exculpatory efforts seemed moderately successful: "They were persuading the demos," Xenophon writes.[100] Nonetheless, the assembly meeting ended without any decision being made, and in the coming days, popular feeling against them grew, particularly after the Apaturia, a civic festival that was transformed into a show of mourning for the lost sailors.

At a second assembly meeting, things came to a head. Callixeinus proposed that the generals be tried collectively for failing to rescue the sailors: "Since the Athenians have heard in the previous Assembly both those accusing the generals and the generals' own defense of themselves, they should all now vote according to tribes . . . and if they [the generals] are judged to be guilty, they should be sentenced to death."[101] As Debra Hamel has noted, this motion put the generals at a distinct disadvantage. Not only would they be given no further opportunity to speak in their own defense, but, given inevitable variation in assembly attendance, "some percentage of the men tasked with convicting or acquitting the generals would do so without having heard their arguments."[102] Here the corporate and shifting nature of the demos contributed to perceived unfairness and irregularity in the decision-making process.

One Euryptolemus rose to indict Callixeinus for having made an illegal proposal (a *graphē paranomōn*). On Xenophon's account, the majority of the assembly responded sharply, crying out that it would be "a terrible thing if someone prevented the people from doing whatever they wished."[103] Euryptolemus continued to press his point that to try the generals immediately and collectively would not be "just and lawful," warning that the assembly might later regret its decision and suggesting other procedures for trying them and holding them to account on an individual basis.[104] While Euryptolemus was nearly successful, in the end, the Athenians chose to try the generals collectively; they were found guilty and the six present were put to death. Nor was this the end of the matter. As Xenophon writes, "Not a long time later, the Athenians regretted the affair and decreed that those who had deceived the demos be prosecuted, and that securities be set down until they were tried; and among them was Callixeinus."[105] Callixeinus was found guilty, although he escaped before his trial during the tumultuous period of oligarchic revolution. He is reputed to have starved to death upon his return to Athens under the restored democracy's amnesty, apparently universally detested for the role he played in the affair.[106]

As Sara Forsdyke has noted, Xenophon's depiction of the demos rejecting all restraints on doing "whatever they wished" recalls "the traditional portrait of the tyrant who can do whatever he wants without being held to account," which can be traced back to Herodotus.[107] The strangeness of the anecdote—did the "majority" of those sitting in the assembly, some three thousand individuals, really shout out in unison?—highlights the comparison Xenophon is seeking to make between demos and tyrant. Xenophon is clearly trading on stock accusations against tyrants (e.g., Plato's claim that they will execute whomever they wish to, without proper trial) and his use of language and phrases typically reserved for tyrants underscores his disapproval of the demos' actions here.

The trial of the generals is often taken as an uncharacteristic failure on the part of the Athenian demos, a uniquely unfortunate event in Athenian history. George Grote's discussion of the trial in his *History of Greece* set the stage for much scholarly opinion to come. He deplores the generals' condemnation as "an act of violent injustice and illegality, deeply dishonouring the men who passed it, and the Athenian character generally."[108] Yet he continues, "Against the democratical constitution of Athens, it furnishes no ground for censure—nor against the habits and feelings which that constitution tended to implant in the individual citizen. Both the one and the other strenuously forbade the deed: nor could the Athenians ever have so dishonoured themselves, if they had not, under a momentary ferocious excitement, risen in insurrection not less against the forms of their own democracy, than against the most sacred restraints of their habitual constitutional morality."[109] If Grote is right, a reading of the aftermath of Arginusae that focuses solely on the fate of the generals leaves the Athenian demos looking unaccountable, and even tyrannical, but only for a moment: the trial was an aberration, and the tyrannical treatment of the generals was the exception, not the rule.

More recently, Steven Johnstone has analyzed the Arginusae trial in the context of Athenian approaches to collective liability. Johnstone suggests that it may have been common practice, in both Athens and other poleis, for "members of groups" to "be held liable collectively."[110] He explicates the "logic of the single vote," which "seems to respond to the unified actions of the board." Given the indicted generals all acted as one, "multiple trials or votes could create potential unfairness if some were convicted and others excused for collective decisions and actions."[111] Johnstone also cautions that while there was usually only a single defendant in an Athenian trial, "we know of no law establishing the single defendant as a universal norm."[112] While acknowledging that aspects of the trial were irregular and even unfair, Johnstone argues that the trial's interest lies less in Xenophon's claims that it was illegal and more in what it reveals about the dynamics of collective liability in Athens and the limits of delegation. The generals were unable persuasively to argue that the delegated trierarchs were to blame and so were collectively held accountable for the collective failure.

Johnstone's argument helpfully focuses on the *logic* of Athenian accountability practices revealed in Xenophon's depiction of the trial, including the controversial decision to try the generals collectively. But even if Johnstone is right that collective liability had a place in Athens' system of accountability, it is instructive to see its limits. Here it is useful to turn our attention away from the Athenians' treatment of the generals and whether that treatment was "tyrannical" and toward the role of Callixeinus and Euryptolemus in Xenophon's narrative.

Xenophon portrays Callixeinus and Euryptolemus as the demos' advisers. Euryptolemus makes this understanding of his own role explicit in his speech: "I have come up here . . . to give my advice [*sumbouleusōn*] about what seems best to me for the entire city."[113] Euryptolemus continues, "I advise you in those matters to follow a course whereby you cannot be deceived—either by me or by anyone else—and whereby, with full knowledge of the facts, you may punish the wrongdoers (either all together or each one separately), by any penalty you wish to inflict: namely, to give them at least one day, if not more, for them to make their defense, not trusting in any others but yourselves."[114] Euryptolemus' speech and effort to stop Callixeinus' motion by means of a *graphē paranomōn* suggest two ways in which asymmetrical accountability structures the relationship between the demos and its advisers. Consider first Euryptolemus' use of the *graphē paranomōn*. We can view the institution as a check on the ability of a demagogue to persuade the demos to resolve on an unlawful or otherwise unwise course of action. As Harvey Yunis has argued, "By invoking the *graphē paranomōn*, politicians, concerned citizens, and sycophants could hinder a demagogue in the assembly from turning his advice into official policy."[115] Euryptolemus' efforts serve as an (admittedly ineffectual) attempt to exercise this function, and as Grote wrote of his attempt to forestall the trial, "nor was there ever any proposition made at Athens, to which the Graphe Paranomon more closely and righteously applied."[116] Euryptolemus' intervention stands as an example of the *graphē paranomōn* being used by the advisers of the demos to keep each other in check.

Yet if we look at the way in which Callixeinus was punished, we see another side to the *graphē paranomōn*: it was structured to leave the decision-maker, the demos, unaccountable while holding only its advisers to account. Collective liability at Athens might have applied to boards of magistrates and even, to some degree, to the *boulē*, as Johnstone has argued.[117] But as I argued in chapter 1, ordinary citizens acting together in the assembly and the courts were unaccountable. Xenophon calls into question this limitation by dramatizing a case where accountability and responsibility seem to come apart. For it seems uncontroversial that the demos was responsible for the decision to try the generals collectively; indeed, the assemblymen's response to Euryptolemus, that they should not be prevented from doing what they wished, suggests that the members of the assembly viewed themselves as the responsible agents, at least at this point in time. Similarly, Euryptolemus' attempt to show them that they might have cause to regret the illegal trial presumes that they are responsible. Nonetheless, when the decision to try the generals collectively comes to be recognized as a poor one, the demos is not held accountable.[118] Instead, the demos holds others to account: the proposers of the decree are charged with deceiving the people. Callixeinus is prosecuted for advising the assembly to try the generals collectively, even though it is the demos that accepts his proposal and acts on it.[119]

IV. Conclusion: The Demos-Tyrant Analogy and the Democratic *Sumboulos*

The two faces of unaccountability—the *idiōtēs* and the tyrant—reflect Athenian ambivalence about the power of the demos. Insofar as jurors and assemblymen exercised unaccountable power in the city, they were a conspicuous exception in a political system that placed great ideological and practical weight on the principle that power ought to be exercised accountably. Given the close association of unaccountable power with the figure of the tyrant, the unaccountable power of the demos could not but be a worry for democrats and a target for their critics. Athenians could attempt to explain and justify the unaccountability of jurors and assemblymen by adverting to the discourse of the justifiably unaccountable *idiōtēs*. But such an identification was tenuous enough that the counterclaim—that the demos' unaccountability more closely resembled the unaccountability of the tyrant—was always available to make.

As both Aristophanes' *Wasps* and Xenophon's depiction of the trial of the generals suggest, the demos-tyrant analogy was not deployed merely as a polemic. Both writers use it to help them—and their audiences—think more generally about the nature of unaccountable power and the effects of its exercise. We might think Aristophanes' primary goal in portraying Philokleon as a pseudotyrant is to make his audience laugh. But he also implicitly invites his audience to consider the role many of them might play in Athenian politics as unaccountable jurors deciding on central political questions in the popular courts and to ask themselves what, if anything, stops them from abusing their own considerable power. And while Xenophon clearly analogizes the demos as a tyrant in order to undermine the legitimacy of the Arginusae trial, he is also making a broader claim about how asymmetrical accountability structures function in practice.

When we see claims in our sources that the demos is acting like a tyrant, it might seem like the natural question to ask in response is, "Over whom does the demos exercise its supposedly tyrannical rule?" This is generally how scholars frame the issue, and they offer two answers. Sometimes the analogy is deployed to criticize Athens' imperial rule over subject cities and allies, as when the Corinthians in Thucydides' work accuse Athens of being a *turannos polis*.[120] On the other hand, sometimes the motivating thought behind the accusation is that the *dēmos turannos* plays the tyrant at home, ruling tyrannically over the elite in the city.[121] It is this latter claim in particular that is rejected as merely polemical. In neither the fifth nor fourth century was Athenian democracy characterized by the generalized, blatant misuse of arbitrary power that the Greeks took to be constitutive of tyrannical rule.

But in the analysis above, I have tried to show that the demos-tyrant analogy can be cashed out not only in terms of rule but also in terms of other relationships that were deeply shaped by Athens' structures of asymmetric accountability. And here the unaccountability of both demos and tyrant allowed for the creative and analytical, rather than purely polemical, deployment of the metaphor. Aristophanes' *Wasps* and Xenophon's account of the aftermath of Arginusae focus our attention on the interaction between collective bodies of citizens and the individuals who come before them to speak and persuade, either as *sumbouloi* in the assembly or as prosecutors and defendants in the courts. Xenophon's account of the aftermath of Arginusae implicitly poses the question "What is it like to be a *sumboulos* to the demos?" The answer he gives relies on a basic similarity between the demos and the tyrant or king: in both regime types, the decision-maker is unaccountable, and this fact structures the relationship between those decision-makers and their accountable advisers. In the following chapters, I turn to a series of texts, across multiple genres, which place that structural relationship at the center of their attempts to grapple with the theory and practice of political counsel in both democratic and autocratic regimes. I begin with Herodotus' depictions of advice-giving in the courts and councils of Persian monarchs.

3

The Accountable Adviser in Herodotus' *Histories*

Introduction

Advice is a central motif in Herodotus' *Histories*; a man who finds himself in "difficult circumstances" is seemingly never lacking for a second opinion on what he should or should not do.[1] Advice arrives from all corners—in letters from distant kings and messages concealed in the body of a hare; in oracles and dreams; from daughters, wives, and sons; from stable boys on campaign and notables in the courts of tyrants.[2] Its very ubiquity might tempt us to treat it as a *given*: in Herodotus' world, we might think, a powerful man such as a king or general is simply supplied, deus ex machina, "with counselors to stand by him and give him general advice, good or bad, or to suggest a particular way of meeting a certain situation."[3] Advisers glom onto situations as if by some law of history or narrative structure: "A certain situation calls for, it may even create, a sage; an impending catastrophe produces a tragic warner, a problem or a proposed stratagem, a practical adviser. Any available wise man will serve, if tradition does not already record one."[4]

Yet as scholars have come to realize, Herodotus' counsel scenes do not simply advance his historical narrative (or serve as entertaining digressions therefrom). Nor should we merely regard Herodotus' counselors as exemplars of the literary archetypes of the "tragic warner" and "practical adviser."[5] Herodotus treats political counsel as an intricate and dynamic process that can be attempted in diverse ways by both political decision-makers and their advisers. Herodotus' text confronts the reader with characters wrestling with fundamental political questions: How and when can political decision-makers safely rely on the logos of others? How can those without the power to decide nonetheless influence politics? What practices are conducive to the exchange of sound political counsel, and which undermine it? Reading the *Histories* as engaged in sustained reflection on these questions allows us to see Herodotus as offering an analysis of counsel as a political problem and as contributing to a political theory of its practice.

In claiming Herodotus as a theorist of political counsel, I do not suggest that he offers programmatic answers to the questions posed above. A theory of counsel embedded in historical narrative and the depiction of speeches will resist simple, formulaic answers to the questions it provokes. In Herodotus' world, politics is contingent and unpredictable (at least from the human perspective, if not from the perspective of fate). Logos can help humans confront that contingency but also has its limits. Herodotus' dramatization of counsel illustrates at once the necessity of, and the difficulties attendant on, relying on the advice of others.

Herodotus' treatment of political counsel makes extensive use of the vocabulary of advice (words such as *sumbouleuein, sumboulos, sumboulia*).[6] Indeed, his use of such terms is among the earliest in extant Greek literature.[7] In what follows, I focus primarily on Herodotus' depiction of the relationship between powerful political decision-makers and their accountable advisers. Most such scenes consist in Persian kings taking (or refusing to take) counsel from their advisers, and as we shall see, advice in these scenes misfires as often as it succeeds. It is therefore tempting to read Herodotus as making sweeping claims about the differences between "Greek" and "barbarian," or free and autocratic, political discourse. This is a move I want to resist. James Redfield offers an example of this approach to Herodotus when he traces the difference between Greek and Persian political discourse to different political institutions and *nomoi* (customs and laws). Among the Greeks, "matters to be determined are referred *es to koinon* or *es meson*—that is to the community at large. A tyrant cannot be talked to (3.80.5); free institutions, by contrast, proceed by talking."[8] Redfield's view—that counseling tyrants in Herodotus is an exercise in futility—is echoed in much of the literature.[9] More recently, however, scholars such as Christopher Pelling[10] have cautioned against reading Herodotus as simply attacking Persian modes of speech while valorizing Greek political discussion by showing the ways in which Herodotus depicts some Greek political discussions as dysfunctional and problematic.[11] Whatever Herodotus is doing with his theory of political counsel, then, it is not simply equating successful deliberation and counsel with free, Greek politics.

I also want to resist readings of the *Histories* that see all counsel, and the very possibility of applying logos to politics, as ultimately futile. On such readings, the human capacity to react to and control the flow of events on the basis of advice and deliberation and to learn from the advice of others and their own past experience is extremely limited. Such a view would imply that there is little point to a close analysis of Herodotus' scenes of counsel. For example, it would not be worth considering the ways in which the politics of the Persian regime might have served as an obstacle to taking good counsel if Herodotus, in recounting such scenes, merely wished to show that the invasion of Greece was fated to fail.

Readings that emphasize the general futility of counsel or the impossibility of counseling tyrants may obscure more than they reveal in their push to find an overarching Herodotean lesson in the text. Of course, there is something to both views. In Herodotus' portrayal of the Persian courts, the power disparities between *sumbouloi* and kings render counsel dangerous and difficult. The application of logos to political questions does not in itself guarantee success. Yet Herodotus' depiction of the relationship between accountable advisers and powerful political actors is considerably more nuanced and varied than is usually understood. The text pushes its readers to learn from logos' success as well as its failures, in part by depicting political actors doing just that.

I begin in section I with a reading of Astyages' reliance on his Magi dream interpreters. I use the scene to introduce a number of the themes Herodotus explores throughout the work, including the accountability of advisers, potential conflicts between advisers and decision-makers, and Herodotus' recognition of both the importance and the limitations of advice. I argue that while sections of the text like the Astyages narrative offer resources for constructing the pessimistic readings of advice in Herodotus that I wish to resist, they are only one side of the story. In section II, I turn to alternative scenes of counsel, involving Cyrus and Darius, to argue that the text offers no programmatic conclusions but instead works its effect by exploring the *dynamics* of giving and receiving advice. In section III, I continue this line of argument by looking in depth at Herodotus' depiction of Xerxes' interactions with his advisers. I argue that Herodotus uses the Xerxes narrative in part to explore how decision-makers can learn to appreciate the value of advice. I conclude with the suggestion that Herodotus' analysis, while centered on autocratic politics, has clear implications for considering the politics of advice in democracies as well.

I. Astyages and the Magi

Early in the *Histories*, Herodotus tells us that Astyages, the king of the Medes before Cyrus' rise, was troubled by a pair of dreams (1.107–8). In one, he saw Mandane, his daughter, urinating "so copiously that she filled up his city"; in the second, "he saw a vine growing from his daughter's genitals and covering all of Asia."[12] Astyages consults with the expert dream interpreters among the Magi to try to understand the disturbing images. The Magi offer interpretations in exact detail (*auta hekasta*; 1.107), indicating that Mandane's son will come to be king in Astyages' place. Astyages takes the Magi's warning seriously and arranges with his agent Harpagus to have her infant son, Cyrus, killed. Harpagus attempts to evade responsibility for the murder by assigning the task to a cowherd. As luck would have it, the cowherd's wife had just given birth to a stillborn baby and they decide to raise Cyrus as their own.

Some years later, Cyrus, unaware of his true parentage, is playing a game with other boys in which he is appointed king for the day (1.114). He proceeds to organize the other children into a minimonarchy, even ordering a flogging for one boy who refuses to follow his orders. When the flogged boy complains to his prominent father, Cyrus is brought for punishment to Astyages, who recognizes the boy as his presumed-dead grandson. Astyages calls on his dream interpreters to reconvene. Has Cyrus' playacting as king fulfilled the prophecy? Or does the boy still pose a threat to Astyages' rule? He asks the Magi for counsel: "Advise me [*sumbouleusate*], after considering the matter well, what is likely to be the safest course of action for my house—and for you" (1.120).[13]

In light of Cyrus' assumption of the role of King of the Boys, the Magi now interpret the dream as harmless: sometimes, prophecies "connected with dreams turn out to be completely trivial in the end" (1.120). The Magi take what could be interpreted as a veiled threat from Astyages—"offer me good advice, or face the consequences"—as a reminder that the king and the Magi share the same overriding interest—the preservation of his rule: "While you reign securely as our king and fellow citizen, we have our share of your rule and receive from you great honors [*kai archomen to meros kai timas pros seo megalas echomen*]. Thus, we must by all means preserve you and your rule" (1.120). They advise Astyages to let Cyrus live, and the king follows their advice. Unfortunately for Astyages, the benign interpretation of the dream is proven false when Cyrus revolts. More unfortunately for the Magi, they bear the brunt of Astyages' anger. He impales "the dream interpreters of the Magi who had advised him to send Cyrus away" (1.128).[14]

The story of Cyrus' rise and Astyages' (and the Magi's) fall is wonderfully Herodotean, replete with salacious details, byzantine plot twists, and (more than) a hint of the supernatural. Yet the details of the story also offer a window into how Herodotus conceives of the dynamics of political advice. Decision-makers in Herodotus seek counsel because they lack something—a perspective, a piece of information, a framework for understanding—crucial to making a decision, which they hope their adviser can provide. The Magi are skilled at interpreting dreams, knowledge that Astyages lacks but believes he requires and must therefore rely on others to provide. But turning to others for advice is a tricky matter, and asking for help is no guarantee of a good outcome. It is not only that the Magi fail to interpret the dream "correctly" and thereby to recognize the danger Cyrus poses to Astyages' rule. Rather, in fixating on the question of whether the dreams' prophecy had been fulfilled in a harmless way by Cyrus' game, they neglect another, more troubling possible interpretation of the game itself. In playing king, Cyrus reveals himself to be a natural leader. Herodotus' description of the game is replete with words for organization and command, as Cyrus goes about "setting each [boy] to his task" (*hōs hekastōi ergon prostassōn*; 1.114).[15] Cyrus is even able to persuade the other children to seize and flog a boy who refuses to play along; the boy is described as the son of a well-reputed man (*andros dokimou*), suggesting the threat Cyrus poses to established authority.[16] Perhaps another adviser, less focused on the niceties of prophetic dreams and the technical terms of their fulfillment, might have interpreted the game as lending credence to Astyages' worries about his grandson. Advice is at best an imperfect guide to the future, and the Magi will not be the only figures in the *Histories* whose words lead rulers astray.

The narrative also emphasizes Astyages' and the Magi's motives and interests. Each party is keen to show the other that they share an interest in getting the dream interpretation right. Astyages stresses that the Magi will do better so long as he remains king, and the Magi reaffirm their commitment to him. Yet these explicit affirmations also suggest that this alignment of interests cannot be taken for granted. Indeed, the Magi's claim to be co-citizens with the king and to have a share in his rule reads as ironic in light of their subsequent brutal treatment. In many of his counsel scenes, Herodotus explicitly explores the ways in which advisers and rulers seek to assure for themselves, and even to construct, an alignment of interest and trust.

Finally, there is the Magi's fate to consider. They are made to bear the consequences of their dream interpretation, even though Astyages found it persuasive. Asymmetrical power relationships structure a number of Herodotus' scenes of counsel, and the accountability of advisers is a leitmotif that runs throughout the text. It is a crucial element of Zopyrus' deception of the Babylonians when he claims to have been punished gruesomely by Darius for advising poorly (3.156).[17] Only Artabanus' status as Xerxes' uncle prevents the king from punishing him for advising against invading Greece (7.11),[18] and after the Persian defeat at Salamis, Mardonius expects to be punished for persuading Xerxes to invade Greece (8.100). Nor are the dangers of counsel limited to the courts of Persian kings. Pausanias, the king of Sparta, comes close to punishing Lampon for suggesting that the Greeks pay the Persians back for atrocities in kind (9.79). The Athenians stone to death one Lycides for advising them to accept Mardonius' offer of peace (9.5; for good measure, the women of Athens join in and stone his wife and children to death too).[19]

Holding advisers accountable follows a certain political logic. The vulnerability of the adviser to punishment is inseparable from the vulnerability of the decision-maker to the adviser. In turning to others for advice, decision-makers leave themselves open to manipulation and deception, in addition to the consequences of following bad advice offered in good faith. From this perspective, holding advisers accountable is in part a mechanism for keeping them honest and working in the interests of the autocrat. The Magi's elaborate claims to share interests with Astyages reflect an awareness of this. In trying to show they can be trusted, the Magi are not only concerned with persuasion—that is, with getting Astyages to accept their interpretation of the dream and to follow their advice. They are also concerned about what will happen to them should things go wrong. In claiming to have Astyages' best interests in mind, they are suggesting that even if their advice turns out to be poor, they should not be held accountable for aiming to deceive or otherwise manipulate. Herodotus does not abstract away from power asymmetries in his counsel scenes; he dramatizes them to provoke reflection on their implications.

This is not to say that Herodotus thinks such power asymmetries are always and everywhere present. Elsewhere in book 1, Herodotus offers a story about advice under a very different set of circumstances. In Babylon, Herodotus writes, people "do not use physicians." Instead, the sick are carried to the agora where others "approach the sick person and advise [*sumbouleuousi*] him about his illness." Herodotus continues, "Some may themselves have suffered from the same illness that the sick person has, or have seen someone else who did. They go to the sick person and give advice, encouraging him [*sumbouleousi kai paraineousi*] to do whatever they themselves or others they may know have done to be cured of a similar illness. And it is not permitted for anyone to leave the side of a sick person before having inquired what illness he suffers from" (1.197). Herodotus considers this marvelous institution the "second wisest" of the Babylonians' customs. Here is a practice of advice-giving that is participatory and antihierarchical.[20] In Babylon there are no doctors; everyone who passes by the sick person is seen as a potential source of wisdom by virtue of his direct experience and what he has learned from others. The questions posed sharply by Astyages' reliance on his expert Magi dream interpreters do not arise. No one has any interest, it seems, in deceiving the sick man; nor do the sick seem to worry that their advisers have anything but their best interests at heart. The law requires engagement with the sick from all who visit the agora. But once they have said their piece, or even if they have no advice to give at all, they are not held to account for their comments or suggestions (or lack thereof). This practice of advice-giving, while taking place in public, is curiously private and even apolitical. The stakes are high only for the sick person, and there is nothing he can do for (or to) the passersby. This is perhaps why the law has to require participation from everyone. They have no incentive to deceive but also have no incentive to advise other than sympathy for the sick and a recognition of their common humanity. The *requirement* to inquire about the sick man's suffering may itself be a tacit recognition that benevolence alone is not enough spontaneously to sustain a practice of freely given, disinterested advice.

Astyages' court is a world apart from the agora of Babylon. It is tempting to generalize from the fate of the Magi, and similar stories in the *Histories*, to a Herodotean critique of the very possibility of successful counsel in autocratic settings. As I discussed in the previous chapter, Herodotus' text explores the ways in which unaccountability enables arbitrary, hubristic behavior. The tyrant's unaccountability, we might think, will always threaten to undermine practices of advice-giving. Consider Xerxes' blunt remarks to Pythius late in the *Histories*, uttered in the context of meting out a horrible (and undeserved) punishment to one of Pythius' sons: "A person's feelings dwell in his ears, and when this seat of the emotions hears something good, the body fills up with delight, but when it hears the opposite, it swells with rage" (7.39).[21] Xerxes here makes a broad claim about the visceral human response to speech, a purported tendency to delight in good news and be angered by the opposite. Yet whatever the truth of the matter, not everyone is in a position to give free rein to his temper. It is Xerxes' position as king that makes his desire to hear good things and anger at hearing bad things dangerous for those who attempt to advise him. This form of "accountability" serves neither tyrant nor adviser. A tyrant merely lashing out in anger is not using accountability as a tool for controlling his advisers. Such an attitude threatens to subvert advice-giving altogether. An adviser confronted with such an agent would do better to offer flattery in place of sound (but painful) advice, lest one finds oneself the victim of the king's wrath.

Cambyses' interactions with his advisers represent perhaps the limit case of this dynamic. Insofar as Cambyses is interested in what others have to say, it is primarily for the pleasure of being praised.[22] He is volatile, even dangerous, in the face of criticism, and so those who wish to advise him typically do so carefully—and obliquely.[23] Croesus at one point does advise Cambyses forthrightly and frankly, warning him that should he continue to rule tyran-nically he will encourage revolt. In offering such frank criticism, he appeals to the authority of Cyrus: "Your father Cyrus often ordered and instructed me to admonish you and to suggest to you [se noutheteein kai hupotithesthai] whatever advice I found noble and good" (3.36). Cambyses responds angrily to Croesus' admonishment and sends him running for his life.[24]

The tyrant's power distorts speech: "No one, especially no wise person, will tell a man like this [i.e., a tyrant] that he is likely to behave badly, and to bring himself as well as others down . . . speech itself is distorted, as the wis-est of humans finds that they cannot talk straight."[25] But this need not imply that advising tyrants is always futile. The power asymmetry between adviser and decision-maker conditions speech, but does not determine it (let alone render it impossible). Even with a figure like Cambyses, there is variation in how advice plays out. Cambyses' advisers try out multiple strategies in dealing with him, from flattery to ambiguity to outright criticism. Of course, Croesus' more direct efforts are met with violence. Yet even still, this suggests a more complicated picture. Indeed, Croesus' admonishment of Cambyses itself pro-vides another model for autocrat-adviser relationships. Croesus presents his criticism as ultimately solicited by Cyrus, the previous king. Herodotus, then, juxtaposes Cambyses' unwillingness to take criticism and advice with Cyrus' farsighted efforts to secure it—even across generations.[26]

In the following section, I turn to scenes from the reigns of both Cyrus and Darius in which Herodotus depicts decision-makers aware of the ways their power inhibits their ability to get good advice and explores the tactics they and their advisers deploy in navigating their relationships. Far from offering a simplistic conclusion, the Histories, in dramatizing the process of advice-giving, furnishes readers with resources for thinking about—and practically confronting—the problem.

II. Securing Counsel and Counseling Securely: Cyrus and Darius

In book 1 of the Histories, Cyrus, after securing the conquest of Babylon, turns his attention to the Massagetae, a nomadic people to the east of his empire. Cyrus arrives at the river Araxes, separating the Persians from the Massage-tae, and begins the task of bridging the river to cross with his troops to the far side. Tomyris, queen of the Massagetae, sends Cyrus a message. She advises him not to fight but recognizes that he is not likely to listen. She therefore simplifies matters, offering Cyrus a choice of venue for the coming battle: either he should retreat deeper into Persian territory, allowing the Massagetae to cross over for the battle, or he should cross unharried and meet the Massagetae on their own turf.

Faced with this choice, Cyrus' first action is to call a council to solicit advice: "Hearing these things, Cyrus called to council the first men of Persia, and when he had gathered them together, he placed the matter before them [*es meson*], seeking counsel as to what he should do [*sumbouleuomenos hokotera poieēi*]" (1.206).[27] His Persian counselors unanimously urge him to allow Tomyris to cross and to meet the Massagetae on Persian ground. Croesus is the lone dissenter, urging Cyrus instead to attack the Massagetae and offering a plan for how the Persians might defeat them in battle. Cyrus follows Croesus' counsel. While the plan of attack appears to work well at first, Cyrus is ultimately defeated and killed.

Scholarly attention to this episode has focused primarily on the *failure* of Cyrus' expedition. Does this imply that Croesus' advice was incorrect? If so, what are the implications for Croesus' reputed wisdom—or even the possibility of applying wisdom to human affairs at all?[28] Less remarked on is the *process* by which Cyrus makes his decision. Herodotus' language in setting the scene suggests an openness to the proceedings. Cyrus places the matter *es meson*—"in the middle"—the same term, we will remember, that Redfield associates with open, "Greek" debate. Of course, Cyrus' war council is not an assembly of equals. Cyrus retains sole control over the decision, and the other attendees of the council function merely as advisers.[29] But the repetition of *sun-* words—*sugkaleō, sunageirō, sumbouleuō*—reinforces the impression that Cyrus is genuinely soliciting the advice of others to help him decide what he should do.[30] Opposing viewpoints are aired and debated. Croesus alone dissents from the consensus view, which might suggest that the other Persian *sumbouloi* are unwilling to offer frank advice and instead seek safety in numbers. Yet nothing Cyrus has done up to this point has been anything but encouraging of advice. If some Persian kings, such as Cambyses, are shown as impossible to advise, Cyrus is depicted as open to counsel.[31]

Of course, there is a limit to Cyrus' openness. In spite of the care he takes in listening to his subordinates, he is impervious to the advice offered by his adversary, which may have been the best counsel of all. As Tomyris tells him, "Cease your labors; you cannot know whether this project will prove to be advantageous to you. So stop; be satisfied with reigning over your own people and endure the sight of me ruling over the subjects that I have now. However, I assume that you will not follow my advice, as you would find anything preferable to living in peace" (1.206). While Cyrus focuses his council on whether to fight the battle on one side of the river or the other, the prior question of whether this is a sensible battle to fight at all is quietly dropped.[32]

We could see this failure as in part an inability to recognize that Tomyris was less an enemy than Cyrus realized. Her attempt to establish a kind of common interest between herself and Cyrus—both should be content with ruling over their own subjects (and only their own)—fails to change his course. Herodotus remarks earlier on Cyrus' eagerness to lead his army against the Massagetae, stemming from his victory in past wars and the extraordinary circumstances of his birth (1.204). As with other characters in the *Histories*, the growth of empire for Cyrus is nonnegotiable. Given the failure of Croesus' advice, Cyrus' inability to recognize the wisdom behind Tomyris', and his bloody fate, it might be tempting to read the seemingly positive description of Cyrus' council as ironic, wholly undermined by its limitations and subsequent events. But this would be to overlook Herodotus' genuine interest in the process itself. There is something praiseworthy about Cyrus' conduct in the war council, even if it did not lead to the desired outcome.

Herodotus' attention to the process of advice-giving also comes through in other scenes that focus on the potential clash of interests between *sumboulos* and ruler. Earlier in the work, Cyrus comes to Croesus for advice in dealing with the Lydians, the latter's former subjects, who have rebelled against Persian rule (1.155). Turning to Croesus for advice in this instance is a strange choice, and the analogy Cyrus deploys in explaining the problem underscores this. Cyrus compares himself to someone who has killed the father but spared the children in removing Croesus from power but leaving the Lydians free. Cyrus asks Croesus whether he ought not therefore reduce the Lydians to slavery.

In responding to Cyrus' request for advice Croesus does what he can to preserve his "children." He placates Cyrus, redirecting the king's anger toward himself and the leader of the rebellion, Pactyes. He concludes by offering a counterproposal to slavery, a plan to neutralize the Lydians by removing their capacity to make war and rebel: "Order them to wear tunics under their cloaks and soft boots, instruct them to play the lyre and the harp, and tell them to educate their sons to be shopkeepers. If you do this, sire, you will soon see that they will become women instead of men and thus will then pose no danger or threat to you of any future rebellion" (1.155).

The scene functions in part to reinforce deep Herodotean themes: the dependence of military prowess and freedom on nomoi, and luxury's corrosive effects on political virtue (see also 9.122). Yet to view the counsel scene simply as a vehicle to make this point would be a mistake. The text draws more attention to the political dynamics of the scene than to the content of the advice. Herodotus proceeds to offer a didactic explanation, in his own voice, for Croesus' counsel:

Croesus gave this advice [*hupetitheto*] to Cyrus because he realized that these conditions would be better for the Lydians than those which they would face if they were enslaved and sold. He knew that if he did not put forth a compelling case, he would not be able to persuade Cyrus to change his mind [*ouk anapeisei min metabouleusasthai*], and he was worried that even if the Lydians did manage to emerge unharmed from their present danger, they might someday rebel from the Persians again and then they would certainly be destroyed. (1.156)

As with Cyrus' war council before his invasion of the Massagetae, his imperial ambitions frame the limits and possibilities of advice. Croesus cannot simply advise Cyrus to grant the Lydians independence. Yet he can influence Cyrus in ways that serve his own interests as well as the king's. He does so by balancing competing goals: to get what he wants, he must also appeal to Cyrus. In this case, the proposal is successful. Cyrus is delighted, his anger abates, and he calls on a subordinate "to order the Lydians to carry out the steps which Croesus had advised" (1.156).

Elsewhere Herodotus depicts advisers and decision-makers negotiating a straightforward exchange of honest advice in return for honors and favor. In book 4, a Greek named Coës wishes to suggest an alteration to Darius' plan for a bridge over the river Ister. Herodotus has Coës first attempt to learn whether Darius "would welcome the opinion of someone who was willing to offer it to him" (4.97).[33] Coës is also careful to portray himself as offering advice with Darius' interests in mind: "Someone might say that I am telling you this for my own sake, so that I may remain behind [i.e., not accompany the army on campaign], but the real reason that I am presenting my opinion to you is because I found it to be a proposition in your own best interests, sire, and I shall in fact follow you—I would never be left behind" (4.97). In addition to securing the right to speak, then, Coës seeks to demonstrate to Darius that their interests are aligned. Coës' efforts to negotiate a space for giving good advice pay off for both him and the king. Darius is pleased with Coës' counsel and makes him the tyrant of Mytilene in reward. As for Darius, it is only Coës' advice to keep the bridge over the Ister as an escape route that prevents the total loss of the Persian army when they are forced to retreat (4.141).[34]

Scholars have read scenes such as this, where speakers must ask "permission to speak," as evidence of restrictions on speech in Herodotus' depiction of Persian courts.[35] I rather read them as showing Herodotus' interest in how advisers and autocrats can navigate their relationships. Herodotus' depiction of counsel is thus far from one-dimensional. His portrayal of figures such as Cambyses and Astyages and their relationships with their advisers must be read alongside his depictions of figures such as Cyrus and Darius. Rather than offering a single message—something along the lines of Redfield's "tyrants cannot be talked to"—Herodotus is engaged in exploring *how* tyrants can be talked to. Herodotus makes the conditions of advice-giving a matter of explicit discussion and depicts powerful political actors and *sumbouloi* as self-consciously aware of—and attempting to work through—the problems attendant on their asymmetric relationship.

Herodotus' exploration of the problem of counsel finds its fullest elaboration in the portrayal of Xerxes in the final books of the *Histories*. Xerxes' evolving engagement with counsel and attitudes to his advisers suggest that rulers can learn from advice—but also underscore the limits to that process.

III. Xerxes and His Advisers

Book 7 of the *Histories* begins with Darius' death and Xerxes' succession, and the narrative turns immediately to the question of Greece. While Xerxes is initially reluctant to invade, Mardonius, who "had more influence with the King than all other Persians," advocates for war (7.5). Mardonius argues for the need to take vengeance on the Athenians and other Greeks but also sweetens the deal by portraying Europe as a fertile and beautiful land. Mardonius does not offer this advice because he believes it to be in the king's (or Persia's) interest but rather because he hopes to be made the satrap of Greece after the conquest. The Peisistratid exiles ally themselves to Mardonius' efforts at persuasion, promising to reward Xerxes if he would restore them to their place in Athens. Onomacritus, a crooked collector of oracles, aids in the effort by reciting for Xerxes only the oracles portending a favorable result, leaving those predicting failure unspoken. Herodotus portrays a persuasive apparatus marshaled to seduce Xerxes into war without due consideration of the risks and whether such a plan is truly in his interest (7.5–6).

It is only after Xerxes has already been persuaded by Mardonius to invade that Herodotus gives us one of the great set-piece counsel scenes in the *Histories* (7.8–11). The council does not get off to an auspicious start. As Herodotus puts it, "[Xerxes] made a council of the best of the Persians, so that he could learn their opinions and say to all of them what he wished to do" (7.8).[36] The deficiencies of the council to come are already on display. The decision has been made, and listening to the opinions of his counselors is subordinate to his goal of telling them what he wants to do. Rather than turning to the council for advice, Xerxes presents his plan as already well conceived, making no reference to Mardonius' and others' roles in influencing the decision: "I have thought hard and discovered [*phrontizōn de heuriskō*] a plan to win us both glory and additional land that is in size and fertility no worse than what we possess now—and, at one and the same time, vengeance and punishment." As he concludes, "These are the things that must now be done. But so that I do not appear to you as self-counseling [*idiobouleuein*], I place the matter in the middle [*es meson*] and urge whoever wishes among you to give an opinion" (7.8).[37]

Xerxes' speech is rich in irony. Pelling has described it as laying the groundwork for a "travesty of debate, at least as Greeks would understand it." He notes the ways in which "several phrases in that sentence [Xerxes' closing lines] capture mantras of Greek, especially democratic debate," including the phrase "in the middle [*es meson*]."[38] John Lombardini has argued that the phrase *es meson* takes on different connotations under conditions of political equality and in autocratic regimes. In the former case, "all have a share in deciding what is placed *es meson* in Herodotus."[39] By contrast, as we have already seen in the case of Cyrus' council, when an autocrat places an issue *es meson* he reserves the right of decision for himself. Autocrats like Xerxes and Darius also "retain control over what it is permissible for others to share and discuss. . . . Under a monarchy or tyranny, public deliberation is a privilege that the ruler can extend, but also take away."[40]

Yet even within autocratic regimes, Herodotus seems to be drawing important distinctions. Cyrus and Xerxes both retain control of decision-making and the privilege of speaking, but they exercise it in different ways. When Herodotus describes Cyrus as placing a matter *es meson*, he uses the term to capture the real, if imperfect, openness of debate that Cyrus seeks to establish. To place a matter *es meson* is to make it subject to *contestation*; Cyrus does so, even if he reserves the right to judge the outcome of the contest for himself.[41] On the other hand, when Xerxes claims in his own voice to be placing the matter *es meson*, he is doing something altogether different. No contestation is possible when the decision-maker has already made up his mind before the debate has started. If Xerxes' council is a travesty of debate by Greek standards, Herodotus portrays it as a travesty of at least some Persian standards too. Other verbal echoes of earlier scenes of counsel are prominent and reinforce the point. Xerxes is not the only political actor in the *Histories* who takes decisive action after "thinking hard and discovering" a plan (or at least claiming to). For example, Cyrus responds to Harpagus' advice to revolt by considering how to get the Persians on his side; he considers the matter and discovers a "solution perfectly fitted to the circumstances, which he duly put into action" (1.125).[42] Xerxes' claim to have given the matter of invasion much thought and to have arrived at a coherent plan is thus called into question by comparison with other instances of well-considered deliberative action in the text.

Particularly suggestive, too, is Xerxes' acknowledgment that he asks for his counselors' opinions only so that he might not *appear to be* "self-counseling." "Self-counseling" translates *idiobouleuein*, an extremely rare Greek word; Herodotus' is the only attested usage of it before the Roman era. In Xerxes' choice of words, he seems to recognize that there is something odd about the council he has called. His desire not to appear self-counseling suggests that he recognizes a norm that an important decision such as whether to invade Greece would ordinarily only be made after taking counsel with others. Even here Xerxes may not have adequately diagnosed the problem. Xerxes is not truly self-counseling in this instance; he has taken counsel—but only from Mardonius and other supporters of the invasion. His desire not to appear to be self-counseling obscures the real problem: that he has chosen to follow a bad adviser who will lead him into the ill-fated invasion of Greece.

Mardonius is the first to respond, and given the start to the debate (and his own role in persuading Xerxes to invade), it is no surprise that his response is long on flattery and short on critique: "My lord, you are the best of all Persians . . . Everything you said was right on the mark" (7.9). Mardonius discounts the possibility that the Greeks will offer much resistance to the invasion, calling into question their resources, martial prowess, and courage. Mardonius' speech does not aim to help Xerxes understand whether his decision was the right one or to offer an alternative. His goal is instead to make Xerxes' proposal seem plausible (7.10). Xerxes, then, might appear as another Cambyses in his interactions with his advisers. At the end of Mardonius' flattering speech, Herodotus writes, "The rest of the Persians remained silent and did not dare to express an opinion in opposition" to the proposal (7.10).

It is at this point that Artabanus, Xerxes' uncle, intervenes, offering advice to a king who seemingly has no desire to hear it. He begins by attempting to instruct Xerxes on the value of advice: "O King, unless opposing opinions are aired, it is not possible to choose and select the better one. Instead, one can only use the opinion voiced. Just as we cannot distinguish pure gold by itself, but when we rub it against another piece of gold, we can determine the better, so of things said" (7.10).[43] He proceeds to offer a striking critique of the invasion plan. He frankly reminds Xerxes of Darius' failures in fighting the Scythians and praises the Greeks as the Scythians' superiors by land and sea. He stresses how risky an invasion would be, again drawing on Persia's past failures: just as the Persian invasion of Scythia was dangerously dependent on the bridge over the Ister, the Persians will be vulnerable once they cross the Hellespont. Yet Artabanus is also aware of the difficulty of his task of persuasion. He continues with a striking plea: "Dissolve this gathering now. Later, when it seems best and you have considered things for yourself, announce publicly what seems best to do. For I find that deliberating well [*to eu bouleuesthai*] is a great gain" (7.10).[44] Artabanus' advice threatens to dissolve into incoherence. He first stresses the need to make decisions only after testing multiple opinions against one another. He concludes by recommending that Xerxes ignore all advice and consider the matter on his own.[45] In Artabanus' partial endorsement of being "self-counseling" lies a deep recognition of the limits of advice. Proper counsel requires that multiple opinions be aired and considered. Absent that, Artabanus suggests, it might be better not to take counsel at all. At least in this case, he implies, it would be better for Xerxes to decide independently than to fall under the influence of a single interested party.

Artabanus' analysis of the problem of slander reflects a similar judgment that no advice might be preferable to the wrong kind of advice. In response to Mardonius' disparagement of the Greek ability to resist Persian imperialism, he calls attention to the ways in which such attacks are intended to encourage Xerxes to wage war. Here again, it is the one-sidedness of the account that is most troubling: "The one who slanders commits an injustice against the one who is not present, while the person who listens to him does wrong by believing him before learning if his claims are accurate" (7.16). Artabanus attacks both Mardonius and Xerxes here in ways that reinforce his earlier point.[46] Xerxes has listened only to Mardonius thus far, committing himself to one person's view before hearing both sides of the debate. Throughout his speech Artabanus stresses the value of contestation. An open debate need not imply the subversion of the decision-maker's control; conducted correctly, it reinforces it.

Xerxes initially responds to Artabanus with anger and threats: "You are the brother of my father, and that will protect you from paying the penalty your foolish words deserve, though for your cowardice and lack of nerve I shall impose upon you the disgrace of not accompanying me on my campaign against Hellas" (7.11). Yet once alone, he changes his mind, persuaded by Artabanus' warnings (7.12). In turn, his new resolve not to invade is undermined by a recurring dream in which a mysterious figure warns him that failing to invade will be his downfall. Artabanus offers a rationalizing interpretation of the dream: "Most of the visions visiting our dreams tend to be what one is thinking about during the day" (7.16). But he also accedes to Xerxes' request that he put the dream to a test: if he himself has a similar vision when sleeping in the king's bed, then he will accept it as a divine portent. The vision appears to him too, warning him not to attempt to "avert what is destined to happen," and Artabanus, "who before had been the only one to publicly oppose Xerxes, now openly and eagerly encouraged him" (7.17–18).

The war council scene might seem to lend itself to the lines of interpretation I am trying to resist in this chapter. Just as Cambyses would not listen to Croesus' advice and responded to his counsel with violence, Xerxes, we might think, has shown himself to be the kind of ruler whom it is both fruitless and dangerous to advise. And the ultimate futility of Artabanus' advice in the face of Xerxes' dream may call into question the very idea that human advice can be efficacious at all. As such, it is tempting to see Artabanus' intervention as a total failure.[47] But just as in the case of Cyrus' war council before the decision to invade the Massagetae, we should not evaluate the process of counsel solely by its outcome. Even if Artabanus' advice did not forestall Xerxes' invasion of Greece, it may nonetheless have influenced Xerxes' understanding of the value of counsel.

We can see Artabanus' influence at work in Xerxes' treatment of Demaratus. As Xerxes prepares his fleet and army for the invasion of Greece, he calls on Demaratus, the exiled king of Sparta, for advice. Xerxes' purpose is to learn just how much resistance he can expect from the Greeks. He tells Demaratus his own view of the matter: the Greeks, recognizing how badly outnumbered they are, will not be willing to stand and fight. Yet he also asks Demaratus for his view of the matter (7.101). Given how he organized his war council and his resistance to Artabanus' advice, one might wonder whether Xerxes is altogether serious in his inquiries. Accordingly, Demaratus puts Xerxes' motives to the question: "Sire, shall I tell you the truth or shall I say what will please you?" Xerxes orders him to tell the truth (7.101). The space for giving and receiving good advice is secured by Demaratus ascertaining what Xerxes is really asking for—does he want comforting lies or honest advice?— and by Xerxes' attempts to reassure Demaratus that he will not be punished for speaking frankly. Throughout their conversation, Demaratus frames his advice with invocations of their agreement that honesty is the order of the day (e.g., 7.102). After Xerxes expresses incredulity at Demaratus' claim that the Spartans will resist the Persian invasion no matter how outnumbered, Demaratus again reminds the king of the terms of their discussion: "Sire, from the beginning of this conversation I knew that if I told you the truth you would not like it. But since you compelled me to speak the absolute truth, I have told you how things stand with the Spartans" (7.104). The king is not angry with this reply; instead he laughs and sends him on his way (7.105).[48]

Xerxes' desire to hear from Demaratus speaks to the way in which Artabanus' earlier interventions have partially transformed the king. Demaratus' warnings to Xerxes are not so different from Artabanus' own. Both, for example, stress that the Greeks are excellent fighters.[49] Moreover, Demaratus cannot even seek security in his status, in the way that Artabanus might have found the confidence to speak up by virtue of being Xerxes' uncle. Yet Xerxes does not respond to Demaratus with anger or violence. The king now recognizes the value of honest counsel, even if he finds it in this instance difficult to believe.

Artabanus' warnings about the dangers of slander and the need to hear multiple perspectives on an issue also find reflection in Xerxes' later dealings with Demaratus. Demaratus' accounts of Spartan courage and steadfastness are borne out by the Spartan performance at Thermopylae. Now recognizing him as a trustworthy counselor, Xerxes' calls on Demaratus for advice on his next steps in dealing with the Spartans. Demaratus advises Xerxes to send a portion of his ships and troops to occupy and fortify Cythera, the island off the coast of Laconia that the Athenians would later occupy during the Peloponnesian War. If the Spartans are directly threatened in this manner, Demaratus claims, they will quickly abandon the defense of the rest of Greece and surrender without a fight (7.235). Xerxes' brother Achaemenes takes a different view, advising Xerxes to keep his navy together. He attempts to bolster his argument by attacking Demaratus' motives as a "man who envies your success or perhaps is even acting treacherously against you and your interests. For these are exactly the sorts of things that Hellenes delight in doing. They envy prosperity and hate whoever is better and stronger than themselves." (7.236). Xerxes rejects Achaemenes' slander while accepting his advice: "Achaemenes, you seem to me to speak well and I will do these things. But Demaratus also said to me what he deemed to be best; his advice [*gnōmēi*] was just inferior to yours. But I do not believe that he is not well inclined to my affairs" (7.237).[50] He goes on to explain the basis for his trust in Demaratus: "I reckon this from earlier things he said to me—and also from this: a citizen is often jealous of a fellow citizen's doing well and so is hostile in silence. If a citizen approaches one of his fellows asking for advice, his fellow citizen would not suggest what seemed to him to be the best unless he had come up high into virtue, and such men are rare. But a guest-friend [*xeinos*] is well disposed to a flourishing guest-friend, and being asked for advice, he will advise the best [*sumbouleuomenou te an sumbouleuseie ta arista*]" (7.237).[51] This argument is striking from the Greek perspective, since it rests on a claim that it is co-citizens who are least trustworthy when it comes to giving advice. Xerxes' reasoning here may reflect differences between Persian and Greek understandings of citizenship,[52] but the exchange suggests that Xerxes has thought about whom to trust as an adviser. Moreover, the way in which he orders everyone to cease slandering Demaratus suggests that he has taken Artabanus' advice about slander to heart.

Of course, it is not immediately clear to anyone that Xerxes really has changed. Not even Demaratus fully trusts him. When a fellow Greek reports to Demaratus that he has seen an omen foretelling Persian defeat, Demaratus warns him not to pass on the news to anyone else, least of all Xerxes, fearing how he will respond to the bad news (8.65). Yet Demaratus' fear that Xerxes cannot be relied upon to receive information and advice with a cool head is soon shown to be unwarranted.

As Xerxes prepares his naval forces for what will become his defeat at Salamis, only Artemisia, the tyrant of Caria, dissents from the unanimous view that a naval encounter with the Greeks is desirable (8.68).[53] Herodotus reports that Artemisia's friends were concerned that her dissent was unwise and believed that "she would suffer some punishment from the King for telling him not to wage a battle at sea." Her enemies at court, on the other hand, "were delighted by her response to the question, thinking that she would perish for it" (8.69).[54] Both groups are proven wrong: Xerxes is impressed with Artemisia's opinion and comes to value her even more highly as an adviser (8.69). While he does not follow her advice, he nonetheless subverts the expectations of many in his court by not punishing her for it. Pelling offers the following reading of the episode: "Courts, like Greek states, do not always fit the stereotypes we build of them—even the stereotypes which the narrative has encouraged."[55] But at this point in the narrative, Herodotus has already done as much to undermine these stereotypes as to encourage them. Herodotus depicts Cyrus and Darius as autocrats open to, actively soliciting, and rewarding honest advice. Artabanus' counsel has helped make Xerxes more like these other rulers.

Of course, there are limits to what Xerxes has learned. After the defeat at Salamis, Xerxes calls once more on his advisers. Herodotus notes that Xerxes decides to include Artemisia in his counsels: "He decided to summon Artemisia to join the consultation [es sumbouliēn], because she had obviously been the only one before who had correctly perceived what should be done" (8.101). Artemisia advises Xerxes to return to Persia, leaving Mardonius with the army. In this case, Xerxes accepts her advice. But Herodotus undermines the sense of a successful counsel scene by noting that, in his view, Xerxes only accepted her advice because it corresponded with his own wishes. His fear of the Greeks was the motivating factor in his retreat, not Artemisia's words.[56] Xerxes proves himself, in the end, to be "self-counseling." There is a limit to the power of the adviser: a decision-maker who has already made up his mind may not be amenable to counsel. But this is not the only attitude to counsel we have seen depicted in Herodotus' work.

IV. Dramatizing Advice

Throughout the *Histories*, Herodotus depicts rulers and their advisers working through the problems inherent to their asymmetrical relationship. The scenes of counsel I've analyzed above do not offer simple, programmatic lessons for confronting these problems but rather give the reader a sense of the relevant considerations. To decide matters without counsel—to act *idiobouleuein*—is unwise. And indeed, few actors in the *Histories* reject counsel altogether. Yet listening to good advice does not guarantee that a ruler will follow it, and accepting advice—good or bad—is no guarantee of a good outcome. Herodotus dramatizes the process of counsel throughout his work but offers no promises as to its ultimate efficacy.[57]

A similar conclusion holds for Herodotus' depiction of the motives and interests at play in the politics of advice. In their own ways, Cyrus' discussion with Croesus about the fate of the Lydians and Xerxes' reliance on Demaratus, buttressed by their guest-friendship, represent attempts by autocrats and their advisers to understand whether and how their interests might be aligned. In Herodotus' world, this kind of trust is constructed through speech and action; there is no assumption that the interests of *sumbouloi* and rulers will always be aligned. Nor is it easy for rulers to ascertain when they are. Conversely, there is no sure way for an adviser to portray himself as trustworthy. Herodotus depicts these issues as open-ended problems, and he explores the different ways autocrats and their advisers work through them with varying degrees of success.

For other problems—such as the tendency of the power imbalance between autocrats and advisers to encourage flattery—Herodotus' depictions of rulers and their advisers suggest a number of possible outcomes. We see attempts by would-be advisers such as Coës and Demaratus to negotiate a space for offering honest advice and kings such as Darius and Xerxes acceding in those attempts. We also see figures such as Croesus, Artabanus, and Artemisia taking the risk of speaking frankly to Cambyses and Xerxes, even where they and others have reason to expect that such advice may be met with anger. Herodotus' varied portrayals of the ways in which autocrats and advisers interact tell against readings that make sweeping generalizations about the impossibility of speaking truth to power in Herodotus' world.

Pelling's interpretation of Xerxes' council prior to the invasion of Greece is telling in this regard. He stresses the indirectness of Artabanus' advice in this instance: "Artabanus himself has to tread so very carefully and present his advice so very indirectly."[58] But Pelling's interpretation here clashes with Herodotus' own judgment of Artabanus' conduct. Referring to that same scene later in the text, Herodotus claims that Artabanus gave his opinion "freely" in that instance (7.46). The only other character in the *Histories* singled out by Herodotus for speaking "freely" (*eleutherōs*) is Socleës of Corinth, who rallies the Greeks against tyranny (5.92–93). While that description of Socleës is frequently remarked on and marshaled as evidence for a Herodotean endorsement of the link between Greek ideas of freedom and open debate, the same description of Artabanus is passed over.[59] Frank speech in a tyranny is not impossible: the question is how an autocrat can be made to see its value, and whether and how advisers can be encouraged to supply it.

Of course, in the meeting of the Greeks, Socleës approaches his audience as an equal; Artabanus speaks to Xerxes as a subordinate. There are a number of scenes in the *Histories* depicting Greeks from multiple poleis coming together as equals and discussing their plans for coordinating against the Persians. These settings for counsel have their own dynamics, and Herodotus' interest in process and problems can be found in these scenes as well. Christopher Pelling's analysis of the Greek debate before Salamis makes this point well. He contrasts the "regulated nature of the Persian debate" with "the confusion of the Greek assembly." Pelling argues convincingly that the Greek debate features a distortion of logos no less troubling than the examples we have seen in autocratic courts. Themistocles is unable to convince the assembled Greeks of the threats the Persians pose, and the possibility that the Athenians and others will leave with their ships and return home is ever present. Ultimately, Themistocles is only able to carry the day by trickery. As Pelling puts it, this is a "travesty of logos . . . born of freedom rather than of fear of a master."[60] Pelling thus identifies one strand of problematic Greek discourse, where the problems of distorted logos are a function of Greek freedom and equality rather than of unequal power relationships.

Yet I want to close by cautioning against pushing this line of thought too far. Notice that it recapitulates the free/autocratic distinction between kinds of political discourse, even if it denies that one mode is always superior. This emphasis on difference may prove misleading, for the dynamics of Greek discourse—even democratic discourse—in Herodotus sometimes follow a structure parallel to the Persian cases. Consider first Lampon's proposal to Pausanias, the Spartan general, that the Greeks mutilate Mardonius' corpse (9.78).[61] Pausanias rejects his advice: "As for you, do not ever again approach me with such a suggestion or try to advise me [*mēte sumbouleusēis*], and be thankful to leave here without suffering harm" (9.79). Leaving aside the merit of Lampon's proposal, Pausanias' threat suggests that the dynamics of accountability at play in the relationship between Persian kings and their advisers may have analogs in the Greek world.

Nor are such incidents limited to interactions between powerful generals and subordinates, where unequal power relationships might be expected. In the lead up to Plataea, Mardonius sends peace proposals to the Athenians through an intermediary, Alexander. The Athenians reject the proposals and remain determined to fight. When, a short time later, Mardonius resends his proposals, a remarkable scene unfolds:

> One of the members of the Council, Lykidas [Lycides], declared his opinion that the better course would be to accept the offer of Mourychides and present it to the people. Whether he had received money from Mardoni[u]s or actually liked the idea, this, at least, was the proposal that he publicly expressed. The Athenians, both those in attendance at the council and others outside, at once grew so indignant when they found out about this proposal that they surrounded Lykidas and stoned him until he died. But they sent Mourychides of the Hellespont away unharmed. Now with all the commotion going on at Salamis concerning Lykidas, the Athenian women found out about what had happened, and word of it passed from one woman to the next as they recruited one another, until, on their own initiative, they all went to the home of Lykidas and there stoned to death his wife and children. (9.5)

Pelling glosses the story as evidence of the Athenians' "peculiarly, indeed chillingly, clear commitment to liberty."[62] I am not sure this gets at what is most of interest in the story. By contrast, Sara Forsdyke reads the Lycides episode as a "striking example of joint participation in an instance of popular justice by the members of an official body and a crowd of bystanders."[63] Forsdyke points out that it was primarily elite citizens who were the targets of stoning, which was typically reserved as punishment for "tyrants, traitors, and military commanders thought guilty of misconduct."[64] Herodotus does suggest that Lycides might have been bribed, and so this alleged act of treason might explain his stoning.

Yet I do not think this exhausts the meaning of the episode. After all, Herodotus is not even sure that Lycides was bribed; he leaves it open that Lycides simply approved of Mardonius' proposals. Nor is this idea so farfetched. Xerxes had proposed peace on quite generous terms: an amnesty for "all the wrongs" the Athenians had done to the Persians, the return of Athenian land, whatever extra territory the Athenians might want, and perhaps most importantly, self-government (8.140). It is hardly out of the question that Lycides simply thought that making peace with the Persians was the best thing for the Athenians to do.

Let me propose, then, a second way of understanding Lycides' fate. As Forsdyke notes, "It is perhaps significant, moreover, that Herodotus employs the same term used of heckling in the courts and other civic contexts to describe the noise that attended Lycides' stoning: 'a commotion (*thorubos*) arose . . . around the person of Lycides'. Herodotus' use of this term indicates that he viewed the collective uproar against Lycides as conceptually analogous to collective verbal ridiculing of speakers in civic contexts."[65] Now I think we are getting closer. As Forsdyke here suggests, the proper context for understanding Lycides' punishment is not only how Athenians treat traitors but also how the Athenians treated those men who came before them to persuade them in the assembly and the courts. Lycides' stoning underscores something important about the relationship between Athenians and their advisers. This is not to say that Athenians were in the habit of stoning to death the men who spoke before them in the assembly. But it is to recall the important fact that advisers in the assembly were always accountable for the advice they gave. Lycides' stoning from this perspective is a kind of spontaneous, popular *graphē paranomōn*.[66]

Christopher Pelling has argued that the scenes in which the Athenians treat Persian peace envoys with patience and respect are meant to contrast with how autocrats receive advice: "Democratic Athenians *listen* to unpalatable views."[67] Other scholars have offered generalized versions of the claim: "Herodotus does not record any restrictions concerning [freedom of speech] in the parts of the *Histories* that deal with democracies."[68] John Lombardini has argued that Herodotean *isonomia* signals the *absence* of unequal power relationships: "The equalization of *archē* means that no individual or group possesses *archē*, or *kratos*, in the same way a monarchical or oligarchical ruler does."[69] The Lycides story undercuts such claims. Indeed, the issues and problems Herodotus elucidates in his depiction of counsel in the autocratic case have clear parallels in democratic Athens, obliquely if graphically hinted at in the Lycides story.

4

Responsibility and Accountability in Thucydides' Mytilenean Debate

Introduction

In turning from Herodotus to Thucydides, we move from the councils of Persian kings to the mass meetings of the Athenian assembly. Yet the change of context belies a similarity in the way these texts approach problems of counsel and deliberation. Like Herodotus, Thucydides uses historical narrative and dramatizations of counsel scenes to give readers insight into the circumstances under which political actors might succeed—and fail—in their attempts reliably to make use of the logos of others. The problem of logos in politics cannot be treated merely abstractly. Even where Thucydides' characters offer broader theoretical reflections on logos, counsel, and deliberation, they do so in particular circumstances and for particular ends, and the narrative itself sometimes works to undermine or qualify their claims. The Athenian demos relied on the logos of others to aid in deliberation, in the persons of *sumbouloi* speaking in the assembly. And just as in Herodotus' depiction of counsel in autocratic regimes, Thucydides' depictions of assembly debate raise the question of how accountability relationships structure practices and dynamics of deliberation and advice.[1] Thucydides treats these questions most richly, and explicitly, in the Mytilenean debate.

In 428 BCE, the poleis on the island of Lesbos, led by the Mytileneans, revolted from the Athenian empire. When Mytilene was recaptured, the leaders of the revolt were brought to Athens. The ensuing action constitutes one of the most dramatic episodes in Thucydides' narrative. The Athenian assembly meets to deliberate on the Mytileneans' fate. Furious, the Athenians (at Cleon's instigation) "decided to kill not only the ones there in Athens [Mytileneans previously identified as the leaders of the revolt] but also the whole adult male population of Mytilene, and to enslave the women and children" (3.36).[2]

A ship is dispatched to Mytilene to order the army to carry out the decision. The next day, the Athenians change their minds and call a second assembly to reconsider. A vigorous debate ensues. Cleon, whom Thucydides describes as the "most violent" (*biaiotatos*) and "most persuasive" (*pithanōtatos*) Athenian of his day, argues for the Athenians to stand by their original decision (and his original proposal). Cleon was one of the chief exponents of Athenian imperial policy at the time and an advocate of harsh treatment for allied cities. He is opposed by Diodotus, who proposes restricting the harshest measures to the leaders of the revolt.[3] In a close vote, the Athenians choose Diodotus' proposal. A second ship is sent to countermand the original orders, arriving just as the Athenian general Paches has begun preparations for the executions. "So close," Thucydides writes, "did Mytilene come to disaster" (3.49).

At the heart of the debate between Cleon and Diodotus is the problem of identifying and acting on *aitiai*—that is, questions of responsibility, cause, and blame.[4] Who was ultimately responsible for the Mytileneans' revolt? Does the *aitia* lie with a handful of conspirators? The oligarchic class most opposed to Athens? Or does responsibility reach further, as Cleon explicitly argues, to include the Mytilenean demos and ultimately the city as a whole? Questions of causation and responsibility arise throughout Thucydides' work.[5] Invocations of *aitia* often have a subjective framing: the narrative pays close attention to *actors*' understandings of responsibility.[6] Here in the Mytilenean debate they come in for extended treatment, linked directly to questions of accountability and advice.

Such questions may appear backward-looking and hence irrelevant to the Athenian demos' chief concern. Surely the question the Athenians should focus their deliberations on is "What should we do with the Mytileneans here and now, with an eye to our own future good?" Diodotus frames the question in just this way in his response to Cleon, accusing him of focusing on questions of justice and the past rather than offering advice about Athens' interests and the future (3.44). Cleon's speech might therefore be read as somehow missing the point—or even an abuse of constitutional form, an attempt to turn a deliberative matter into a forensic trial.[7]

But assessments of responsibility and blame are rarely *solely* backward-looking. Understanding an actor's motives and reasons, and assessing who is responsible for actions and outcomes, is one way we grapple with how the same or similarly situated agents might act in the future. Assessments of responsibility are also central to the politics of accountability; to hold actors accountable is usually taken to imply that they are responsible agents who could have acted otherwise. Here, too, assessments of responsibility are not merely retrospective. In holding political actors to account for their past actions, accountability holders mean to influence and control how they and other accountable agents will act in the future. As both Cleon and Diodotus recognize, assessing responsibility for the Mytilenean revolt—and appreciating how other actors will assess it—is crucial to deciding on an effective response to a potential strategic crisis: the revolt of Athens' tribute-paying allies. Cleon and Diodotus will clash over how other cities will perceive responsibility for the revolt and whether Athens is able to influence the choices of other responsible actors. Grappling with *aitia* for the revolt is thus inseparable from the deliberative choice the Athenians face: should the city primarily try to deter future revolts (Cleon's argument) or prioritize bringing them to a satisfactory conclusion (Diodotus')?

The dispute over how to assess the *aitia* for the Mytilenean revolt is paired with a second strand of debate: how to diagnose the deficiencies of Athenian decision-making in the assembly. Both Cleon and Diodotus offer far-reaching critiques of how the Athenians listen to and make use of advice in their deliberations. Scholars have long recognized this dual character of the debate: "The quarrel between Diodotus and Kleon is as much about how to conduct debate in the *ekklēsia* as about the fate of Mytilene."[8] But they have struggled to make sense of it: Why is the debate over the fate of Mytilene linked, in this seemingly artificial way, to a second debate over Athenian practices of public deliberation? As I will argue, this second debate, too, plays out in part as a conflict over assessing *aitia*—who or what is responsible for Athens' failures in deliberating and listening to advice? In their focus on *aitia*, the two strands, otherwise seemingly disconnected, display an underlying unity.

Cleon's advice is both more coherent and more plausible than many scholars recognize. In both parts of his speech, Cleon's advice to the Athenians relies on a consistent account of how the assessment of responsibility can be linked to political action. He promises the Athenians that *aitiai* are transparent and that policy and action will follow simply and directly once responsibility and causality are adequately discerned. Diodotus offers in exchange a view that is less simple and less certain. It recognizes limits on political actors' abilities to assess *aitia* and act on those assessments both in domestic politics and in foreign affairs. As Diodotus stresses, however, a vision of politics where assessments of *aitia* are de-emphasized is in tension with the Athenian commitment to holding advisers accountable for their advice. It is unclear whether the Athenians will be able to accept Diodotus' vision of a prudent city that recognizes the limits of a politics of responsibility and accountability, even if his motion carried the day in the debate over Mytilene.

In what follows, I begin with Thucydides' ambiguous framing of the *aitia* for the Mytilenean revolt in the narrative leading up to the debate, setting the stage for Cleon and Diodotus' clash. I then analyze Cleon and Diodotus' speeches in turn. I argue that paying close attention to how they approach the problem of assessing responsibility reveals a basic coherence to the two parts of each speech. In the conclusion I consider the Mytilenean debate in the context of later episodes in Thucydides' narrative, including the Sicilian expedition and Athenian reprisals against other rebellious allies, such as Scione and Torone.

I. Assessing *Aitia* for the Mytilenean Revolt

Thucydides himself says little explicit about the causes of, and responsibility for, the Mytilenean revolt.[9] The revolt is introduced in the opening narrative of book 3: "Immediately after the Peloponnesian invasion all Lesbos, except Methymna, revolted from Athens. They had been wanting to do that before the war began, but the Spartans were not then willing to receive them as allies" (3.2). In lumping the Mytileneans together with the other poleis on Lesbos, Thucydides offers us little insight into the driving force, domestically, behind the decision to revolt.[10] Throughout most of the narrative "The Mytileneans" are referred to as a unitary actor. This might suggest a high degree of consensus but is also the standard Thucydidean way to refer to a polis acting on the international stage.[11] Thucydides reports some resistance, or at least misgivings, during the early stages of the revolt: the Athenian *proxenoi* at Mytilene were keeping Athens informed of Mytilene's plans (3.2). But Thucydides tells us nothing of whether they had much, or even any, popular support. Further moments of internal dissensus are equally ambiguous. At a critical moment in the Mytilenean bid for independence, hoped-for Spartan aid fails to materialize. The Spartan envoy at Mytilene therefore decides to distribute hoplite armor to the Mytilenean demos. Once armed, the ordinary citizens show themselves to be independent actors. They demand control of the distribution of food and threaten to make a separate peace with the Athenians should their demands go unmet (3.27). The demos' actions here might imply that they only participated in the revolt while they lacked the means to resist the commands of those in charge. But it is equally possible that they simply realized, earlier than the Spartan envoy and the Mytilenean elites, that the revolt had failed and therefore attempted to position themselves advantageously for the coming reckoning with Athens.[12]

In contrast to Thucydides' authorial reticence, the actors in the narrative seek to assess *aitia* explicitly. The Mytileneans themselves offer an account of the "reasons and causes" (*prophaseis kai aitias*) for their revolt when they send an envoy asking for assistance from the Spartans (3.13). The Mytileneans attempt to exculpate themselves by shifting responsibility for the revolt to Athens' imperial abuses. When the Athenians began to treat the other allies as subjects, the Mytileneans could no longer trust them: "It seemed unlikely that men who had subjugated our fellow allies, protected though we all were by treaty, would not deal with the rest of us the same way if they ever had the power to do so" (3.10.6). What kept the Mytileneans in check was a "balance of fear" and the recognition that they had little to gain from aggression (3.11.2). When the balance of fear was disturbed, the Mytileneans took their chance: "We were constrained to remain allies more by fear than friendship; whichever of us was first emboldened by a sense of security was also going to be the first to transgress in some way" (3.12.1). Here any sense of Mytilenean agency and choice recedes as they present their decision to revolt as practically necessitated by Athens' transformation into an imperial power. On their account, Athens, rather than the Mytilenean demos or oligarchs, is truly responsible for the cities' falling out.

The Athenians, too, work to identify the responsible parties for the revolt, and unsurprisingly have a rather different view of the matter. In the wake of Mytilene's capitulation, the Athenian general Paches begins the process of assigning responsibility and blame. He initially singles out "those of the Mytileneans who had been most involved in the negotiations with the Spartans" along with "anyone else who seemed to him implicated in the revolt [*aitios edokei einai tēs apostaseōs*]" (3.28, 3.35) to send back to Athens. It is also clear that the question of responsibility remains on the Athenians' mind as they deliberate—and deliberate again—over the Mytileneans' fate. Thucydides attributes the Athenians' change of mind to the recognition that it would be "savage and extreme . . . to destroy an entire city rather than just those directly responsible [*tous aitious*]" (3.36).

Thucydides' reticence, and the ambiguity of the narrative, thus contrast with his portrayal of actors keenly interested in assessing *aitia* for the revolt. A number of scholars have argued that Thucydides makes no explicit authorial statement about the Mytilenean demos' complicity because the question was ultimately of secondary interest to him: "By depriving us . . . of the information required to form a firm opinion one way or the other, he insures that our response to the ensuing debate will turn on more fundamental issues."[13] I rather think that he has crafted the narrative precisely to draw attention to the problem of making such assessments of responsibility in politics. As Hornblower notes, Thucydides likely had available a further account of the origins of the conflict, which he makes no mention of in the narrative.[14] Aristotle offers a simple story—presumably current when Thucydides was writing as well—tracing the revolt to a dispute over heiresses. One Mytilenean, a *proxenos* of Athens, wished to marry his sons to the two wealthy daughters of a recently deceased prominent citizen. When his suit was rejected he provoked the *stasis* and called on Athens to intervene.[15] Aristotle's account, in which a single actor is ascribed primary responsibility for the revolt, works a very different effect on the reader than Thucydides' narrative. Canvassing multiple possibilities and explicitly endorsing none, Thucydides has left the right way to understand responsibility for the Mytilenean revolt open to competing interpretations. The uncertainty in Thucydides' narrative is reflected in the Mytilenean debate itself: assessments of responsibility and motive will be crucial to Athens' deliberations. Cleon and Diodotus offer the assemblymen—and Thucydides' readers—fundamentally different orientations to questions of responsibility. These orientations structure both their approach to the problem of Mytilene and their reflections on Athenian debate, the politics of advice-giving, and the proper way for a decision-maker to make use of the logos of others.

II. Cleon's Speech

Cleon takes *aitia* seriously. He addresses the question of the responsibility for the revolt directly: "Let them now be punished, therefore, in the way the crime deserves, *and do not let the blame fall on the ruling few, while you absolve the people [kai mē tois men oligois hē aitia prostethēi, ton de dēmon apolusēte]*. They all of them joined in attacking you, though if they had taken our side they could now be back in possession of their city. They judged, however, that siding with their rulers presented the safer option and so joined in the revolt with them" (3.39.6, emphasis mine). Cleon's insistence on the shared responsibility of the Mytilenean demos for the revolt is one of the outstanding features of his speech. Maurice Pope has argued that Cleon here commits himself to a "holistic view" of the demos meaning the "whole citizenry," and that it is this commitment that drives his argument for punishing the entire city.[16] Yet throughout his speech, Cleon makes distinctions between elites and ordinary citizens (as we will see, both in Mytilene and in Athens). In this passage, too, Cleon comfortably distinguishes between the Mytilenean demos and the *oligoi*. Cleon is not advancing a claim that since Mytilene qua polis acted, all the inhabitants of Mytilene are therefore ipso facto responsible. Rather, he is arguing that the demos, understood separately from the *oligoi*, is equally responsible because they *joined in* the revolt (*xunapestēsan*) with the few.[17] Far from assuming a holistic account of responsibility, Cleon argues directly for it. He does so, as we shall see, because getting such assignations of responsibility right is central to his understanding of politics.

As scholars have long noted, Cleon's speech represents an attempt to bring together considerations of justice and advantage. His claim about the Mytileneans' shared responsibility for the revolt is central to both sides of his argument. Consider first Cleon's use of the language of punishment. As Edward Harris has argued, throughout his speech Cleon adopts the tactics and forensic rhetoric of a prosecutor.[18] The invocation of responsibility is crucial to Cleon's case: all of the Mytileneans *deserve* the death penalty because they were all responsible for the revolt. Cleon recognizes excusing conditions that generally absolve agents from responsibility and blame, such as compulsion (3.39.2).[19] But he is at pains to argue that these do not apply in the Mytilenean case. The demos willingly joined the revolt, calculating that it would be to their advantage: "They did us harm not through some involuntary deed but in a deliberate act of conspiracy, and one only pardons what is involuntary" (3.40.1).

The Mytileneans' joint responsibility for the revolt also features as a core premise of Cleon's second, future-oriented argument that destroying the city and executing the Mytilenean demos would be advantageous to Athens. Cleon stresses that there is far more at stake here for Athens than the fate of one city. What Athens does with Mytilene will send a clear signal to the other allies: "Think of your allies too. If you impose just the same penalty on those who choose to revolt [*tois hekousin*] as on those who are forced to do so [*tois te anagkastheisin*] by the enemy, who is there, do you think, who will not revolt on the slightest pretext [*bracheiai prophasei*], when the reward for success is liberation and the penalty for failure is easy to bear?" (3.39.7). Cleon's argument from advantage is a classic statement of deterrence theory.[20] But notice that the logic of deterrence depends crucially on the voluntariness of the Mytilenean demos' participation in the revolt, which also (as we saw in his discussion of the justice of their punishment) grounds their responsibility for it. If Athens' aim is to deter the demos in other allied and subject cities from choosing to participate in future revolts, then it must neatly sort rebels into the categories of "willing and responsible" versus "involuntary and coerced." It must then send a strong signal by punishing harshly those in the first category. This is the logic behind Cleon's claim that the Mytilenean demos must be made to suffer the consequences of their voluntary actions: what is at stake is not only punishment but a successful policy of deterrence with respect to other allied poleis.

As I suggested above, Cleon's interest in *aitia* also structures the first half of his speech, where he offers a critique of Athenian assembly debate. Tying the two halves of the speech together is a coherent theory of responsibility threaded through both. To see that though, we first have to isolate what exactly Cleon's critique of Athenian public deliberation is.

Cleon's speech has come in for its share of criticism from scholars and commentators. Cleon is considered an opponent of intellectualism, a crude demagogue and populist, a rhetorician and manipulator of the emotions of the crowd—in short, an enemy of democratic deliberation and the use of lo-gos in politics.[21] These claims all capture something of the spirit of his speech. Cleon is unafraid to endorse "ignorance" over "cleverness"—at least if the former is paired with "moderation" (*amathia te meta sōphrosunēs*) and the latter with "intemperance" (*dexiotēs meta akolasias*; 3.37.3). His claim that the "unsophisticated" (*phauloteroi*) are, for the most part, better managers of the city's affairs than their "intellectual superiors" (*tous xunetōterous*) is a classic piece of populist rhetoric (3.37.3); William F. Buckley was channeling Cleon when he said, "I would rather be governed by the first 2000 people in the Boston telephone directory than by the 2000 people on the faculty of Harvard University." Cleon urges the Athenians to recall their initial an-ger at the Mytileneans and to vote to punish them severely in what looks like a manipulative and cynical appeal to emotion: "Recall as closely as you can how you felt then and how you would have given anything then to beat them. This is your chance to pay them back" (3.40.7). Moreover, as we shall see, while Cleon's speech contains a critique of rhetoric, commentators note that he is happy to make use of the very techniques he abjures in a kind of "rhetoric of anti-rhetoric."[22] Cleon's opposition to reconsidering the Mytilene-ans' punishment—"I myself haven't changed my mind at all"—is, of course, in part self-interested: as the proposer of the original punishment, his repu-tation and policy are at stake in the decision to reopen debate (3.38).[23] Yet his obstinacy also makes him appear to be an enemy of deliberation and perhaps even the use of logos in politics. Certainly Diodotus is happy enough to paint him in such a light. Diodotus frames his opening response to Cleon around the value of logoi: "As for words, anyone who argues seriously that they should not guide our actions is either stupid or has some personal interest at stake: stupid, if he thinks there is any other way to explore the future in all its uncertainty; self-interested, if he wants to argue some discreditable case but concludes that though he cannot speak well enough to carry a bad cause he can slander well enough to intimidate both the opposing speakers and the audience" (3.42.2). The criticism is aimed squarely at Cleon. Diodotus is responding directly to Cleon's accusation that anyone who would speak in favor of Mytilene at this point must either be overconfident and arrogant or else have been bribed (3.38.2) and is repaying him in kind: Cleon must either be self-interested or stupid. But does it hit the mark?

Scholars who follow Diodotus in labeling Cleon an enemy of deliberation and a foe of logos in politics have, in my view, failed to understand what Cleon is arguing and the force of his position. Here turning to the Spartan ephor Sthenelaidas' speech to the Spartan assembly, to which Cleon's is often compared, is instructive.[24] Cleon's speech contains verbal echoes of Sthenelaidas', but the differences between the two are just as revealing. In book 1, the Spartans consider whether to declare war on Athens. Corinthian and Athenian delegations speak for and against war before the Spartan assembly, followed by the Spartan king Archidamus, who urges caution. Sthenelaidas then gives a short speech in favor of taking immediate action against Athens. Sthenelaidas begins his speech with a disdainful dismissal of logoi: "The Athenians spoke a great deal but I have no idea what they meant" (1.86.1). Here Sthenelaidas aligns himself with Spartan practices of *brachulogia* ("succinct speech"), but his mistrust of speeches also resonates with Cleon's attacks on his fellow orators' clever rhetoric. Sthenelaidas frames his short speech around the injustices committed by the Athenians and the Spartan need to punish them for their crimes against Sparta's allies and the people of the Peloponnese.[25] He thus shares a vocabulary with Cleon's accusations against Mytilene (although, unlike Cleon's deterrence theory, Sthenelaidas does not explicitly link the discourse of wrongdoing and punishment to an argument about Sparta's future-oriented interests). Sthenelaidas invokes Spartan steadfastness—"We, however are the same now as we were then" (1.86.2)—just as Cleon will claim, with respect to Mytilene: "I haven't changed my mind at all." Sthenelaidas concludes his main line of argument by questioning the value of deliberation altogether: "Don't let anyone tell us that it is fitting to deliberate [*prepei bouleuesthai*] while we are being treated unjustly. It is much more fitting for those who are about to commit injustice to spend a lot of time in deliberation" (1.86.4).[26] Sthenelaidas sees no need for the Spartans to deliberate at all. While the Athenians might need to carefully think things through as they hatch their unjust plots, the correct response to Athenian aggression is simple and clear: "With the gods on our side let us advance on the wrongdoers" (1.86.5).[27] The Spartans need not carefully weigh and consider their options, and it is far from clear that in Sthenelaidas' view logoi would be of any help in doing so (see 1.86.3).

   In contrast with Sthenelaidas' brute rejection of deliberation, Cleon's argument is considerably subtler. The difference between their positions is neatly captured in Cleon's withering criticism of his fellow citizens: "You sit here more like an audience of spectators at a performance of sophists than men deliberating about matters of state [*peri poleōs bouleuomenois*]" (3.38.7).[28] Far from rejecting deliberation, as Sthenelaidas does, Cleon accuses his fellow citizens of *failing to deliberate*. Seemingly paradoxically, this is so even when they reconvene the assembly, ostensibly to deliberate *again* about the Mytileneans. How are we to understand Cleon's argument here?

It is clear that Cleon is not telling his audience that they should strive to participate more actively as *speakers* in the assembly's debates. He has nothing but scorn for those citizens who wish to emulate the orators (3.38.6). But that does not mean, as Noémie Villacèque has concluded, that Cleon's argument here amounts to a "brutal calling into question of the *ekklēsia*, which is to say of democracy itself. For Cleon does not content himself with critiquing *isēgoria*; he castigates, more broadly, democratic deliberation."[29] His claim instead is that deliberation is not first and foremost a matter of *speaking*. It rather requires attending to advice, to the logos of others, and doing so *in the right way*. Cleon's claim is that when the Athenians sit in the assembly, they may decide matters, but they fail to adopt the practices and postures appropriate to deliberation and judgment.[30] The democratic audience likes to listen—Cleon accuses them of being slaves to the pleasures of the ear—but they do not know what to listen for: "You judge the feasibility of future projects from the performance of good speakers [*apo tōn eu eipontōn*], and the facts of past events from the speeches of clever critics, preferring to believe in what you hear rather than in the deeds you can actually witness" (3.38.4). Cleon here contrasts *erga* and logoi, but not to denigrate the use of logoi altogether. The problem is rather that the Athenians judge matters based on the rhetorical performance of their advisers rather than the content of the advice. Strangely enough for a supposed enemy of logos in politics, Cleon offers an attack on politics as theater that should resonate with contemporary theorists concerned for the *quality* of democratic discourse. Cleon has not offered a wholesale critique of logos in politics so much as a pointed critique of the *ways* in which the Athenians make use of the logos of others—that is, the ways in which they engage with advice.

Cleon's analysis of Athens' deliberative foibles draws a sharp distinction between ordinary citizens, who listen and vote, and those who speak in the assembly to advise the demos and offer proposals. The central claim he makes is that the democratic audience, while unsophisticated, may yet exercise better judgment in political matters than elite orators. He links this claim to a puzzling invocation of "the laws." Clever orators, Cleon argues, always want to appear wiser than the laws. Ordinary citizens, by contrast, "distrusting their own intelligence, judge themselves less learned than the laws and less competent than a fine speaker to criticise an argument. Content to be judges among equals [*apo tou isou*] rather than competing contestants, they are generally the more successful citizens" (3.37.4). Cleon's conclusion from all this is that a city fares better with bad laws that are enforced than good laws that lack authority (3.37.3). How precisely this discussion of the laws is meant to support his argument against revising the decision on Mytilene is not entirely clear. He seems to be suggesting that in light of his analysis, decisions of the assembly should remain firm. Scholars sometimes take Cleon's argument here to rely on an appeal to tradition and a kind of democratic conservatism, "a professed reverence for the past as a restraint."[31] But as they recognize, it is an odd appeal, since it requires identifying the decision to punish the Mytileneans—taken only the day before(!)—with "law" and imbuing it with a hallowed status.[32]

While Cleon's invocations of the law are confusing, I think we can understand him here as making an argument in favor of a kind of *epistemic deference*. Viewed in this light, Cleon's populism seems to appeal to a kind of humility. Ordinary citizens, he thinks, should recognize their own limitations. (Indeed, their great virtue is that they are more capable of doing so than clever elites.) Cognizant of those limitations, they should take advantage of the fact that they do not have to judge alone. Assemblies are collective actors, in which each citizen acts as a judge among equals. To judge oneself as less learned than the *laws*, in this context, might be to show epistemic deference to a previously made majority decision, and to show this kind of epistemic deference is, in Cleon's view, an appropriate response to the difficult tasks of deciding between alternatives and judging competing logoi. This is not an argument against deliberation altogether, or against listening to advice. It may not even be an argument against reconsidering all assembly decisions. But it suggests that in Cleon's view, to reopen the decision on Mytilene demonstrates a lack of self-awareness and appropriate respect for majority rule—particularly if the decision is being reopened for the wrong reasons.

When Cleon summarizes his central arguments, he claims that three things in particular are the most prejudicial to the exercise of rule (*axumphorōtatois tēi archēi*): pity (*oiktōi*), equity (*epieikeiai*), and "taking pleasure in speeches" (*hēdonēi logōn*; 3.40.2). With respect to the third obstacle, we have already seen that it would be a mistake to put the emphasis here on the *speeches*. The problem is the *pleasure* the Athenians take in oratory, not the speeches themselves. As Cleon goes on to argue, "As for the orators who delight us with their speeches, they will have other arenas for display in matters of less moment, not when the city pays a heavy penalty for its brief pleasure while they themselves get a fine reward for their fine speeches" (3.40.3). This is not a claim that orators should be banished from the assembly. It is a claim that the function of oratory in the assembly is to inform action, not to delight.[33] To treat assembly debate as an occasion for listening to pleasurable speeches may work out just fine for the orators, Cleon argues, but not for the polis: "In contests of this kind, however, the city bestows the prizes on others, while she herself bears all the risks [*tous kindunous anapherei*]" (3.38.3).

Even Cleon's disturbing appeals to anger, a powerful tool of demagoguery, need to be read carefully. Here his worries about the power of pity are worth lingering on, since they contextualize his attempts to rekindle the Athenians' original anger at the Mytileneans. It is an oversimplification to say that "Cleon actually advocated making decisions in the heat of passion" as though this were a matter of principle.[34] Rather, Cleon appeals to anger as a countervailing force to the Athenians' pity and compassion, which he argues is dangerously clouding their judgment: "You do not realize that with every mistake they talk you into and every concession you make out of compassion your weakness does more to expose you to danger than to win the gratitude of your allies."[35] It is here that Cleon makes the comparison between the demos and the tyrant explicit: "You do not see that the empire you hold is a tyranny, and one imposed on unwilling subjects who for their part plot against you" (3.37.2). On Cleon's view, the Athenians believe that they can afford to act as mere spectators of speeches, and to give in to the pity they feel for the Mytileneans, precisely because they do not understand the reality of their own rule.[36] More generally, while Cleon's appeal to anger in this instance is in the service of a savage end, it is not obvious that Thucydides means to offer a broad critique of the use of emotional appeals in political discourse. After all, Thucydides praises Pericles directly in the narrative for his ability to modulate the Athenians' emotions in similar fashion (2.65.8–9).

I have offered up to this point a sympathetic reconstruction of Cleon's argument in the interest of drawing out what is at stake in his claims and explaining their power. Nonetheless, commentators are right to treat his speech with suspicion. For Cleon does not rest content with offering a diagnosis of the problems with Athenian deliberative practices; he also identifies the responsible parties. Some of the blame lies with the demos' advisers: orators like him "should . . . not be so carried away by cleverness and contests of wit that we offer you, the public, perverse advice" (3.37.5). Yet primary responsibility lies with the audience of ordinary citizens: "You have yourselves to blame for perverting these contests [*aitioi d' humeis kakōs agōnothetountes*]" (3.38.4). Here is a striking parallel to his analysis of Mytilene's revolt. Cleon there argues strenuously for the collective responsibility of the Mytilenean demos; similarly, he holds the Athenian demos collectively responsible for the failures of Athenian assembly debate.[37] Athens' advisers are simply following the lead of an audience of citizens that rewards cleverness, novelty, and paradox over sound advice. What links the two sections of Cleon's speech together is therefore a certain way of understanding responsibility and its relevance for political action. On Cleon's model of politics, decision-makers best proceed by investigating and assessing responsibility for the problems they face— that is, by identifying the relevant *aitia*—and then acting confidently on that basis. This is done at least in part through listening to advice like Cleon's. And these kinds of assessments are well within the capability of ordinary citizens. Indeed, they can even make these assessments about themselves. They can recognize when they are responsible for their own problems, engaging in practices of self-critique and self-correction (with Cleon's help, of course).

Cleon offers this model presumably because he recognizes that it is powerfully attractive. It would be a mistake to view Cleon as simply trading on the Athenians' anger and desire to punish. Rather, he holds out to his audience the possibility of responding to politics in a straightforward way: responsibility and causality can be easily assessed and acted upon. Consider Cleon's advice for how the Athenians might improve their practices of public deliberation. He calls on his audience to recognize their bad habits—their privileging of performance over substance, thereby reducing politics to spectatorship. Once they come to see their own responsibility for the problem, they can adjust their actions and practices accordingly. Cleon aims to forestall a change of policy toward Mytilene in part by turning the Athenians away from faulty deliberative practices: "These are the habits of mind I am trying to make you abandon [*apotrepein*] when I tell you plainly that Mytilene has wronged you more than any other single state" (3.39.1).

The tenor of Cleon's speech is not flattering, as other scholars have noted.[38] But in assuming that the Athenians are responsible for their own problems and hence capable of solving them simply by changing their practices, he offers a flattering (because inflated) account of their own collective agency and power.[39] This is a superficially attractive and reassuring vision, but it is also a profoundly misleading and even dangerous one. For the soundness of Cleon's advice depends crucially on whether he has assessed *aitia* correctly and, more broadly, on the general transparency of *aitia* to political actors. If the Athenian demos is not actually responsible for the corruption of assembly debate, there is little reason to think that their attempts to change their behavior— say, by simply deciding to act like "deliberators" rather than "spectators"— would have any ameliorative effect. As I will show in the next section, this is a crucial element of Diodotus' critique of Cleon.

Similarly, it is only Cleon's insistence on the transparency of *aitia*, and hence his confidence in unproblematic and simple ascriptions of responsibility, that allows him to bring advantage and justice together in his advice concerning Mytilene. To see this, let us grant to Cleon that the Mytilenean demos really was responsible for the revolt, insofar as they joined in willingly. Let us also grant to him the logic of his deterrence theory. If the allies know that the Athenians punish "willing revolters" harshly, they will duly take that into account when they decide whether or not to revolt. But how they respond to

Athens' signal will depend on whether *aitiai* really are transparent to all. For the allies to get the right message from Athens' punishing Mytilene, they too must recognize that the Mytilenean demos joined the revolt willingly. Otherwise, Athens will look like an indiscriminate punisher rather than a judicious employer of force, and the expected deterrent effect will not materialize. Similarly, imagine members of a demos in an allied polis who believe they could revolt but plausibly deny that they did so willingly (claiming to be coerced or otherwise acting out of necessity). They, too, would not be deterred. The collective nature of the demos as a political actor plays a role here as well. If we decompose the demos into a mass of ordinary citizens who might themselves disagree strongly about a proposed course of action, imputations of responsibility to the demos as a whole might seem even less secure and the signaling game correspondingly more complicated.[40] Finally, judgments of necessity may themselves be as fluid and indeterminate as assessments of responsibility (e.g., the Mytileneans' presentation to the Spartans of the practical necessities they acted under in staging their revolt).[41] Cleon's deterrence theory requires that the Athenians accurately and reliably ascribe responsibility in cases of revolt and that they are able to signal both their ascriptions and the reliability of those ascriptions to other actors. We can see, then, that the logic of the theory requires exactly what Cleon is so eager to loudly proclaim: that judgments about responsibility are uncomplicated and transparent. If they are not, Cleon's advice becomes much less compelling. Of course, a policy of harsh, indiscriminate, collective punishment, regardless of responsibility, might also serve as a deterrent. But Cleon does not advocate directly for such a policy, perhaps because he wants to convince the Athenians that punishing the Mytileneans is not only expedient but also *just*.[42]

We've already been primed by the difficulties of assessing *aitia*, as implied by Thucydides' introduction to the Mytilenean debate, to think that there is something too simple about Cleon's analysis of both domestic deliberation and international politics. Cleon's speech—with his emphasis on facts, deeds, and the harsh demands of empire—"warns us to be wary of those who purvey political fantasies in the place of political realities."[43] But part of the irony of Thucydides' presentation of the speech is that Cleon's arguments themselves ultimately rest on fantasy: that responsibility is easy to assess, that such assessments can be easily translated into the basis for political action, and that the demos is responsible for its own problems and hence can easily adjust its actions and practices. It is this portrait of powerful democratic agency, linked to a simplistic but seemingly attractive model of responsibility, which explains Cleon's demagogic appeal. It is no surprise, then, that Diodotus in reply will aim to undercut Cleon's speech by complicating assessments of responsibility, both in the domestic case and in international affairs.

III. Diodotus' Speech

Diodotus begins his speech with two disclaimers: "I do not censure [*oute . . . aitiōmai*] those who propose to reopen the debate about Mytilene, nor do I commend [*oute . . . epainō*] those who object to deliberating about the greatest matters many times over" (3.42.1).[44] Diodotus' twin refusals—to hold actors responsible and to praise them—are at the heart of his position and signal the terrain on which the deepest disagreements between him and Cleon lie. In contrast to Cleon's hunt for *aitiai*, Diodotus counsels his audience to resist both the urge to ascribe responsibility and blame and the urge to praise those whose actions and advice they find most congenial.

Cleon attacked his opponents with slander and accusations of bribery, and Diodotus responds by arguing that such tactics have corrosive effects on the practice of advice-giving: "When the charge is malpractice the speaker becomes an object of suspicion if he succeeds, and is thought dishonest as well as stupid if he fails. The city too loses out in this situation, since fear robs it of its counselors [*phobōi gar apostereitai tōn xumboulōn*]" (3.42.3–4). We might therefore think that Diodotus does assess *aitiai*, blaming Athens' advisers rather than the demos for the pathologies of assembly debate. Orators like Cleon, whose slanderous tactics put speakers' motivations under intense scrutiny, create a climate of fear and distrust.

But as Diodotus develops his argument, he does not focus on blaming Athens' advisers. Instead, he proceeds to offer an alternative description of successful assembly debate with attention to the practices of both advisers and their audience: "The good citizen should not want to frighten his opponents, but should want to prove the better speaker from a position of equality [*apo tou isou*]. A moderate city [*sōphrona polin*] should not pile honors on the one who regularly gives good advice, but nor should it take away those he has. And the city should not punish the speaker who happens not to win the debate—indeed, it should not even dishonor him" (3.42.5).[45] Diodotus' portrait of the "moderate city" is one where the stakes of speaking in the assembly are dramatically lowered. Speakers whose advice is found persuasive should not be held in higher esteem and rewarded more than those whose advice is rarely followed. The consequences for failing to persuade should be similarly low. Diodotus does not deny that in some sense speakers are competing with one another. Each should offer the best advice he can, and where there is disagreement, an adviser should try to persuade his audience that he is right and his opponent is wrong. But in the moderate city, such competition is structured so that both the benefits of winning and the consequences of losing are minimized.

This is the key to understanding why Diodotus ascribes these practices to a "moderate city." The citizens of such a city would have enough self-control or self-knowledge to recognize that sustaining practices of good advice-giving requires restraint in how they reward and punish their advisers. It might seem only natural for a decision-maker to encourage and reward the advice he finds congenial and persuasive and to disincentivize bad advice. But Diodotus explains why this is a self-defeating practice that will quickly distort the practice of advice-giving if left unchecked, even if decision-makers begin by rewarding only genuinely good advice. If persuasive advisers are routinely rewarded and the unpersuasive ignored (or worse, punished), the successful will be tempted to speak against their own judgment (*para gnōmēn*) and instead to gratify (*pros charin*) in order to continue to win favor. The unsuccessful speakers will resort to similar kinds of flattery in imitation (3.42.6). And the problem is not only speaking *pros charin*—slander and accusations such as Cleon's are also a predictable result of the high-stakes incentives built into assembly debate.

Clifford Orwin has argued that Diodotus' "proposed reform" is "utopian," "a spurious solution that serves to clarify a genuine problem." But I am not convinced that Diodotus is offering a "proposed reform," exactly, nor that he is quite so utopian as Orwin makes him out to be. Orwin attacks Diodotus for advocating the impossible: "To enact someone's advice *is* to honor him. . . . The habitually persuasive enjoy great repute (which in turn enhances their persuasiveness), while those who go always unheeded get none. This is not a matter of positive law, and no law or usage can hope to oppose it."[46] But surely Diodotus' suggestion is that this a matter of degree. Recall Xerxes' response to Achaemenes' slander of Demaratus: "Achaemenes, you seem to me to speak well and I will do these things. But Demaratus also said to me what he deemed best." Xerxes proves himself capable (at least at this moment) of the kind of deliberative practice Diodotus ascribes to the moderate city: he makes a distinction between Demaratus' advice (which he finds unpersuasive) and his esteem for and trust in Demaratus as an adviser (which remains undiminished). The deliberative practices of the moderate city may never be fully realized but might still serve as a kind of regulative ideal, to be recognized as a good and achieved when and where and to the degree possible.

The real problem with the moderate city's deliberative practices, from an Athenian perspective, is not that they are fundamentally unrealizable owing to the limits of our all-too-human nature.[47] Rather, they imply a deep challenge to Athenian accountability politics. Diodotus recognizes that in Athens—in contrast to his vision of the moderate city where the stakes of speaking are low—advisers are accountable to the demos for the advice they give: "In matters of great importance like the present one, however, we should be expected to take a rather longer view in what we say than the limited attention you give matters, especially since we as advisers can be held responsible in a way that you as listeners are not [*hupeuthunon tēn parainesin echontas pros aneuthunon tēn humeteran akroasin*]" (3.43.4).[48] Diodotus shows an awareness of the logic of holding advisers accountable for their advice. The audience of ordinary citizens, not unlike Herodotus' Persian kings, are dependent on advisers for the advice they give. Diodotus acknowledges that holding advisers responsible for their advice might work to incentivize them to offer the best advice they can—to exercise careful forethought. But the asymmetry of accountability has, perhaps, an unintended consequence. As he continues, "If those who gave advice and those who followed it suffered the same consequences you would make your decisions more carefully. But as it is, in the mood of the moment, when things go wrong you punish the single judgment of your adviser not the multiple judgments on all your own parts that were implicated in the same error" (3.43.5). Here Diodotus offers an analysis of the distribution of rewards and risks under Athens' current set of deliberative practices that differs markedly from Cleon's. Recall that on Cleon's view, when deliberation is treated as a spectator sport, "the city bestows the prizes on others [the orators], while she herself bears all the risks" (3.38.3; see p. 115 above). Diodotus by contrast pays close attention to the asymmetric structure of Athenian accountability practices (note in particular the contrast between advisers who are *hupeuthunoi* and the demos as *aneuthunos* at 3.43.4). This leads him to make the opposite claim: ordinary citizens, as unaccountable voters in the assembly, are insulated from the consequences of their decisions, while accountable advisers suffer punishment. Diodotus accepts that asymmetric accountability might incentivize advisers to take their role seriously.[49] And by outsourcing responsibility for assembly decisions to their advisers, the Athenian demos may hope to limit their liability for their decisions and exposure to the consequences.[50] Yet Diodotus' worry is that this licenses an unserious approach to deliberation and decision on the part of the democratic audience. Athenian accountability practices are incompatible with the deliberative practices of the moderate city: the accountable adviser is an agent susceptible to punishment and reward in precisely the ways that Diodotus finds troubling. Diodotus' warnings against hunting for *aitiai* thus strike at the heart of Athens' accountability politics.

There is a sense in which Diodotus' critique here nearly converges with Cleon's. Both are concerned that the audience of decision-makers in the democratic assembly may fail to take their deliberative duties seriously (Cleon expresses this concern in the language of spectatorship, Diodotus in the language of irresponsibility). Yet Diodotus never takes the further step of *blaming* the demos—of making a final assessment of *aitia*—for the problem. His unwillingness to assign responsibility to a single party is underlined by his claim that the demos and its advisers "share in a fault" together (*xunexēmarton*), insofar as anyone is at fault at all (3.43.5). In refusing to offer a simple assessment of responsibility for the current state of affairs, he likewise offers no clear path forward.[51] In this he remains consistently opposed to Cleon, who so sanguinely identified both responsibility for the pathologies of assembly debate (the demos, acting more like spectators than deliberators) and a proposed solution (the demos should simply change their habits and practices and the rest will follow). Diodotus has sketched for the assembly a different model of deliberation and an *explanation* for why Athenian assembly debate does not conform to this model—their commitment to a politics of accountability, including accountability for advice. But Diodotus offers no suggestions for how the Athenians might change their practices. There is no explicit injunction to "adopt the practices of the moderate city" akin to Cleon's injunction to adopt the practices of "deliberators" over those of "spectators." Perhaps Diodotus can be read as suggesting the Athenians should adopt a set of institutions that would promote coaccountability between decision-makers and advisers. But just how to institutionalize such a plan is far from clear. As I argued above (chapter 1), reciprocal accountability is difficult to achieve given the constraints of mass democratic politics.

When Diodotus turns to the Mytileneans, he continues to differentiate his analysis from Cleon's primarily through the lens of his understanding of *aitia* and its relevance in decision-making. Diodotus directly attacks Cleon's theory of deterrence. He offers a picture of human nature in which hope and desire are more powerful motivators than fear.[52] Cities will run great risks to achieve great aims, including their freedom (3.45.6). This has important implications for any theory of deterrence: "It is a fact of human nature—and it is very naïve of anyone to believe otherwise—that when people are really committed in their hearts to doing something they cannot be deterred by force of law or by any other threat" (3.45.7). If Diodotus is right, Cleon's search for the *aitia* turns out to be idle, since Athens should not assume it has the power to deter allies' revolts no matter how harshly it punishes.

Instead of aiming to identify the *aitia* accurately, the Athenians would be better served by treating the concept as malleable and wielding it to political effect. If the goal of Athens' foreign policy is to deter future rebels, identifying those responsible and punishing them severely would make sense. But given his skepticism about the possibility of deterrence, he offers a different goal: to make subject cities accept their status with minimal destruction and waste of resources. Athens should work to prevent rebellions to the degree possible. And when cities do rebel, the penalties should be selective, primarily limited to the oligarchic class, so that the reconquered city can continue to contribute to the empire. All of this involves taking a consciously narrow view of responsibility: "After suppressing any revolt we should limit the blame [*tēn aitian*] as much as possible" (3.46.6). Diodotus does not go so far as to claim that assessments of responsibility are entirely subjective. He accepts Cleon's distinction between allies who rebel willingly and those who are coerced into doing so (3.47.2–3). Yet he counsels the Athenians not to focus on the truth of the matter, even insofar as it can accurately be identified. In dealing with the demos in a rebellious city, Diodotus counsels, "What you should do, even if they were guilty, is pretend that they were not, to prevent the only faction still loyal to us from becoming hostile" (3.47.4). Assessments of *aitia* can be useful fictions, made more with an eye to influencing future actions than accurately representing past ones.

Cleon's arguments stand and fall with his imputations of responsibility, and Diodotus accordingly undermines them by showing the Athenians the limits of a politics of assessing responsibility and blame. He offers a sketch of what a different politics might look like, both at home and abroad. Diodotus' advice may appear superior, since it does not hinge on making difficult, even illusory, assessments of *aitia*. But his analysis may nonetheless be hard to act on. As we have seen, he offers no simple solutions to improve Athenian deliberative practices. Nor are the practical implications of his foreign policy advice obvious. Whether the Athenians will be able to learn from his advice and put his logoi to use is unclear.

At the end of Diodotus' speech, the Athenians turn to vote: "Such was Diodotus' speech. These contrary arguments were quite evenly matched, but the Athenians had to decide between them and though on a show of hands the voting was very close the view of Diodotus nonetheless prevailed" (3.49.1). Diodotus' motion carries the day, but what is the reader to make of this result? Viewed from one perspective, Diodotus appears in the narrative as a kind of savior: the "gift of Zeus" who saves the Mytileneans from total destruction— and perhaps the Athenians from their own worst selves.[53] Yet in keeping with Thucydides' unwillingness to assess *aitiai*, the narrative is compatible with other views. It is plausible that a majority of the Athenians had already made up their minds in favor of a more lenient policy when debate was reopened.

Indeed, the narrative points in this direction insofar as "the greater part of the citizens" (*to pleon tōn politōn*) wanted a chance to reconsider (3.36.5). It is possible, then, that neither Cleon's speech nor Diodotus' had much of an effect on the Athenian audience. And we can push this line of thought still further: the results of the vote are also compatible with the thought that Cleon, not Diodotus, actually offered a more persuasive speech on that day. We do not know how many Athenians were already hoping to vote for a lesser punishment before either Cleon or Diodotus spoke. But if a solid majority of Athenians were in favor of reversing the decision before the second vote was called, the closeness of the final vote might suggest that Cleon's speech was more effective. The question "Who was responsible for saving Mytilene?" is ultimately no easier to answer from Thucydides' narrative than the question "Who was responsible for the revolt?"[54]

The ambiguities are compounded when we consider the debate in light of subsequent events in Thucydides' telling of the war. As Athens' fortunes in the war ebb and flow, other cities follow Mytilene's path in revolt. In the summer of 421, when the Athenians take the rebellious city of Scione by siege, they enact the original punishment intended for Mytilene on Scione's inhabitants: "[They] killed all the adult males, took the women and children into slavery, and gave the Plataeans the land to occupy" (5.32.1). The proposer of the motion to destroy Scione, which the Athenians "immediately" pass, is Cleon (4.122.6). The rebellious city of Torone suffers a similar punishment (5.3). Cities such as Mende are treated differently, but their fates still reflect Athenian judgments of responsibility. After the Mendean demos assists Athens in recovering the city, the Athenians tell the Mendeans "to go on managing their political affairs as they were used to doing and to pass judgment among themselves on any they considered responsible for the revolt" (4.130.7).[55] If Diodotus succeeded at Mytilene, it nonetheless seems that the Athenians come closer to adopting Cleon's advice as a consistent long-term policy. Assessments of responsibility remain central to how the Athenians conceive of, and conduct, their imperial policy.

IV. Conclusion

I want to close with a discussion of the Sicilian expedition, the Athenian defeat that serves as the climax of Thucydides' narrative. Thucydides' portrayal of the debates over the decision to invade Sicily both confirms and undermines Diodotus' and Cleon's analyses of Athenian discursive practices. In 415 BCE, at the urging of their allies the Egestans, the Athenian assembly votes to send an expedition—led by Alcibiades, Nicias, and Lamachus—to Sicily to aid the Egestans in a conflict against the Selinuntians (6.8). Notwithstanding this pretext, Thucydides claims that they were really motivated by a wish "to rule over the whole island": to expand their empire into the western Mediterranean (6.6.1). This was an ambitious and audacious plan, not least because, although now at peace with the Spartans (since 421 BCE), relations were still unstable. Without even knowing it—Thucydides stresses Athenian ignorance of Sicily's population and size—Athens was committing itself to a second "war on almost the same scale as that against the Peloponnesians" (6.1.1). A second assembly meeting is held to discuss the outfitting of the expedition, and here Thucydides records the speeches of Nicias and Alcibiades. Nicias speaks against the expedition, urging the Athenians to reconsider "whether it is right to send the ships at all" (6.9.1); Alcibiades speaks in favor. When it looks as though the Athenians will follow Alcibiades' advice, Nicias takes a risk: "realising that he could now no longer deter them by repeating his original arguments but that he might perhaps change their minds by stressing the scale of the resources required" (6.19.2), he proceeds to describe the immensity of the undertaking (6.19–23). As Thucydides writes, "The result was just the opposite of what he had expected—they thought that he had given them good advice and that now the safety of the enterprise would be fully assured. Everyone alike had fallen in love with the voyage. . . . And so, in the face of this extreme passion on the part of the majority, anyone who felt otherwise was afraid of seeming disloyal if he voted against and therefore held his peace" (6.24). The assembly subsequently votes to send a massive expedition to Sicily. The Athenians are ultimately thoroughly defeated with a tremendous loss of resources and lives. As Thucydides' concludes the Sicilian narrative, "Few out of many returned home" (7.87.6).

Scholars have long seen parallels between Thucydides' depiction of the Sicilian debate and Herodotus' depiction of Xerxes' war council before the invasion of Greece (analyzed above, in chapter 3). The decision to invade Sicily, like Xerxes' decision to invade Greece, is the result of an overwhelming (even tyrannical?) desire for empire.[56] Both debates take place "after a decision has already been made."[57] Alcibiades and Mardonius are each cast in the role of agitator, attempting to persuade a decision-maker to undertake an invasion that may not be in their best interest. Each does so in part out of personal motives: Mardonius wishes to become governor of Greece, and Alcibiades believes that his successful command of the expedition will "promote both his personal wealth and his reputation" (6.15.2).[58] Both Mardonius and Alcibiades call into the question the ability of the Greeks and the Sicilians, respectively, to unite together to resist aggression. Artabanus and Nicias, on the other hand, seek to dissuade their decision-makers from pursuing these policies in similar ways, urging Xerxes and the Athenian demos to take their opponents seriously and calling into question the wisdom of this kind of imperial expansionism. As scholars have demonstrated, Thucydides' depiction of the Sicilian expedition offers substantive, structural, and literary echoes of Herodotus' text.

What makes these parallels possible is precisely the institutional structure of decision-making common to both regimes: both scenes dramatize the relationship between an unaccountable decision-maker and the accountable advisers who seek to persuade it. This is underscored by reading the Sicilian debate in conjunction with the one over Mytilene. Cleon's concerns that the Athenians allow fantasy to trump reality in their deliberations finds reflection in the spell the prospect of the expedition casts over the Athenians. The older citizens believe in the inevitability of success, and Thucydides describes the younger ones as "yearning to see these far-off sights and spectacles" (*tēs te apousēs pothōi opseōs kai theōrias*), directly echoing Cleon's contrast between spectators and deliberators (6.24.3). Similarly, Nicias' warning to the Athenians not to allow Alcibiades to convince them to engage in a war in which he would benefit "at the risk of the city's safety" (6.12.2) recalls Cleon's claim that the city runs all the risks when its deliberative processes are subverted.

Yet as I argued above, the Mytilenean debate offered contrasting claims about the distribution of the benefits and risks attendant on Athens' bifurcation of decision-making into two roles, advisers and audience. If Nicias echoes Cleon's view, the narrative in the wake of the Sicilian expedition might seem to echo Diodotus'. After the failure of the expedition, the Athenians "turned their anger on the orators who had joined in promoting the expedition—as if they had not voted for it themselves—and were also furious with the oracle-mongers, seers and all those whose divinations at the time had raised their hopes of conquering Sicily" (8.1.2). Their reaction in part validates Diodotus' claim that the individual adviser bears the brunt of the blame for collective decisions at Athens.

But Diodotus also claimed that the trouble with democracy is that advisers and those they persuade do not equally suffer the consequences of bad decisions. The tragedy of the Sicilian expedition is that—contrary to Diodotus' claim—the Athenians *do* suffer the consequences of their decision to invade Sicily. Indeed, while an individual adviser like Alcibiades may be able to escape punishment for his role in the Sicilian expedition by going into exile, the Athenians bear the costs of the expedition's fate directly, measured in ships, treasure, and lives. Cleon's warning—that the Athenian demos, not its advisers, runs the greater risk when deliberating about central matters of state—proves prophetic.

The connections between the politics of accountability dramatized in the Mytilenean debate and the Sicilian expedition were made more explicit by later ancient historians. The first century BCE historian Diodorus Siculus, drawing on the work of earlier historians, recounts a meeting of the Syracusan assembly after the Athenian invaders of Sicily had been rounded up and captured. Diodorus depicts the speeches of two figures: a Syracusan, Nicolaus, who had lost two sons in the war with Athens, and the Spartan envoy Gylippus. Nicolaus argues (to the surprise of his audience) for leniency toward Nicias and the captured Athenians; Gylippus argues in favor of a proposal to kill the Athenian generals and put the soldiers to work in the quarries (where many would ultimately die). This "Athenian debate" in the Syracusan assembly mirrors Thucydides' depiction of the Mytilenean debate: now it is the fate of the Athenians being decided, with Gylippus assuming the role of Cleon and Nicolaus the role of Diodotus.[59] In an echo of the Mytilenean debate's focus on *aitia* and the asymmetric responsibility of advisers and audience, Gylippus directly attacks the idea that advisers, not decision-makers, should ultimately be held responsible for political actions:

> [One might say], "Yes, but it is not the mass of the Athenians that is to blame [*ouk aition to plēthos tōn Athēnaiōn*], but Alcibiades, who advised [*sumbouleu-sas*] the affair." But we will find that advisers in most cases try to figure out the wish of their audience, such that the voter suggests to the orator an argument suitable to his own purpose. For the speaker is not sovereign over the masses [*ou gar ho legōn kurios tou plēthous*], but the demos, in deliberating well, accustoms the orator to speak in favor of the best. If we give pardon to those who commit desperate injustices when they pass on the responsibility to their advisers, we will furnish the wicked with an easy defense. This is simply the most unjust of all: in the case of good services not the advisers but the demos receives the gratitude of those treated well, while in cases of wrongdoing they transfer the punishment to the orators.[60]

Gylippus stresses the bad incentives created when decision-makers are able to pass off responsibility on their advisers. Speaking before the Syracusan demos, the Spartan lays out for them what he takes to be the logic of democracy: if the demos is sovereign (*kurios*), not the orator, then responsibility for decision-making rests with the ordinary citizens. Cleon's logic, so appealing to the Athenians in the Mytilenean debate, is turned against them.

This debate in Syracuse is not portrayed in Thucydides' text. (Indeed, parts of his narrative directly contradict it.) But even without a trial in Syracuse to make the point explicit, the Athenians do not get off lightly. The Athenian demos is not held accountable in the way an adviser would be. Hobbes, one of the most astute readers of Thucydides, also had to confront the question of the potential consequences of unaccountability in his own political theory. While the Hobbesian sovereign is accountable to no one, he is nonetheless obliged to follow the natural law. Should he depart from it, he will find himself susceptible to "Naturall Punishments":

> He that will do any thing for his pleasure, must engage himself to suffer all the pains annexed to it; and these pains, are the Naturall Punishments of those actions, which are the beginning of more Harme than Good. And hereby it comes to passe, that Intemperance, is naturally punished with Diseases; Rashnesse, with Mischances; Injustice, with the Violence of Enemies; Pride, with Ruine; Cowardise, with Oppression; Negligent government of Princes, with Rebellion; and Rebellion, with Slaughter.[61]

Hobbes' list of natural punishments that the sovereign may be forced to suffer is not so far off the Athenians' own experience of the war. The demos, if formally unaccountable, is not in the final analysis insulated from the consequences of its decisions.

5

Parrhēsia across *Politeiai*

Introduction

In the Mytilenean debate, Diodotus praises the moderate city, where the stakes for assembly debate are low. Under such circumstances, successful speakers will least feel the need to speak against their true opinion (*para gnōmēn*) and to gratify (*pros charin*) in an effort to garner ever greater honors (and avoid punishment).[1] Diodotus denies that Athenian assembly debate regularly conforms to this model. Indeed, he goes so far as to claim that far from encouraging truthful, frank speech, in the Athenian assembly, even an adviser who wishes to counsel well "must lie to be credible."[2] In the debate over the Sicilian expedition, Nicias, too, invokes the specter of counsel that does not reveal the adviser's true opinion, if only to deny he would ever offer such advice. In the opening lines of his speech, he declares to the Athenians, "I have never in the past sought preferment by speaking contrary to my real beliefs [*para gnōmēn*], nor do I do so now. I shall just speak in whatever way I think best."[3] Without explicitly naming it, both Diodotus and Nicias here appeal to a central tenet of Athenian democratic ideology: *parrhēsia*, or "saying everything."[4]

The word *parrhēsia* was deployed in fifth- and fourth-century sources in two broad senses. On the one hand, when used pejoratively, it could connote thoughtless, careless, impudent speech. Isocrates in the *Aeropagiticus*, in comparing the fourth-century democracy unfavorably with the regime founded by Solon and Cleisthenes, lists *parrhēsia*—along with license (*akolasia*), lawlessness (*paranomia*), and a general sense of entitlement among the citizens to do whatever they please (*exousian tou panta poiein*)—as lamentable features of contemporary Athenian life.[5] On the other hand, used positively, *parrhēsia* could connote free speech as a privilege granted by a political regime to its citizens and the practice of frank speech even (or especially) in the face of personal risk.

Parrhēsia was a paramount democratic cultural value. In the *Republic*, Socrates describes the democratic city as "full of freedom and freedom of speech [*parrhēsia*]."[6] Modern scholars have followed suit in their depictions of democratic Athens.[7] Arlene Saxonhouse, stressing *parrhēsia*'s link with shamelessness, sees it as fundamentally connected to democracy as the regime that "breaks from the reverence for what has been and focuses rather on the present and the future."[8] For her, *parrhēsia*, "so central to democratic Athens' self-conception," is fundamentally antihierarchical and egalitarian.[9] Sara Monoson, emphasizing *parrhēsia*'s democratic overtones, contrasts a picture of a democratic city teeming with outspoken purveyors of sharp, critical insight with an inverse image of the cowed subjects of a tyrant. Once again, Plato's *Republic* offers a window onto this view: in Socrates' description of the tyrannical regime, one of the tyrant's first acts is to dispose of his former allies on the grounds that they "speak freely [*parrhēsiazesthai*] to each other and to him, criticizing what's happening."[10] The supposed absence of *parrhēsia* under tyranny and its flourishing in democracy can thus be linked to the general antityrannical ideology in fifth- and fourth-century Athens: "The practice of *parrhēsia* in politics and personal life at Athens was treated as a sign, indeed as proof, that the Athenians had defeated tyranny at home . . . and were now in fact living as free citizens."[11]

As Monoson suggests, the value of *parrhēsia* and its place in Athenian democratic ideology needs to be understood in comparative perspective. The relevant comparison is not only to tyrannical but also to oligarchic regimes. The fourth-century Athenian orator Aeschines explicitly associated free and frank speech with democracy as opposed to oligarchy: "For in oligarchies not whoever wishes but only those in power speak in public, while in democracies whoever wishes can speak *and can say what seems best to him*."[12] If the openness of public speech in Athens invokes the principle of *isēgoria*, the equal right to address the assembly, Aeschines' emphasis on the ability to say what one really thinks—to speak frankly—implicitly invokes *parrhēsia*. As discussed above (chapter 1), oligarchic and tyrannical regimes restrict the right to speak in assemblies to officials and other political elites even when they allow ordinary citizens to come together and participate in decision-making. Even outside of assembly settings, frank criticism of the regime, particularly in public, where it could rally opposition to the rulers, might be experienced by oligarchs as a threat to regime stability.[13] For example, Thucydides recounts a period of political turmoil in Mende in 423–422.[14] The Spartan general Polydamidas was tasked with assisting the Mendean oligarchs, who for the moment had the upper hand. As Polydamidas organized the Mendeans to fight an Athenian force threatening the city, "someone on the people's side objected that he wasn't going out and saw no need for war, whereupon Polydamidas grabbed the protestor by the arm and shook him about. The people at once picked up the arms in great anger and turned on the Peloponnesians and the opposition party that had been working with them."[15] It is Polydamidas' violent *response* to the unnamed member of the demos' *parrhēsia* that is the immediate catalyst for democratic resistance. But even without Polydamidas' hubris adding fuel to the fire, the *parrhēsiastēs*' (frank speaker's) intervention might well have been enough to turn the city against the oligarchic faction and its Spartan supporters. (Presumably this is why Polydamidas responds so forcefully, even if he miscalculates the effects of his actions.)

It is thus no surprise that ordinary Athenians would view the protection of their own privilege to speak frankly and openly in Athens as an important democratic accomplishment. The hierarchical reservation and enforcement of a privilege to speak frankly to an elite few would entail banishing ordinary citizens from the "deliberative circle."[16] As a character in a fragment from a work by Nicostratus, the fourth-century comic poet, asks, "Don't you know that *parrhēsia* is the arms of poverty [*tēs penias hoplon hē parrhēsia*]? If someone were to lose this, such a man has thrown away the shield of life."[17] The speaker in the fragment suggests that the equal social standing of poor citizens in a democracy is bound up with their ability to speak their minds: not only does the protection of their *parrhēsia*, and their own practice of it, count as evidence of the equality they have achieved in a democratic city; *parrhēsia* is also instrumental to its preservation.

Parrhēsia's place in Athenian democratic ideology and civic culture found legal and institutional support. While there was nothing like a First Amendment right to free speech, Athenian slander law and other restrictions on speech were limited in scope: in the main, Athenian citizens were legally free to criticize one another in public and private contexts.[18] *Parrhēsia* was closely linked to the comic theater, where shameless frank speech—including, as we have seen, political criticism (see chapter 2)—found institutional support and flourished.[19] Scholars also claim that *parrhēsia* found an institutional home in the assembly. *Parrhēsia* is thought to have played an important role in political debate, serving as a possible antidote to the dangers of expert and potentially deceptive rhetoric and helping secure the epistemic properties crucial to a successful debate.[20] And the extant record of Athenian sumbouleutic and dikastic rhetoric is filled with references to *parrhēsia*, direct and indirect.[21] Yet as I will argue in this chapter, *parrhēsia*'s relationship to the assembly is ambivalent and complex. This complex relationship is obscured in much of the literature on *parrhēsia* and assembly debate by a tendency to treat democratic norms and practices as exceptional. Consider, for example, Sara Monoson's account of the role *parrhēsia* played in assembly debate: "The association of critical parrhesia with Assembly debate helped establish confidence in the collective wisdom of the demos. A vote taken after speeches delivered in a spirit of parrhesia could represent not simply the *preferences of the majority*, but *the considered judgment of the demos*. Such a decision could reasonably be thought wise, worthy of the confidence of the demos."[22] Note in particular the contrast Monoson draws between the (mere) "preferences" of the majority and the "considered judgment" of the entire demos after speeches made with *parrhēsia*. Such language seems to reflect an importation of contemporary deliberative democratic theories and ideals back into Athenian democratic theory and practice.[23] In a similar vein, Elizabeth Markovits has linked *parrhēsia* to contemporary deliberative democrats' interest in sincerity as a requirement of democratic deliberation.[24]

Given the tight link between *parrhēsia* and democracy in the minds of many scholars and given their assumption that democratic modes of discourse and advice need not be compared with advice in other regimes, it is no surprise that the literature contains little sustained consideration of *parrhēsia*'s place in nondemocratic regimes.[25] This is unfortunate for two reasons. First, our understanding of *parrhēsia* is incomplete when we focus only on the democratic context. Just as importantly, a consideration of how *parrhēsia* was thought to function in autocracies can and should be the occasion to supplement and clarify our understanding of how it functioned in Athenian democracy.

My analysis of *parrhēsia* is predicated on the asymmetries of accountability between *sumbouloi* and decision-makers, which, I have been arguing, was characteristic of both democracies and autocracies. My focus in this chapter is on fourth-century rhetoric, but as will become clear, it also builds on the explorations of the dynamics of advice found in the fifth-century historical sources. *Parrhēsia*, I argue, was a practice employed by speakers addressing an audience that had the power to reward or sanction them for their advice. Insofar as this is true, *parrhēsia* was not so much a norm for *deliberation*—understood as equals jointly and freely deciding on a plan of action by discussing and weighing the possible options—as it was a norm for *counsel*, understood as an individual offering advice to a decision-maker, individual or collective.[26] As such, it could be practiced, in both democracies and autocracies, as a *remedial* virtue, necessitated by a structural feature common to both autocratic and Athenian democratic decision procedures: at the center of both regimes was an unaccountable decision-maker able to hold advisers to account. The remedial status of this form of *parrhēsia* is underscored when we contrast it with another usage of the term: *parrhēsia* could also refer to a *privilege* of speaking frankly with relative impunity—one that could be either granted or denied by rulers.[27] Athenian democratic ideology celebrated democracy as a regime that consistently granted this privilege to its citizens. But the fact that Athenian *sumbouloi* had to cultivate the *virtue* of risky *parrhēsia* strongly suggests that the *privilege* of speaking with impunity was not consistently protected. If it were, why would political speech have been risky in the first place? Speaking with *parrhēsia* in the assembly—offering bold counsel in the face of significant personal risk—was a virtue in part because the demos itself was structurally similar to a tyrant (at least in its relationship to its advisers).

The argument of the chapter proceeds as follows. In the first section, I explore texts in which *parrhēsia* is explicitly discussed in autocratic contexts. I show that theorists such as Isocrates thought that *parrhēsia* was important in autocratic as well as in democratic settings: *parrhēsia* could serve as a possible counterweight to flattery, which was itself engendered by the autocrat's position as sole, unaccountable decision-maker with the power to reward and punish his advisers. I place Isocrates' invocations of *parrhēsia* in autocratic settings in the context of his wider interest in the problem of political counsel and in the figure of the *sumboulos*—in Isocrates' words to Nicocles, the most "kingly" (*turannikōtaton*) possession.[28] In the second section, I turn to an analysis of *parrhēsia* and flattery in democracies. I show that while Isocrates sometimes seems to argue that the nature of political counsel differs markedly across political regimes, he diagnoses similar potential problems in both autocracies and democracies. He makes similar claims about who should serve as a *sumboulos* and the need for *parrhēsia* in both regime types. Nor is Isocrates alone in working with the demos-tyrant analogy in this way. In Demosthenes' speeches too, the discourse surrounding *parrhēsia* and flattery is predicated on important similarities between the assembly and an autocrat. Isocrates' discussions of *parrhēsia* were not appropriations and distortions of democratic ideology by an elite critic: they share much with how democratic practitioners thought and spoke about their own practice of *parrhēsia* in the assembly.

I. *Parrhēsia* in Autocracies

In spite of *parrhēsia*'s democratic pedigree and associations, there are a number of discussions in fourth-century Athenian literature of *parrhēsia* in autocratic settings. Aristotle's *Constitution of Athens*, for example, contains a single reference to *parrhēsia*, which, strikingly, is divorced from the democratic context. As Aristotle tells it, a farmer was busy working one day on a plot of marginal land when the tyrant Peisistratus happened by: "Peisistratus saw someone working an area that was all stones, and, being surprised, told his attendant to ask what the land produced. 'Aches and pains,' the farmer replied; 'Peisistratus ought to take his 10 percent of the aches and pains too.' The man made the reply not knowing that he was speaking to Peisistratus, while the latter was delighted at his frankness [*parrhēsia*] and industriousness, and exempted him from all taxation."[29] Scholars who have commented on this passage tend either to downplay its importance or to move quickly to interpret it within the context of democratic Athens. Sara Monoson sees it as playing on the incongruity of *parrhēsia* being found in a tyranny at all, while Arlene Saxonhouse believes it to reveal more about the values of Aristotle's fourth-century Athenian contemporaries than the prevalence of "frank speaking" under Peisistratus' fifth-century tyranny.[30] On one level, Saxonhouse is surely right. If we take the story as a tale that fourth-century Athenians told themselves, it says as much or more about their own self-image as it does about how *parrhēsia* might have functioned in tyrannies: the Athenians are proud of their reputation for boldness and frankness. We cannot extrapolate much from the anecdote. Yet the story opens the question of *parrhēsia*'s function in nondemocratic regimes and of the attitudes of autocrats toward its practice. The tyrant in Plato's *Republic* thought *parrhēsia* a danger to his regime, a practice he could not tolerate. Why did Peisistratus, in contrast, find the farmer's frankness delightful?

Two letters, written by Isocrates to autocratic rulers, suggest that perhaps Peisistratus had good reason to be delighted with frankness.[31] In these letters—one to Antipater, who served as Philip's regent in Macedon, and the other to Nicocles, a king on the island of Cyprus—Isocrates reflects on the proper relationship that should obtain between a ruler and his *sumbouloi*. The letter to Nicocles makes advice a central theme; the shorter letter to Antipater is a recommendation written on behalf of a former student, Diodotus, commending him as a suitable adviser for Antipater. In both letters, *parrhēsia* plays a prominent role. The letter to Antipater contains this passage: "For it is likely that because of men who always choose to say what is pleasing [*tous aei pros hēdonēn legein proairoumenous*], not only are monarchies unable to survive when they inevitably encounter many dangers but citizen governments [*politeias*] cannot endure either with such men around. Yet because of those who speak openly in the interest of what is best [*tous epi tōi beltistōi parrhēsiazomenous*] many of these are preserved, even when their affairs seem headed for ruin."[32] Those who are accustomed to thinking of *parrhēsia* as a peculiarly democratic practice will be surprised by Isocrates' claim that *parrhēsia* is a requirement for both autocratic and democratic regimes; indeed, Isocrates seems to be claiming that *parrhēsia* is even more important for the former. His argument relies on the contrast between those who speak "to please" and those who speak with *parrhēsia* in favor of what is best. The advice of the former leads to "dangers," while the advice of the latter is salutary.

On Isocrates' account, while monarchs should listen to frank speakers, they are often seduced by flatterers. In the letter to Antipater, Isocrates illustrates this tendency by recounting Diodotus' experience advising "some leaders in Asia." Diodotus, "because of his frankness [*dia to parrhēsiazesthai*] with them about their own interests," was deprived of the honors he had expected for his faithful service while "the flatteries of inconsequential men counted for more with them than the good services of this man."[33] Similarly, Isocrates notes in the beginning of his letter to Nicocles that since most associates of kings consort with them "to gain favor [*pros charin*]," kings are rarely exposed to the kinds of *parrhēsia* and criticism crucial to good education.[34]

Nicocles and Antipater should be particularly interested in advisers willing to speak with *parrhēsia*, then, because the default tendency of most advisers is to flatter the autocrat. This flattery is itself invited by the autocrat's position as sole, unaccountable decision-maker, with the power to reward and punish his advisers. Given this position, those under his power are more likely to tell him what they think he wants to hear rather than to run the risk of giving him what they think is the best advice. Isocrates' analysis of the relationship between autocrat and adviser thus recalls Herodotus' depictions of vulnerable, accountable *sumbouloi* in the *Histories*. Speaking to the autocrat is a risky endeavor, and Diodotus' experience with the Asian potentates highlights that risk: one's audience may not appreciate what one has to say. Herodotus depicts Xerxes as warning his would-be advisers that if one "hears something good, the body fills up with delight, but when [one] hears the opposite, it swells with rage."[35] Isocrates identifies a similar predilection for pleasing flattery among autocratic rulers of his own day. The desire to hear only what is pleasurable, coupled with the power asymmetry between adviser and autocrat, gives rise to a particularly pernicious form of advice-giving: flattering speeches, aiming not at "the best" but "to gratify." This form of speech nullifies the immediate dangers to the speaker, since the result—if the speech is successful—is a gratified audience. Nonetheless, it is ultimately, in Isocrates' view, destructive for the ruler: "monarchies cannot endure" when advice aims at gratification and not good policy. We can imagine that, at the limit, the flattery endemic to such asymmetric power relations produces a vicious circle: advisers, fearing for their positions, tell the autocrat what he wants to hear; the autocrat rewards those who gratify and flatter him, rein-forcing the incentive to flatter. The process feeds on itself, with advice tending further and further away from good policy until the autocrat's rule collapses.

Isocrates' letters offer two potential ways out of the vicious circle, ver-sions of which can also be found in Herodotus' *Histories* as well. First, the autocrat can try to mitigate the problem by creating a climate favorable to *parrhēsia*—that is, by allowing and even encouraging his advisers to offer him their best advice frankly rather than to flatter him. Cyrus' war council in book 1 of Herodotus' *Histories* stands as an example of this practice.[36] Where autocrats do not unilaterally attempt to create conditions supportive of frank speech on the part of their advisers, *sumbouloi* can also attempt to negotiate with their rulers a space for giving frank advice or otherwise encourage au-tocrats to view *parrhēsia* more favorably.[37] Isocrates' advice to Antipater and Nicocles can be read as just such an intervention. As Isocrates tells Antipater, "Those who state the truth should be more highly valued by all monarchs than those who say everything with a view to pleasing but, in fact, say nothing that should please."[38] Nicocles, too, is advised to encourage frank speech. He is counseled to regard as trustworthy not those who praise everything he says and does, but those who point out his mistakes. He should "grant *parrhēsia* to those with good judgment" (*didou parrhēsian tois eu phronousin*)—that is, allow and encourage those with good judgment to speak freely and frankly— and distinguish between "artful flatterers and those who serve with goodwill" (*tous technēi kolakeuontas kai tous met' eunoias therapeuontas*).[39] Isocrates thus counsels both Nicocles and Antipater to make frankness less risky by granting the privilege of free speech (*didonai parrhēsian*) to at least some ad-visers and by esteeming and rewarding those who speak frankly rather than those who flatter.

Yet in recounting the story of Diodotus, who took it upon himself to practice *parrhēsia* even in an inhospitable context, Isocrates offers another, distinct possibility: an adviser can speak up for the best even in situations where it is likely that the autocrat does not want to hear it. In such cases, the adviser's actions recall the practice of figures such as Artabanus and Arte-misia in the *Histories*, who offer frank advice to rulers even when there is good reason to think that the advice will not be met with pleasure. Here the adviser willingly takes on a degree of risk in deciding to speak truth to power. It is also worth flagging that there is a democratic analog to this practice. Consider, for example, Demosthenes' characterization of his own *parrhēsia* in the *First Philippic*: "I have spoken my plain sentiments with parrhesia. Yet, certain as I am that it is to your interest to receive the best advice, I could have wished that I were equally certain that to offer such advice is also to the interest of the speaker. . . . But, as it is, in the uncertainty of what the result of my proposal may be for myself, yet in the conviction that it will be to your interest to adopt it, I have ventured to address you."[40] In bravely speaking up in favor of "the best" rather than "speaking to please," the autocrat's adviser, like Demosthenes in Athens, can choose to engage in risky but salutary critique. Moreover, in both cases, the *parrhēsiastēs'* willingness to take on the risk of speaking frankly may itself serve as possible evidence of his trustworthiness (as Isocrates suggests to Nicocles and as Demosthenes suggests to his democratic audience).

There are therefore two distinct, if related, meanings of *parrhēsia* at work in these passages, which imply different ways to think about the relationship between *parrhēsia* and risk. To grant *parrhēsia* to one's advisers, as Isocrates advises Nicocles to do, is to commit oneself publicly to a policy of openness to advice. This is an attempt to *minimize* the risks associated with speaking truth to power. On Isocrates' analysis, the reason the autocrat would want to do this is clear: those risks are the cause of one of the chief forms of pernicious advice-giving.[41] If reward and punishment were not contingent on pleasing the autocrat, the motive to flatter would be absent. Isocrates seems well aware that the riskier frank speech is, the less likely one is to get it. On the other hand, even where *parrhēsia* is not granted from above, it can still be practiced—as the cases of Diodotus, Artabanus, and Artemisia (and Demosthenes as well, in the democratic context) all suggest. To do so, however, is to take on considerable risk: where a powerful decision-maker has not signaled openness to advice, frank counsel can be dangerous. There is some suggestion that the element of risk may itself be salutary: that an adviser is willing to speak under such conditions might imply that he is trustworthy and speaking with the decision-maker's best interests in mind. But of course, there is no guarantee that the autocrat's advisers will willingly take on the risk of speaking frankly.

In this section, the focus has been on *parrhēsia* in autocratic contexts. But the parallels I drew between Demosthenes' invocations of *parrhēsia* in the *First Philippic* and the risky speech of Isocrates' Diodotus should prompt us to see how far this Isocratean analysis of *parrhēsia* can travel beyond the autocratic case. This might seem an unpromising line of thought. David Konstan, for example, has offered a reading of Isocrates on *parrhēsia* and counsel in monarchical settings that resists any comparison to the democratic case. In his analysis of Isocrates' letter to Antipater, Konstan notes that "frankness is a virtue in a counselor, who must risk the ire of princes foolish enough to be offended when contradicted, even if the advice is in their own interest." Understood as such, frankness might be considered a virtue of a counselor across regime types. Yet Konstan blunts the comparative force of his insight insofar as he understands the relationship that obtains between frank speaker and prince to be a form of friendship: "To dare to speak the truth in such a context represents the genuine fidelity of a friend and is to be prized."[42] Konstan's focus on friendship, then, leads him to de-emphasize the structural similarities between the practice of *parrhēsia* in democracy and autocracy.

In the letters to Nicocles and Antipater, Isocrates folds his reflections on *parrhēsia* into a broader discussion of counsel in autocratic contexts. In places, he seems to draw a sharp distinction between the adviser-autocrat relationship and the adviser-demos relationship, particularly insofar as he portrays the demos in a negative light. Isocrates claims that democratic audiences delight in pleasurable fictions rather than useful advice: "Clearly those who wish to do or write something to please the masses do not seek the most useful speeches but those that are full of fictions [*muthōdestatous*]."[43] The result, Isocrates suggests, is that in a democracy, "those who wish to persuade their audiences have been shown that they must steer clear of reprimand and advice [*nouthetein kai sumbouleuein*] and say such things they see will be most delightful to crowds."[44] Here Isocrates' criticisms of the demos share much with both Diodotus' and Cleon's arguments in the Mytilene debate. Yet Isocrates also uses these criticisms to draw a distinction between kingly and democratic rule: "I have made these points because I think that you, not being one of the many but ruling over many, should not have the same understanding as others. You should not judge serious matters or sensible men by the criterion of pleasure, but should value them for their useful actions."[45]

The association of good counsel with monarchical government in the letter to Nicocles is neatly captured in Isocrates' counsel to "value and cherish those who have intelligence and are more insightful than others, for you know that a good counselor is the most useful and most kingly [*turannikōtaton*] of all possessions."[46] The description of the *sumboulos* as a "kingly" or even "tyrannical" possession might seem to imply a privileged relationship between good counsel and monarchical government. The point is reemphasized in his *Nicocles*, which is written from the perspective of Nicocles himself. In comparing democracy and oligarchy with monarchy, "Nicocles" notes that "the former attend to the commonwealth as if it were someone else's, the latter as if it were their own, and on these matters the former use the most aggressive citizens as advisers, while the latter select the wisest of all. The former honor those who can speak to a crowd; the latter, those who know how to manage affairs."[47]

Yet interpreting such claims requires some care. Isocrates' purpose is not simply to present an idealized portrait of the relationship between autocrats and their advisers. Nor is he drawing an absolute contrast between democracies and monarchies, in which "the king-advisor relationship is marked by freedom, whereas the orator-demos relationship is marked by flattery."[48] It is true that Isocrates presents his own relationship with Nicocles as marked by frankness, not by flattery (although his extravagant praise of Nicocles might suggest otherwise). And as he acknowledges in the *Antidosis*, it might sometimes be necessary to "pay court" to the demos at Athens. There Isocrates claims that one of his students, the general Timotheus, failed in his trial before the demos precisely because he refused to flatter them.[49] Yet if Isocrates taught his students that it was at least sometimes necessary to flatter the demos, he also recognized the same need in autocratic contexts.[50] For every Timotheus, who failed at democratic politics because of his refusal to pay court to the demos, Isocrates offers a Diodotus, whose *parrhēsia* and refusal to flatter autocrats caused equal trouble. The point is made quite generally in the letter to Antipater: "Some rulers, who have a noble dignity of soul, honor this frankness [*parrhēsia*] as a useful thing; other rulers, whose nature is weaker than their circumstances would require, are displeased by it since it forces them to do something that they do not choose to do. They are not aware that those who dare to disagree with them about what is advantageous can, in fact, give them the most power to do what they want [*pleistēn exousian autois tou prattein ha boulontai paraskeuazousin*]."[51] *Parrhēsia* is here depicted as of extraordinary benefit for an autocrat. Advisers willing to disagree can give rulers great power "to do what they want."[52] But the frankness that can come to characterize the relationship between an autocrat and his advisers is by no means a given. As Isocrates makes clear, some rulers will be able to tolerate the criticism that frank advice often entails, while others will not.

Yet even if Isocrates is not offering a fully idealizing account of advice in autocratic settings, it is still not clear how this discussion of *parrhēsia* in autocracies might bear on the democratic experience. After all, much seems to differentiate the practice of *parrhēsia* in democracies and autocracies. In a democracy, the assembly is the decision-making body, while in an autocracy, a single man decides. There is also the question of *who* gets to speak with *parrhēsia*: the circle of advisers to an autocrat is smaller than the set of possible advisers to a democratic assembly (even accepting the fact that the right to speak at the assembly, while guaranteed to all citizens, would have been exercised by relatively few). Isocrates' recommendation to Nicocles to grant *parrhēsia* to those with good judgment, not to all his subjects, reinforces the idea that autocratic *parrhēsia* is more limited in scope than its practice in a democracy.[53]

Perhaps, then, *parrhēsia* in the autocratic setting tells us little or nothing about its practice in a democracy. Isocrates may well have looked to democracy for inspiration for his advice in the letters.[54] Yet this would not necessarily mean that we could move in the other direction, from autocracy to democracy. Perhaps Isocrates was simply transferring some Athenian political know-how to a foreign regime or two—if *parrhēsia* had been so successful at ensuring good decision-making at Athens, then a form of it, suitably adapted to the less egalitarian climate of an autocracy, could work just as well in other regimes.[55]

Yet I think these lines of argument too quickly dismiss the significance of *parrhēsia* as it was theorized in the autocratic case for understanding its place in Athens. For we have already seen the important role that power asymmetries and risk play in structuring the practice of *parrhēsia* and the problem of flattery in Isocrates' analysis of autocracy. Given the accountability of democratic *sumbouloi* to the unaccountable demos, we should not be surprised to find parallels to the autocratic experience that run quite deep.

II. Democratic *Parrhēsia*: Isocratean Ideals and Demosthenic Practice

Recall that there were two ways in which *parrhēsia* could feature in the autocrat-adviser relationship, given the power asymmetry between the two. *Parrhēsia* could be granted from above, as when Isocrates urges Nicocles to "grant *parrhēsia*" to his trusted advisers. *Parrhēsia* could also be practiced independently of such a privilege, as when Diodotus spoke frankly to the "Asian potentates" he advised, even though to do so carried the risk that he would be ignored, unrewarded for his efforts, or worse, punished for his frankness. In this section, I argue that *parrhēsia* at Athens could feature in the orator-demos relationship in the same two ways.

Isocrates' *On the Peace* directly addresses the question of the possibilities and limitations of counsel in democratic Athens. Isocrates imagines critically rebuking his fellow citizens: "I know that it is dangerous to oppose your views and that even though we live in a democracy, there is still no freedom of speech [*parrhēsia*], except here in the Assembly for those who are foolish and do not care about you [*tois aphronestatois kai mēden humōn phrontizousin*] or in the theater for the comic poets."[56] Isocrates identifies the cause of this state of affairs in the preceding passages of the speech, echoing the language of his warnings to Nicocles and Antipater. The Athenians have refused to hear speeches from anyone except those who assent to their desires.[57] The Athenians recognize the dangers "flatterers" (*tōn kolakeuontōn*) pose in their personal lives but "clearly trust them more [*mallon toutois pisteuontes*]" than their franker fellow citizens in public affairs.[58] As Isocrates argues, "You have made speakers practice and study not what will help the state but how they might say what pleases you. And even now, most of them have rushed to speak such words, for it is clear to everyone that you will be more pleased by those who urge you to war than by those who recommend peace."[59] Thus just as in autocratic regimes, a vicious circle arises, with political advisers telling the demos what they think it wants to hear and the demos reinforcing this habit by only listening to those speakers. Isocrates had advised Nicocles to "grant *parrhēsia*" to trusted advisers; in noting that there is almost no *parrhēsia* in Athens, he stresses that the demos has failed to do so. The consequences for the democracy are potentially grave: in the case Isocrates has in mind, the Athenians refuse to listen to speakers advocating peace with their enemies and instead are persuaded to carry on a costly policy of aggression and empire. The institutional context is also worth stressing: Isocrates claims that *parrhēsia* does not exist because the demos—freed like the autocrat from the burdens of being held accountable and able to punish and reward its advisers at will—has begun to fall prey to the kind of rhetoric that such insulation from accountability breeds.

Yet Isocrates does not leave his analysis at that. Throughout *On the Peace*, he attempts to make clear to his Athenian audience that a good adviser is a useful possession not only for a king but for a democracy as well. Isocrates' goal, just as with his letters to autocrats, is to help those in power recognize who is giving them good advice, even (or especially) when that advice contains criticism:

> Of necessity, those who advise the state and those who attack it use similar words, even though their intentions are diametrically opposed. Thus, it is not always right for you to take the same attitude toward those who say the same things; you should hate those whose criticism is harmful, for they are hostile to the city, *but you should praise those who give you helpful advice and think them the best citizens; and among this latter group, you should praise especially that one who can most clearly show the wickedness of your actions and the troubles that result from them.* For this man will most quickly make you hate what should be hated and desire better things. And so that is what I have to say to you about the harshness of the words I have spoken and what I am about to say.[60]

Isocrates thus identifies parallel problems of counsel in democracy and autocracy and offers similar solutions in both regimes. While parts of the letter to Nicocles may imply that there is no hope for offering good counsel in democracies, the argument of *On the Peace* leaves that possibility open.

In his lectures on *parrhēsia*, Foucault interprets Isocrates' critique of the lack of *parrhēsia* in contemporary Athens as a sign of a "crisis of democratic institutions." In Foucault's view, by Isocrates' time, *parrhēsia* had ceased to function properly. Flattering orators, telling audiences only what they wanted to hear, left no space for the "honest orator" who "has the ability, and is courageous enough, to oppose the *demos*." There is a fundamental opposition between the will of the demos and the best interests of the city; because of this, "real *parrhesia*, *parrhesia* in its positive, critical sense, does not exist where democracy exists."[61] Foucault's interpretation identifies many of the key features of Isocrates' argument, including the problem of flattery and the tension between the will of the people and what Isocrates takes to be the best interests of the city, but his conclusion strikes me as misguided. Isocrates' speech is better read not as evidence for the decline of *parrhēsia* in the fourth century but as highlighting an important way in which it operated: *parrhēsia*—understood as the virtue of bold, risky speech—was necessary precisely because the unaccountable demos was unwilling to grant it to orators—that is, to guarantee them the privilege of speaking frankly. Our understanding of *parrhēsia* as a cornerstone of democratic ideology should be supplemented by the recognition that, at least in the assembly, it was often a remedial practice necessitated by the institutional power of the demos.

This recognition underscores the need for a reappraisal of the role of risk in the practice of *parrhēsia* in Athens. The dangers of speaking in the assembly are often portrayed in contemporary scholarship as a necessary and even salutary concomitant of a system in which advisers were accountable to the demos for the advice that they gave.[62] This line of thought goes back at least to George Grote. Reflecting on Thucydides' remark that the Athenians "turned their anger on the orators who had joined in promoting the [Sicilian] expedition—as if they had not voted for it themselves," Grote writes, "The adviser of any important measure always makes himself morally responsible for its justice, usefulness, and practicability; and he very properly incurs disgrace, more or less according to the case, if it turns out to present results totally contrary to those which he had predicted. We know that the Athenian law often imposed upon the mover of a proposition not merely *moral*, but even *legal*, responsibility; a regulation of doubtful propriety under other circumstances, but which I believe to have been useful at Athens."[63] Here Grote offers only a cautious endorsement of legal accountability for advice as of "doubtful propriety" but nonetheless "useful at Athens" for unstated reasons. Contemporary scholars such as Sara Monoson, Elizabeth Markovits, and others have built on Grote's claims, arguing that when an orator speaking with *parrhēsia* willingly shouldered those burdens of risk, his willingness to do so counted as evidence for his public-spiritedness. The conclusion drawn, then, is that "the risks [the orators faced] were not thought by the Athenians to undermine or even conflict with the practice of frank speech. Rather, the risks affirmed that the speaker could be held accountable for the advice ventured."[64] My analysis complicates this view. As Isocrates' analysis suggests, the riskiness of speaking to the demos, which was itself the consequence of the power asymmetry between the demos and its advisers, could just as easily lead to flattery as it could to *parrhēsia*. Indeed, Monoson recognizes this problem in the autocratic case: "A tyrant's arbitrary, unaccountable, and absolute power virtually precluded that individuals would risk saying anything other than what the tyrant wished to hear."[65] Given the structural parallels between the tyrant's role and the demos' in accountability politics, we should not be surprised if the discourse surrounding the theory and practice of *parrhēsia* in both regime types converged.

One might argue that Isocrates' presentation of the parallel dynamics of *parrhēsia* in autocracies and at Athens rests on a warped view of the democracy that Athenian democrats themselves would not have accepted. Yet the recognition of these parallels was not limited to critics of the democracy. Demosthenes' analysis of *parrhēsia*'s presence (and absence) in the Athenian assembly shares much with the "Isocratean" view. In the *Third Philippic*, Demosthenes—speaking with *parrhēsia*—complains that Athens, famous for allowing a measure of *parrhēsia* even to slaves and foreigners, nonetheless has banished it from assembly debate. Rather than listening to good advice, the demos is flattered by pleasant speeches, with the result that the city runs great risks:

> I think, men of Athens, that if I speak something of the truth frankly [*meta parrhēsias*], none of you will on that account become angry with me. For look at it this way. In other matters you think it is so necessary for there to be general freedom of speech [*parrhēsian . . . koinēn*] for everyone in the city that you even allow aliens and slaves to share in it . . . but from your deliberations you have banished it altogether. Hence the result is that in the assembly, your self-complacency is flattered by hearing none but pleasant speeches but your policy and your practice are already involving you in the gravest peril.[66]

In this passage, Demosthenes invokes both of the senses of *parrhēsia* analyzed in this chapter. On the one hand, Demosthenes claims that granting the privilege of *parrhēsia* is a practice the Athenians pride themselves on, to the extent that perhaps even foreigners and slaves benefit from it. But Demosthenes also points out that this privilege is not properly secured in the assembly—indeed, it is "banished altogether." As Demosthenes makes clear elsewhere, this is far from ideal: "I suppose it necessary, men of Athens, when deliberating about such great matters, to grant *parrhēsia* [*didonai parrhēsian*] to each of your advisers."[67] In this passage, too, Demosthenes takes *parrhēsia* to be a privilege that can be granted, using the same language (*didonai parrhēsian*) as Isocrates uses in his advice to Nicocles.[68] Of course, that the Athenians have not "granted *parrhēsia*" to their advisers—that they are not making frank speech as safe as possible—does not mean that Demosthenes cannot speak frankly. After all, in the *Third Philippic*, he claims to be offering frank advice even while noting that the Athenians have banished it from the assembly. But it does mean that he has to cultivate a risky practice of the virtue in the face of potential censure and punishment. And it is far from clear that Demosthenes thinks that risk helps ensure good debate; rather, at least in this instance, he is claiming that the demos' attitude toward criticism has encouraged flattery, at least on the part of the other orators.

While their treatments of *parrhēsia* converge, Demosthenes and Isocrates must be distinguished in two respects. Most importantly, unlike Isocrates, who never spoke in the assembly, Demosthenes directly challenges the demos, even under circumstances where such frank speech may not be encouraged and rewarded. In both the *Third Philippic* and *On the Chersonese*, Demosthenes contrasts his own *parrhēsia* with the flattery of his fellow orators. He sees himself (or presents himself) as practicing the virtue of *parrhēsia* that Isocrates merely preaches. Demosthenes willingly takes on the risks of acting as an accountable adviser. Yet while Isocrates declines to speak directly in the assembly, he nonetheless claims for himself the status of *sumboulos*. Isocrates attributes his own reluctance to enter politics to a lack of "sufficient voice and daring" (*phōnēs hikanēs kai tolmēs*).[69] So constrained by "nature"—"of all of the citizens I was born the least naturally suited for political affairs"— Isocrates suggests that he was forced to develop a different model for making himself into a useful counselor for the polis.[70]

Demosthenes also identifies a different cause of the pathologies of assembly debate: the corruption of the demos by the orators. When Demosthenes repeats his critique of assembly debate from the *Third Philippic* almost verbatim in *On the Chersonese*, he blames his fellow orators for the deficiencies of assembly debate: "By persuasive arts and caresses they have brought you to such a frame of mind that in your assemblies you are elated by their flattery and have no ear but for compliments, while in your policy and your practice you are at this moment running the gravest risks."[71] Whereas Isocrates seems to hold the demos primarily responsible for the rise of flattery—in his presentation, the demos has all but forced the orators to deploy flattery— Demosthenes asserts that the orators are to blame.

Demosthenes further explores the dynamics of oratorical corruption of the demos in the *Third Olynthiac*. The problems the Athenians face can be traced back to the "popularity hunting" (*pros charin dēmēgorein*) of some of the orators.[72] Rather than proposing good public policy, the orators ply the demos with questions such as "What would you like? What shall I propose? How can I oblige you?"[73] One might be tempted to take such questions as *support* for an Isocratean analysis of the power asymmetry between demos or autocrat and advisers. The obsequious questions the orators ask could be seen as a natural response to their inferior position: they can profit only by offering the demos exactly what it wants. Strikingly, however, Demosthenes seems to draw the opposite conclusion. Contrasting assembly debate before the process of corruption began with its current state, Demosthenes says the following:

> What is the cause of all this, and why, pray, did everything go well then that now goes amiss? Because then the people, having the courage to act and to fight, were the master [*despotēs*] of the politicians and were themselves the dispensers of all favors [*kurios autos hapantōn tōn agathōn*]; the rest were well content to accept at the people's hand honor and authority and reward. Now, on the contrary, the politicians hold the purse-strings and manage everything, while you, the people, robbed of nerve and sinew, stripped of wealth and of allies, have sunk to the level of lackeys and hangers-on [*en hupēretou kai prosthēkēs merei gegenēsthe*].[74]

The flattery and obsequiousness of the orators, Demosthenes claims, is not a sign of the demos' power but rather of that power's usurpation by a few. To some extent, Demosthenes is exaggerating the powerlessness of the demos here for rhetorical effect: using the image of a debased and weakened demos, Demosthenes hopes to shame the assembly into adopting his activist and energetic policies against the Macedonians. His argument is still ultimately premised on the demos being the chief decision-maker: the obsequious questions of the orators only make sense given this premise, as does the very occasion for Demosthenes to give the speech. If the demos could not change its policies as it saw fit, there would be no point in Demosthenes attempting to persuade it. Yet by highlighting the orators' role in generating the vicious circle of flattery, Demosthenes both minimizes the responsibility that the demos bears for the situation and points to a way forward: if the orators were not out to corrupt and the demos were more jealous of its own sovereignty and mindful of its own good, the vicious circle could be avoided.[75] Demosthenes is also making an important observation here about the power dynamics between a flattering adviser and a decision-maker: at the limit, flattery undermines the ruler's own power. This happens not only because bad advice leads to bad policies but also because once the vicious circle of flattery and its rewards begins, it becomes difficult to say who is really controlling whom. Is the demos using the orators, or is it being used by them?

The ambiguity of the power relationship analyzed in the *Third Olynthiac* is reminiscent of Aristotle's analysis, in book 4 of the *Politics*, of the relationship between the demos and demagogues in the final form of democracy. Yet Aristotle's account, while confirming aspects of Demosthenes' analysis, also points to its limits. In the final form of democracy—of which Aristotle would consider Athens an example—"not the law, but the multitude [*to plēthos*], have the supreme power [*kurion d' einai*], and supersede the law by their decrees."[76] Aristotle goes on to argue that, under these conditions, the power of the demos closely resembles the power of a tyrant and in both regimes flatterers are honored. When the demagogue plays the flatterer to a tyrannical demos, the lines of power become blurred: "For it happens that they [the demagogues] become great because while the demos is sovereign [*kurion*] over all things, they are sovereign over the opinion of the people; for the multitude is persuaded by them."[77] In such regimes, Aristotle suggests, the demos is paradoxically both tyrant and tool of the orators.

Both Aristotle and Demosthenes, then, focus on the problematic ambiguities of the orator-demos relationship. Yet Aristotle's explicit focus on the institutional basis for that relationship seems to preclude Demosthenes' voluntarist solution to the problem. The issue is not that orators must be reined in by the demos; rather, Aristotle claims that any democracy in which such a relationship between demos and orators is even possible is structurally flawed. Aristotle claims that where the demos has unlimited, unaccountable power to judge matters, flattery is the expected result. Aristotle does not explicitly deny that even under such circumstances, good orators might be able to challenge the demos and speak with *parrhēsia*, but neither does he suggest that this would be a likely outcome.

Of course, if Aristotle's solution to the problem of flattery is a "moderate" democracy—subordinate to the law and in which the people do not judge all matters—then his solution is not one that an Athenian democrat could accept. Indeed, a good democrat would reject Aristotle's framing of the problem and counter that the people, judging matters in the courts and the assembly, are the best guardians of the rule of law. Aeschines, at least, argues as much: "Tyrannies and oligarchies are administered according to the tempers of their lords, but democratic states according to their own established laws. Let no man among you forget this, but let each bear distinctly in mind that when he enters a court-room to sit as juror in a suit against an illegal motion [*graphē paranomōn*], on that day he is to cast his vote for or against his own freedom of speech [*parrhēsia*]."[78] Aeschines here calls on the Athenians to defend the rule of law by continuing to hold elites accountable. He may be correct that the *parrhēsia* of ordinary citizens—understood as the privilege of speaking freely and frankly, which Athens prided itself on promoting—depends on the robust popular control of elites, who might otherwise attempt to subvert democratic norms and institutions. But in defending the *graphē paranomōn*, he is also calling for the preservation of an institution that made the practice of frank speech in the assembly rarer, riskier, and more difficult.

III. Conclusion

The contrast between flattery and *parrhēsia* and the parallels between the institutional positions of the tyrant and the demos complicate our under-standing of the theory and practice of *parrhēsia* in Athens. On the level of public culture and in the Athenian ideological imagination, *parrhēsia* may well have served to mark off a boundary between tyrannical and democratic regimes. Yet it is nonetheless telling that the discourse of *parrhēsia* deployed in the assembly often highlighted the similarities between the demos and the autocrat. While both the autocrat and the demos could "grant *parrhēsia*" to their advisers, such freedom was not a foregone conclusion. Absent this privi-lege, advisers could still practice the virtue of risky *parrhēsia* in addressing their audiences, but *parrhēsia* in this sense is a remedial mode of advising unaccountable decision-makers who have the power to hold their advisers to account. The practice of *parrhēsia* was often predicated on inequalities and asymmetries of power. Our understanding of *parrhēsia*'s egalitarian, demo-cratic overtones should accordingly be modified.

Placing that power asymmetry between adviser and decision-maker at the center of the analysis of *parrhēsia* suggests a distinction important for our understanding of Athenian assembly debate more generally. *Parrhēsia* is less a norm for *deliberation* than it is a norm for *counsel*. Athens was not a de-liberative democracy but a democracy with a sovereign demos and a host of advisers. And an analysis of the parallels between autocratic and democratic decision-making, and the kinds of flattering advice they both invite, suggests that the democratic ideals of sound political discussion and strong popular control did not necessarily go hand in hand. Quite to the contrary, there was a potential trade-off between popular control of elites, as institutionalized in the methods for holding orators accountable, and high-quality political debate, if the latter is thought to require a minimum of flattery. It is true that even when the privilege of speaking freely was not granted, *parrhēsia* was still a practice that could help minimize the problem of flattery, but this required an orator to take real risks. And insofar as a supply of orators willing to take those risks could not be guaranteed, flattery was a problem endemic to the assembly. That the Athenians were committed both to popular control of elites and to decision-making informed by sound counsel does not mean that these commitments always fit naturally together.[79]

Demagoguery and the Limits of Expert
Advice in Plato's *Gorgias*

Introduction: Two Objections to Demagoguery

Toward the end of the previous chapter, I briefly turned to Aristotle's analysis of the relationship between the demos and the figures he calls "demagogues" in book 4 of the *Politics*. Demagoguery is a feature of democracies where the judgment of the multitude, rather than the law, is sovereign: "In democracies which are subject to the law there is no demagogue—rather, the best of the citizens are in authority [*en proedriai*]; but where the laws are not sovereign, there demagogues arise."[1] As Aristotle elaborates, "The people become a monarch, one composed of many, and the many are sovereign—not each individual, but all together."[2] Under these conditions, the power wielded by the demos closely resembles the power of a tyrant. Yet the power of both the collective demos and the solitary tyrant is complicated by their relationships with their advisers, demagogues in democracies and flattering counselors in tyrannies: "The demagogue and the flatterer are the same, or equivalents, and each is very powerful [*malista ischuousin*] in their respective cases, flatterers among tyrants, demagogues in democracies of this kind."[3] As we saw, in such situations, power relations become blurred: "For it happens that they [the demagogues] become great because while the demos is sovereign [*kurion*] over all things, they are sovereign over the opinion of the people; for the multitude is persuaded by them."[4] In such regimes, Aristotle suggests, the people have supreme power over political affairs, but their beliefs and opinions are controlled by the demagogues.

The logic of the demos-tyrant analogy would imply that this is not solely a democratic problem: the tyrant, too, could find his power usurped by a flattering counselor whose opinions and advice he trusts. Indeed, elsewhere in the *Politics*, Aristotle describes just such a case from fifth-century Syracuse.

Upon the death of the tyrant Hiero, his brother, Thrasybulus, usurps the authority of Hiero's agreed-upon successor (unnamed by Aristotle, but identified as a son of Gelon and hence a nephew to both Hiero and Thrasybulus).
Strikingly, Aristotle deploys the language of demagoguery here: "Thrasybulus . . . acting like a demagogue to Gelon's son [literally, demagoguing the
son of Gelon], urged him toward the pursuit of pleasure, so that he himself
could rule" (*Thrasuboulou . . . ton huion tou Gelōnos dēmagōgountos kai pros
hēdonas hormōntos, hin' autos archēi*).[5]

The deployment of the language of *demagoguery* in tyrannical (and, as
I discuss below, oligarchic[6]) contexts suggests the need for caution in how
we understand and use the term. Melissa Lane has argued convincingly that
prior to the philosophic interventions of Plato and Aristotle, the term had a
neutral meaning and was not central to diagnosing and analyzing the possible pathologies of democratic rule.[7] Plato, while using a different family of
words (related to the verb *dēmēgorein* as opposed to *dēmagōgein*), was the
first to offer a strong conceptual opposition between the demagogue and the
statesman, emphasizing "the root source of harmful speech in the exercise
of harmful political leadership."[8] Aristotle, following Plato, often deployed
the language of demagoguery pejoratively, particularly in his discussion of
the role of demagoguery in what he views as pernicious forms of democratic
politics.[9] But he also used it to signal political situations where leadership and
influence over a putative decision-maker are mediated decisively through the
powers of speech and persuasion. This captures the two instances of "demagoguery" from Aristotle's *Politics* so far discussed (Thrasybulus' manipulation
of his nephew the tyrant and the orators' relationship to the demos in the
final form of democracy). It also captures what is at stake in Aristotle's discussion of oligarchic demagoguery. On Aristotle's account, while oligarchic
regimes may be threatened when an oligarch appeals directly to the people,
demagoguery can also arise "among the oligarchs themselves [*en autois tois
oligois*]: for though they are very few, a demagogue can still spring up, as in
the case of the Thirty at Athens, where those around Charicles gained power
playing the demagogue [*dēmagōgountes*] to the Thirty; or as in the case of the
Four Hundred, where those around Phrynichus acted in the same way."[10] In
naming Charicles and Phrynichus demagogues, Aristotle calls attention to
the ways in which they (and their associates) used their powers of persuasion
to become leading figures in their respective oligarchic regimes.

The mediating role speech and persuasion play in the relationships
between decision-makers and advisers admits of two distinct, and potentially
difficult to reconcile, worries about democratic politics in particular. We can
start with what we might call *enabling demagoguery*, which gives rise to the

aristocratic objection. On this view, the demagogue fails to exercise his proper role. An orator in a democracy—like a counselor to a monarch—ought to offer sincere advice and attempt to guide political authorities (in a democracy, the assembled demos) in the right direction. By contrast, demagogues and flatterers selfishly pander to the arbitrary whims of the powerful in an effort to aggrandize themselves. Consider the contrast Aristotle draws between the demagogues and the "best of the citizens," whose leadership Aristotle clearly prefers. The contrast calls to mind the analysis of Athenian political history in the Aristotelian *Constitution of the Athenians.* While democratic Athens was tolerably well governed under its earliest leaders, the situation began to deteriorate in the middle of the fifth century; by the end of the Peloponnesian War, the city was run by "an unbroken series of demagogues whose main aim was to be outrageous and please the people with no thought for anything but the present."[11] Moses Finley gives as good a summary of the aristocratic objection as any: "The demagogue is a bad thing: to 'lead the people' is to mislead—above all, to mislead by failing to lead. The demagogue is driven by self-interest, by the desire to advance himself in power, and through power, in wealth. To achieve this, he surrenders all principles, all genuine leadership, and he panders to the people in every way—in Thucydides' words, 'even offering the conduct of affairs to the whims of the people.'"[12] From this vantage point, demagogic politics involves the abdication of leadership and a surrender of control of politics to the people. The demos, not the demagogue, is firmly in control. The aristocratic objection to this state of affairs comes in two forms. A class-based version might dismiss the demagogues themselves as déclassé power strivers and offer critiques of ordinary citizens as passionate, dull, and easily deceived: unfit to manage public affairs. A more sophisticated—we might say philosophical—version of the objection might focus on the need for politics to be guided by reason and virtue. Finley himself did not see much to distinguish these two versions and, in any event, did not think the democrat had to worry too much about either line of attack.[13]

Yet even if we grant to Finley that a committed democrat can avoid the force of the aristocratic objection, Aristotle also develops a second analysis of demagoguery that any democrat would find troubling, regardless of her response to the aristocratic objection. Call this *usurping demagoguery*, which gives rise to the *democratic objection.* Consider again Aristotle's claim that when orators engage in demagogic rhetoric, the rule of the demos may collapse into the rule of those demagogues who are "sovereign over the opinion of the people." The problem here is not a failure to lead, as Finley diagnosed, but a potential usurpation of popular power. This analysis of demagoguery gives rise to a democratic objection to its practice: the demagogue manipulates, deceives, and so comes to usurp the power of his democratic audience. Demagoguery thereby compromises the reality and efficacy of democratic rule. Aristotle's discussion thus seems to point to two very different accounts of demagogic politics. On one description, demagoguery is the perfection of shortsighted, arbitrary popular rule. From another vantage point, demagoguery usurps popular rule and leads to the domination of politics by persuasive orators.

It is tempting to suppose that these are two different political processes that can and should be kept distinct. Yet this way of parsing matters would fail to capture one of the most interesting features of ancient discussions of democratic oratory: the same political phenomena seem readily describable in terms vulnerable to both critiques. Consider Thucydides' famous description of Pericles:

> Being a man of great power both for his dignity and wisdom, and for bribes manifestly the most incorrupt, he freely controled the multitude; and was not so much led by them, as he led them. Because, having gotten his power by no evil arts, he would not humour them in his speeches, but out of his authority durst anger them with contradiction. Therefore, whensoever he saw them out of season insolently bold, he would with his orations put them into a fear; and again, when they were afraid without reason, he would likewise erect their spirits and embolden them. It was in name, a state democratical; but in fact, a government of the principal man.[14]

Under Pericles—that we can even speak of Athens "under Pericles" is suggestive—Athenian democracy was in some way less than real, at least if Thucydides' judgment is to be trusted. On this portrayal, Pericles seems vulnerable to the democratic objection to demagoguery as a subversion of democratic rule (although, of course, for Thucydides this was not necessarily a reason to object to Pericles' political role in the city). On the other hand, consider the judgment of Pericles to be found in the Aristotelian *Athenian Constitution*:

> Pericles became one of the leaders of the people [*pros to dēmagōgein elthontos Perikleous*], first becoming famous when he was a young man and prosecuted Cimon at his *euthuna* as *strategus*. With Pericles, the state became still more democratic; he deprived the Areopagus of some of its powers and turned the state particularly towards naval power, with the result that the masses had the courage to take more into their own hands in all fields of government [*tharrēsantas tous pollous hapasan tēn politeian mallon agein eis hautous*].[15]

Far from describing Periclean Athens as a covert monarchy where the first citizen has usurped the demos' authority, this writer saw Pericles as an enabling demagogue who empowered the demos to take control of the entire constitution (*hapasan tēn politeian*).

Pericles' relationship to the demos, then, was the subject of competing descriptions and analyses: it was possible both to understand Pericles as undermining democracy insofar as he seemed to control the demos and to see Periclean reforms and politics as serving to reinforce popular rule and give the people what they wanted. These competing accounts of democratic oratory—and hence of Athenian politics—have reverberated throughout the history of political thought and in modern scholarship. Let me offer just two examples.

Hobbes (whose translation of Thucydides I used above) presumably has Thucydides—and Athenian democracy in general—in mind when, in the *Elements of Law*, he highlights the likelihood that assembly democracy will collapse into the rule of the putative advisers: "In a multitude of speakers therefore, where always, either one is eminent alone, or a few being equal amongst themselves, are eminent above the rest, that one or few must of necessity sway the whole; insomuch, that a democracy, in effect, is no more than an aristocracy of orators, interrupted sometimes with the temporary monarchy of one orator."[16] Commentators tend to associate this subversion of democracy only with Pericles, perhaps in part because Thucydides encourages his readers to do so: Pericles' successors, "being more on a level with each other and in competition each to be first, began to surrender even the conduct of affairs to the whims of the people."[17] Yet Hobbes' judgment of assembly democracy goes considerably further: not only Periclean democracy but later (perhaps all?) phases of Athenian democracy ran the risk of becoming "merely nominal," whether subverted by an aristocracy of orators or a monarchy of a single ascendant one.[18]

On the other hand, Josiah Ober has done more than any other contemporary scholar to dispel our nagging worries that Athenian democracy was "merely nominal." Like Aristotle and Hobbes, Ober has argued that our assessment of the reality of Athenian democratic rule depends crucially on the relationships between speakers and mass audiences. But Ober interprets that relationship very differently. Stressing the power of the mass audiences over the speakers who came before them, Ober claims that "at the practical level of discourse in the courtroom and Assembly, the orator had to conform to his audience's ideology or face the consequences: losing votes or being ignored."[19] The need for orators always to accommodate their speeches to the beliefs and judgments of the masses meant, in Ober's view, that the orators were never *kurios* over the opinions of the people; rather, the system functioned precisely in reverse.[20]

The clash of judgments here is a tricky matter. For those who might find comparisons between figures from the history of political thought and modern scholars tendentious (in either direction), I would note that Ober claims to find the inspiration for his view in Aristotle's *Rhetoric*.[21] Moreover, Ober sees supporting evidence for his claims that the Athenian demos "really ruled" in what he takes to be the *concurring* judgments of elite critics. Writing of Plato, Aristotle, and others, Ober has claimed that "each of these thoughtful contemporary witnesses assumed that democracy—the political power (*kratos*) of the mass of ordinary citizens (demos)—was real, and that the people of Athens maintained their rule through control of public speech."[22] Yet texts such as the excerpt from *Politics* 1292 with which we began suggest that the story may be more complicated.

Aristotle's accounts of both enabling and usurping demagoguery owe much to the powerful depictions and analyses of both in Plato's *Gorgias*, which I explicate in the rest of this chapter. The dialogue offers competing visions of the power of rhetoric, ranging from Gorgias' claim that the orator can enslave his listeners to Socrates' warning to Callicles that the orator can only gain power in a democratic city such as Athens by effectively enslaving himself to the demos. In presenting these two images, Plato does not privilege one over the other but instead subverts both. Plato's rejection of both claims follows from the analysis of power that Socrates offers in the dialogue, which holds that acting without knowledge of what is really good for human beings cannot be understood as power. Both the assembled demos and the orator fail to meet this standard, and so neither are powerful in the strict Socratic sense. Yet Plato also seems to offer his readers a progression from Gorgias' view to Socrates', and while the former's arguments are criticized and rejected, Socrates' account of rhetoric is never subject to refutation. The dialogue has therefore been read as endorsing the view that the demagogue serves the demos in an uncomplicated way (even if what he provides is not actually good for the citizens).[23]

Ober and others who have endorsed this line of argument are right to stress that the *Gorgias'* grappling with questions of power and control is not exhausted by the Socratic analysis of power. But this does not imply, as they go on to conclude, that the dialogue unequivocally endorses the thesis that the demos is in control after all. Rather, as I will argue, the dialogue proceeds on two levels. Socrates challenges his interlocutors' conceptions of power by contrasting them with one that is tightly linked to a notion of the real good. But he also offers a series of arguments that meet both orators and ordinary citizens on their own levels in an attempt to show them that neither will get what they think they want out of the democratic politics of accountability and advice.

What I am proposing we think of as two separate (or at least separable) lines of argument are often treated in Platonic scholarship as two steps of a single argument. On this line of thought, Socrates' goal is for his interlocutors to recognize that they should spend their time in pursuit of and caring for virtue. His arguments in the protreptic dialogues often take something like the following form. In a first step, Socrates tries to show his interlocutors that doing x (say, addressing the Athenian assembly) will not actually promote some end they think they have (say, becoming powerful). In a second step, Socrates calls into question the end the interlocutors had posited for themselves: becoming powerful isn't the good, but rather philosophy and the care for virtue are.[24] Given the coupling of the two claims, we might think that the first move in the argument is *merely* a first step, entirely subordinate to the central aim of the protreptic, which is to get interlocutors to care for virtue and philosophy. (Plato, in dramatizing the protreptic, may be attempting to get his readers to do the same.)[25] Without disputing that the claims may work together, I argue that in the *Gorgias*, the first step has independent importance. Even where the second step of the protreptic is unsuccessful—where interlocutors are not persuaded to value Socratic virtue and philosophy over other human goods—the first step may prove politically efficacious and normatively valuable.

In the next section, I reconstruct what I call the "Socratic" analysis of power at work in his argument with Polus over whether tyrants are happy. As I argue, Socrates' argument here depends on the premise that tyrants and would-be tyrants, including orators and the demos, are radically ignorant of their own good. (This corresponds to the second step of the protreptic I outlined above, where Socrates attempts to get his interlocutors to see that their understanding of the good is radically deficient.) Whatever the philosophical merits of Socrates' argument, I argue that it is politically inert: he is unable to convince his interlocutors to reorient their lives around a radically alien (to them) conception of the good.

In the following sections, I explore other lines of argument in the dialogue (corresponding to the first step in the protreptic) that may prove more efficacious. In section II, I analyze Socrates' refutation of Gorgias, showing that it works by calling into question not whether the goods the orator seeks to achieve, such as power and wealth, really are *goods* but rather whether an orator is capable of reliably achieving them. In section III, I show that the dialogue similarly seeks to undermine confidence in the demos' ability to use the city's institutions of accountability to promote what they take to be their own advantage. Section IV turns to Socrates' discussion with Callicles. While

some scholars have read this section as implying that the demos, not the orators, are really in control in Athens, I argue that Socrates' shifting accounts of
the power of oratory ultimately work to show the limits of the demos' power
to control public speech. The *Gorgias*, far from univocally acknowledging
(if criticizing) the power of the demos at the expense of the orators, instead
points to the limits of the power of each.

In the conclusion of the chapter, I consider why the dialogue proceeds in
this manner. I argue that, taken as a whole, the dialogue seeks to offer a preliminary answer to a question that Plato saw dramatized by Socrates' own life:
What, if anything, can philosophy say in its confrontation with power? In a
passage that prefigures his trial, Socrates seems to offer a pessimistic account:
a philosopher faced with trying to persuade those who are ignorant of the
good will have nothing to say. If the *Gorgias* limited its discussion of power to
the "Socratic analysis," Socrates' pessimistic judgment would stand. But the
Gorgias also offers another set of reflections on power and politics that might
have offered a way out of Socrates' own political aporia.

I. The Socratic Analysis of Power

On one level, the *Gorgias* offers a simple and straightforward answer to the
question of who truly exercises power when orators interact with their audiences: no one. This is the upshot of the Socratic analysis of power introduced
in his conversation with Polus, the second of the dialogue's three main interlocutors. As I will argue, the Socratic analysis, while (conceivably) philosoph-
ically sound, is politically inefficacious. Socrates' account of power, linked to
knowledge of the good, can be marshaled in the service of an argument that
neither demagogues nor the demos truly exercises power. Yet as the dialogue
dramatizes, these arguments are unlikely to satisfy political agents insofar as
they rely on the premise that political actors are radically ignorant of what is
really good for them.

Socrates introduces his analysis of power as a response to Polus' endorsement of the lives of tyrants and orators.[26] For both the tyrant and the orator,
it is possible to do "in the city whatever seems good to oneself, killing and
expelling and doing all things in accord with one's opinion" (469c).[27] Polus'
argument amounts to something like this:

    a. An agent has power insofar as he can do what seems good to him to do.
    b. Tyrants and orators have the ability to do what seems good to them to do.
    c. Therefore, tyrants and orators have power.

Polus also seems to believe something like the following:

    d. It is good to be able to do whatever seems good to oneself to do (see 468e).

    e. Therefore, it is good to have power and good to be a tyrant or an orator.

Polus' endorsement of the conclusion (e) is plausibly implied by his praise of the Macedonian tyrant Archelaus, who committed many unjust deeds in pursuit of power and personal gain but who, on Polus' account, is to be counted as leading a good life and as happy (471).

Socrates challenges Polus' arguments by offering an analysis of power that links it conceptually to what is *really* good for the agent rather than what seems to him to be good. Relying on Polus' identification of power as a good for its possessor, Socrates asks, "Do you then think it is good, if someone who does not have intelligence does those things that seem to him to be best? And do you call this having great power?" (466e). This is not merely, or even primarily, a challenge to the supposedly powerful's ability to find the appropriate means to their supposed ends. Rather, what is centrally at stake for Socrates is whether political actors have knowledge of what is really good. Polus' praise of Archelaus reflects a strand in Greek (including Athenian) conventional wisdom that sees the tyrant's life as deeply enviable insofar as he is able to appropriate more than his fair share of life's goods.[28] By contrast, Socrates claims that to assess whether Archelaus' position as tyrant is good for him requires, in the final analysis, knowledge of whether he used his position justly. For, as Socrates tells his interlocutors, to their general incredulity, it is better to suffer injustice than to commit injustice; indeed, those who commit injustice are the worst off among humans (473a). This is a specification of what Richard McKim has called the "Socratic Axiom that virtue is always beneficial and vice harmful," even to the agent himself.[29] Socrates thus argues:

    a. Power is good for its possessor (a premise of Polus' that he provisionally accepts).

    b. Doing what seems good to do, without knowledge of what is really good, is not good for the agent.

    c. Orators and tyrants do what seems good to them to do without knowledge of what is really good to do.

    d. Therefore orators and tyrants do not really have power.

Or, to run the argument without recourse to the premise that power is good for its possessor:

    a. Power is the ability to get what you really want, not merely what mistakenly seems good to you.

    b. What humans really want is what is really good for humans, not what merely seems good for humans.

    c. Orators and tyrants do not know what is really good for humans.

d. Acting in ignorance of the real good is unlikely to achieve the real good.

e. Therefore, orators and tyrants are not likely to achieve what is really good for them.

f. Therefore, orators and tyrants do not really have power.[30]

I agree with those commentators who believe that Socrates in the *Gorgias* really is committed to this view of power.[31] It is not merely paradoxical. But whatever its philosophical merits, it is on its face an unsatisfactory political argument. The most troubling premise is that orators, tyrants, and the ordinary citizens who comprise the demos do not know what is really good for them. This is a markedly different claim than merely arguing that they do not know best how to pursue their chosen aims and fulfill their recognized interests—it is a claim that they are radically ignorant about the good.[32] Significantly, Socrates is never able fully to persuade his interlocutors of their own radical ignorance. Consider, for example, the disagreement between Socrates and the other interlocutors over whether it is worse to suffer injustice or to act unjustly.[33] Socrates maintains the latter (e.g., 469c), but he has little success in convincing his interlocutors. Nor is he able to convince them that if one does act unjustly, it is better to be punished and so corrected than to escape punishment.[34] It is not only Polus who finds Socrates' arguments almost incomprehensible.[35] As Callicles demands when he enters the conversation, "Tell me, Socrates, are we to take it that you are now being serious or joking? For if you are serious and these things you are saying now happen to be true, wouldn't the life of us human beings have been turned upside down and don't we do, as it would appear, all the opposite things to what we ought?" (481b–c). If Callicles enters the conversation unconvinced, his subsequent encounter with Socrates does little to change his views (see 513c–d). As Kahn puts it, "The dialogue does not depict episodes of conversion to the philosophic life."[36] To talk someone out of their conception of the good—to convince them of their radical ignorance on this question—seems beyond Socrates' powers, at least this dialogue.[37] The *Gorgias* thus portrays a *failure* of Socratic protreptic, as other commentators have noted.[38]

Socrates' inability to turn his interlocutors toward the care for virtue and philosophy thus threatens to render his entire argument politically inert. For this reason, some commentators have read the dialogue as fundamentally pessimistic. Others have sought to find the dialogue's constructive contribution elsewhere, turning to the political role of the myth that ends the dialogue, the esoteric lessons to which Socrates' failures point, or the ultimate prospects for the success of the protreptic on the *reader*, if not Socrates' interlocutors.[39] Yet this may be to give up on Socrates' refutations of his interlocutors too quickly. The "Socratic" analysis of power is not the only—or, I would argue, even the primary—reflection we get on the question of rhetoric's power in the dialogue. And if the Socratic analysis is politically inert, the other lines of argument are potentially more efficacious. As I will show in the following sections, Socrates argues throughout the dialogue that neither orators nor the demos reliably get what they want from engaging in demagogic politics. Crucially, this argument does not rely on some conception of the good that orators and ordinary citizens may not accept but rather shows how their pursuit of their chosen ends through participation in democratic politics may frequently turn out to be self-defeating or otherwise unrealizable. Accepting such arguments might change political actors' behavior in valuable ways, even if they do not accept the more radical Socratic arguments that entail the wholesale transformation of their values.

II. Gorgias and the Myth of Rhetorical Unaccountability

The first third of the dialogue centers on Gorgias' argument for the power of rhetoric. If Gorgias' claims were true, then democratic politics would look much like Aristotle's depiction of the demos-as-tyrant whose opinions and actions are nevertheless controlled by persuasive orators. Yet as becomes clear in the course of his discussion with Socrates, Gorgias' case for the power of rhetoric is exaggerated. His account of the orator as able to bend his audience to his will is undermined by the ways in which his arguments and actions reveal his own awareness of the limits of the orator's power. In showing Gorgias (and the other interlocutors) those limits, Socrates does not rely on the "Socratic" analysis of power I explicated in the previous section: he shows instead that rhetoric practiced within the institutional constraints of democracy is not the all-purpose means of manipulation and control that Gorgias assumes it to be.

As commentators have long recognized, Gorgias' claims in their conversation are shaped by Socrates' baiting and questioning.[40] Gorgias begins with a series of short claims about rhetoric, in keeping with Socrates' injunction to answer his questions briefly and to the point (449). According to Gorgias, rhetoric is knowledge "about speeches" (449e), it is the art whose "whole action and decisive effect are through speeches" (450b–c), especially speeches about "the greatest of human affairs . . . and the best" (451d). Thus far, Gorgias has said very little (and nothing clearly).[41] Socrates begins putting pressure on Gorgias by summoning into speech a tribunal of experts—the doctor, the trainer, and the moneymaker (452). These men boast of their abilities to provide human goods—health, beauty, and wealth—and challenge Gorgias' claim that rhetoric deals with the "greatest of human affairs . . . and the best" (451d). This challenge induces Gorgias' first extended statement about rhetoric: "[It makes you] able to persuade by speeches judges in the law court, councillors in the council, assemblymen in the assembly, and in every other gathering whatsoever, when there is a political gathering. And indeed with this power you will have the doctor as your slave, and the trainer as your slave; and that moneymaker of yours will be plainly revealed to be making money for another and not for himself, but for you who can speak and persuade multitudes" (452e). In response to Socrates' challenge, Gorgias offers a view of rhetoric that allows its practitioner to enjoy all the goods Socrates had outlined and more. The orator is able to persuade multitudes and thus to exercise power over "political gatherings"—that is, the authoritative institutions of the polis. This also gives the orator power over individuals, making him preeminent in the city. Both the demos and private citizens in the city thereby become instruments of the orator's will. The language of slavery throughout the passage underscores this point: Gorgias presents the power of rhetoric as, in effect, the art of turning humans into tools.[42] Gorgias here expounds what Rachel Barney has called the "*manipulative conception* of rhetoric": the orator is able to get others "to work against their own interests, for the rhetorician's private good."[43]

Having elicited a strong claim for rhetoric's power, Socrates next brings to bear the motivating power of the audience (Gorgias' potential customers[44]) to induce Gorgias to elaborate on rhetoric's scope: "Perhaps some one of those inside happens to wish to become a student of yours. . . . So, being asked by me, consider that you are asked by them too: 'What will be ours, Gorgias, if we associate with you? About what things will we be able to give counsel to the city [*peri tinōn tēi polei sumbouleuein hoioi te esometha*]? About the just and unjust alone, or also about the things of which Socrates was speaking just now [i.e., about preparations for war and civic projects in the city]?'" (455c–d). Socrates here makes clear the basic function of the orator in the assembly: to advise (*sumbouleuein*) the city. Gorgias accepts this framing and asserts that the power of rhetoric is such that it enables the orator to offer persuasive advice in areas beyond his expertise. He cites Themistocles' and Pericles' political successes in support of this view: they—not expert artisans, merchants, or generals—successfully counseled the Athenians to build dockyards and walls (455e).

The significance of the rhetor's ability successfully to advise an audience on almost any topic becomes clear when Gorgias offers as a final example of rhetoric's power his own experience with his brother, a doctor:

[A] On many occasions now I have gone in with my brother and with other doctors to one of the sick who was unwilling either to drink a drug or to submit himself to the doctor for surgery or cautery; the doctor being unable to persuade him, I persuaded him, by no other art than rhetoric. [B] And I assert further that, if a rhetorical man and a doctor should go into any city you wish and should have to contest in speech, in the assembly or in some other gathering, which of the two ought to be chosen doctor, the doctor would plainly be nowhere, but the man with the power to speak would be chosen, if he wished. (456b–c)

I have divided this section of Gorgias' speech into two cases, (A) and (B), since both the similarities and the differences between them are instructive. Gorgias' ability to assist his brother in ministering to patients suggests that the orator can use his influence for the good of those whom he persuades: he *can* serve as a helpful *sumboulos*. Gorgias is presumably guided by his brother's diagnosis and prescribed remedy; here rhetoric comes to the aid of expert knowledge. Why precisely Gorgias' doctor brother requires such assistance is not made explicit in the dialogue, but presumably the patients do not believe him that burning and cutting—"the twin horrors of pre-anesthetic surgery," in Dodds' memorable phrase—will make them healthier.[45] In the second case, cooperation between doctor and orator is replaced by competition. Again, whether through fear or ignorance, the assembly, choosing a doctor, is un-persuaded by the medical man's presentation of his own merits (and those of his cures). This time, however, the alliance between the persuasive orator and the knowledgeable doctor is severed. Gorgias leaves it open whether an orator would seek to supplant the doctor in this way and whether, having done so, he might still rely on the doctor's expert knowledge in offering prescriptions. Nonetheless, the orator's adoption of the role of helpful adviser comes to seem radically contingent. The benevolent use of rhetoric is inseparable from the more troubling "contest in speech" between the rhetorical man and the doctor. The success of the rhetorician in both cases crucially relies on the patients' de-pendence on medical experts for treatment and advice, and their inability to judge and choose medical treatments correctly. Gorgias has thus (implicitly) offered an account of why rhetoric has the power it does. The orator's audi-ence is radically open to manipulation because they are ignorant of the *means* that might promote their good or are unable to judge accurately who would best promote it. Nonetheless, I think it is crucial that the audience accepts that health is a good and that it in principle might require painful treatment. The orator does not try to change their minds about health and its status as a good—he simply convinces them that he can promote that end.[46]

There is a second important difference between the cases. In (A) the orator and doctor pair are advising an individual patient; in (B) the advisee is an
assembly, which Gorgias elsewhere disparages as an *ochlos* (a mob; cf. 454b
and 455a). Gorgias, at least, sees the susceptibility of audiences to rhetorical
manipulation as a particularly democratic problem. The power of rhetoric
finds its natural home in assemblies, courts, and councils—the central democratic institutions (452e). Throughout his conversation with Socrates, Gorgias
tends to limit the scope of rhetoric's effect to interactions with mass audiences: "For there is nothing about which the rhetorician would not speak
more persuasively than any other of the craftsmen *in a multitude* [*en plēthei*]"
(456c6, emphasis mine); "the rhetor has power to speak against all men and
about everything, so as to be more persuasive *in multitudes* [*en tois plēthesin*]
about, in brief, whatever he wishes" (457a–b, emphasis mine). The point is
raised explicitly at 459a:

> SOC: Then you were saying just now that the rhetor will be more persuasive
>   than the doctor even about the healthy.
> GOR: Yes I was—that is, in a mob [*en ge ochlōi*].
> SOC: So then, does the "in a mob" amount to this: among those who don't
>   know? For among those who know, at any rate, I don't suppose he will be
>   more persuasive than the doctor.

The focus on rhetoric's power over democratic audiences in particular may
resonate with the historical Gorgias' own claims. In the *Encomium of Helen*,
Gorgias emphasizes the power of rhetoric over "the mob": "One speech persuades and delights a large mob [*polun ochlon*], written with art, but not spoken with truth."[47] Yet as Dodds rightly notes, there is something odd about
Gorgias' insistence on the collective nature of the audience: "In adding the
restriction [*en ge ochlōi*] Gorgias seems to forget the case he quoted at 456b1
[case A above], or to treat it as exceptional."[48]

Socrates' intervention at 459a thus calls into question Gorgias' restriction
of rhetoric's scope. Neither Gorgias nor Socrates presents an argument denying the possibility that an audience of multiple knowers might be able to
resist rhetoric's power. Nor is there any reason to doubt that a single ignorant individual could be just as vulnerable to manipulation as a democratic
audience. On Gorgias' view, democratic audiences are in a bind. They lack
some knowledge or perspective on an issue (this is, as I've argued in previous
chapters, why they need advice). Yet it is precisely this lack that renders them
vulnerable to manipulation and abuse at the hands of their putative advisers.

On Socrates' view, this bind is a more general problem, intimately tied up with the problem of counsel itself, whether those seeking advice are singular agents or plural.

If the "contest in speech" between the doctor and rhetor stands as a vivid image of the orator's power, it also drives Socrates' refutation of Gorgias. As we have seen, Socrates draws from Gorgias' examples a general claim—the rhetor is better able than an expert to persuade an audience of nonknowers (459a). This turns out to be a dangerous point for Gorgias to insist on, since it implies that orators have great capacity to do injustice. When persuading about the just and unjust, the orator will be able to convince those who do not know about justice to (believe and) do the unjust thing. Gorgias has already shown himself to be concerned about this possibility, claiming that rhetoric, like other competitive skills—such as boxing, wrestling, and fighting in heavy armor—should be used justly (456d–e) and that students of rhetoric who misuse their power should be justly punished (457b–c). When Socrates later interrogates Gorgias on whether he ought to teach rhetoric to those who do not know what is just, Gorgias—presumably fearing to be revealed as an enabler of injustice—claims that he will teach his students justice as well as rhetoric. From this admission, Socrates is able to conclude—using characteristically Socratic premises equating knowledge of justice with being just and being just with doing just things (460b)—that rhetors will never do injustice. With this conclusion, the power of rhetoric is defused and transformed. The rhetor will not make men his slaves or convince mass gatherings to do his will if such actions are unjust. Nor would the rhetor take advantage of his ability to persuade ignorant groups of whatever he wishes.[49]

Socrates' refutation of Gorgias' argument has long been recognized as problematic—indeed, it is marked as such by the other interlocutors in the dialogue. One issue is its reliance on controversial Socratic premises that "knowing" justice entails being and acting just.[50] Yet the problems begin even earlier. Gorgias only accepts the key move in Socrates' refutation—that Gorgias knows about justice and will teach his students about it if they are ignorant of it—out of shame, as Polus makes explicit (461b–c): "For who do you think would utterly deny both that he knows the just things and that he would teach others?" If Gorgias were willing to deny that he teaches justice (which the historical Gorgias, from the available evidence, would have happily done), Socrates' refutation would not get off the ground. As Christina Tarnopolsky has noted, Socrates in the *Gorgias* appears to be "a master of utilizing the psychological compulsion involved in the phenomenon of shame by manipulating his interlocutor's fear of disgrace or dishonor before others."[51] Socrates' constant conjuring of audiences—real and imaginary—is central to his effort to influence the contours and content of Gorgias' argument. In taking the bait, Gorgias shows himself keen to adapt his arguments to his audience.

While other scholars have nicely shown the ways in which the argument is shaped by the dramatic setting and Socrates' manipulations, I want to stress the explicitly political dimension of Gorgias' predicament. Gorgias is not only concerned with attracting customers and avoiding shameful claims. He is also keenly aware of the potential political vulnerability of the orator. And this awareness of vulnerability in itself belies his claims for rhetoric's power. He accompanies his claim that those who misuse rhetoric should be punished with an equally vehement denial that teachers whose students abuse rhetoric are to blame: "If someone has become a rhetorician and then does injustice with this power and art, one must not hate the man who *taught him* and expel him from the cities. For that man imparted it for just use, and the other used it in the opposite way. It is just, then, to hate, expel, and kill the one who uses it not correctly, but not the one who taught it" (457b–c, emphasis mine). Gorgias' concern to indemnify the teachers of rhetoric from the threat of punishment reveals his awareness that "political gatherings" are not merely the tools of orators but potentially have wills of their own. It is the demos, in the assembly and courts, whom Gorgias is counseling to focus their wrath on those who misuse rhetoric rather than on those who merely teach (such as Gorgias himself).

Put another way, one corollary of Gorgias' argument for the rhetor's power is that he can use it with impunity. If the rhetor is truly able to convince a "mob" of anything, then he will be able to convince them of his own goodwill and innocence. Throughout his discussion with Socrates, Gorgias portrays the audience as passive, manipulable, and malleable. He is a "theorist of the persuadable soul," for whom "the soul of the listener remains a passive object," while the "contingency and power in the process remain with the speaker."[52] Within such a conception of rhetoric, the assumption of rhetorical impunity may go unquestioned. Nonetheless, Gorgias' actions suggest that the weakness of the assumption is never far from his mind. Gorgias' attempt to preempt any accusations against the teachers of rhetoric suggests that he recognizes the precariousness of their position and their vulnerability to punishment. Were rhetoric really as powerful as Gorgias claims, he would have no need to be so cautious.[53] Yet his caution makes sense against the backdrop of one of the central facts of Athenian politics, which I have been arguing is deeply implicated in Greek reflections on the politics of advice: the accountability of political elites, including orators, to popular institutions such as the courts and the assembly.

Gorgias' position thus rests on a fiction. We could read Gorgias' arguments, and especially some of the more extravagant claims of the other interlocutors (e.g., Polus at 468e), as fantasies about the power of oratory, fueling and expressing the tyrannical desires of (some) democratic citizens.[54] Or perhaps, more prosaically, these claims merely reflect ignorance of Athenian political realities on the part of noncitizen professional sophists.[55] In any case, the poor fit between Gorgias' model of rhetoric and the Athenian political system is clearly exposed. If the orators were completely unaccountable, and the demos completely passive, then perhaps the former would be able to treat the assembly simply as an instrument of their own power. In reality, though, persuasion in the assembly took place within an institutional structure that held orators accountable to the demos, and the latter could exercise power over the former. It is this fact that Gorgias ignores and that Socrates forces him to confront by continually reminding him of the power of the audience.

This line of argument departs from the "Socratic analysis" of power (discussed in section I) in an important way. It works not by calling into question whether the goods the orator wishes to achieve—say, wealth, security, and domination—are really goods but rather by asking whether the orator in the city is really capable of achieving them reliably. If the power of orators over the demos is always contingent and vulnerable to disruption (or worse), then it is much narrower than Gorgias and his followers would like to believe.

The question of rhetorical impunity resurfaces in Socrates' conversation with each interlocutor in the dialogue. Socrates has to remind Polus forcefully that a rhetor can be made to pay for his unjust actions and that therefore such actions may not be of much use to him. Even if rhetors, "just like tyrants, kill whomever they wish, and confiscate possessions, and expel from the cities whomever it seems good to them," such power is moot when "it is necessary for someone who acts in this manner to pay a penalty" (466c, 470a). Here again, Socrates' strategy is not to argue that orators who manipulate the demos into killing their personal opponents and confiscating their possessions cannot be counted as exercising power unless those actions are *really* good for them. He is making the more basic point that under a democracy, such actions are always liable to the scrutiny, judgment, and potential sanction of the demos.

Importantly, the success of this argument is independent of Socrates' ability to convince his interlocutors to value justice and philosophy above other goods. Jessica Moss and others who read the *Gorgias* as a fundamentally pessimistic dialogue see the encounter with Polus as a failure.[56] Moss argues that "in challenging his interlocutors' conceptions of what is good and of how they should live, Socrates often in effect tells them not to pursue the things they find pleasant."[57] This, she persuasively argues, is a difficult task. Yet insofar as Socrates also offers an argument against the life of the tyrant or the power-seeking orator that does not require a radical reorientation of his interlocutor's conception of the good, the dialogue may leave open a space for effective persuasion.

A parallel line of argument features in Socrates' discussion with Callicles of Athens' reputedly great leaders, such as Themistocles and Pericles, to which I now turn.

III. Socrates and the Limits of Democratic Accountability and Advice

Gorgias first mentions Pericles and Themistocles as paradigmatic cases of successful orators able to "give counsel and victoriously carry their resolutions" about all manner of things (456a). As the dialogue unfolds, Socrates offers a very different account of what successful orators do. A good adviser makes his audience better, and Socrates denies that Pericles and other well-regarded democratic leaders were able to do this (503d). To say that they were unable to improve their audiences is to deny that they were practitioners of the true political art, which Socrates begins to develop here.[58] An orator practicing the true political art will try to instill in his audience justice, moderation, and the other virtues. This, Socrates suggests, is incompatible with gratifying their desires if they are not already good (505b).

As Socrates finds, it is not easy for his interlocutors to apply this standard to actual politics. At 515e, Socrates poses to Callicles the question directly: Did Pericles make the Athenians better, or did he corrupt them? Socrates recounts that he has heard that "Pericles made the Athenians lazy, cowardly, babbling, and money lovers" by virtue of promoting state pay and making the city more democratic. Callicles, however, does not take this to be clear evidence that Pericles failed to meet Socrates' standards of political leadership. He offers the obvious response: these are the common complaints of "the men with cauliflower ears"—that is, suspected partisans of oligarchy within the city.[59] The trouble with Socrates' standard for the good political orator is that it is impossible to apply and evaluate without knowledge of the good, including, inter alia, knowledge of the virtues. The problem diagnosed in section I thus reappears again. How can one judge an orator's success in instilling virtue in his audience without oneself knowing the virtues? Socrates here attempts to solve the problem by appealing to (antidemocratic) public opinion. But Callicles is right to be suspicious: Why accept an oligarch's account of moderation and justice? A democrat might tell a very different story about democracy's relationship to the virtues.[60] Without common agreement on and knowledge of the virtues, Socrates' standards for truly practicing politics provide only an uncertain guide, or no guide at all, to evaluation and action.

Yet Socrates recognizes that this line of argument leads to an impasse. He claims he can do better, as signaled by a contrast between what he has merely heard (the complaints of the oligarchs) and what he distinctly knows: "But the following things are no longer what I hear, but what I distinctly know, and you do too: that at first Pericles was well reputed, and the Athenians voted no shameful judgment in condemnation of him, at the time they were worse. But after they had become noble and good through him, toward the end of Pericles' life, they voted a condemnation of him for theft, and came close to sentencing him to death, clearly on the grounds that he was base" (515e–16a). Socrates argues that this sequence of events strongly implies that Pericles failed to make the Athenians better. If he had made them better, he would have made them more just and therefore gentler (516c). But instead he made them more savage—"and that against himself, against whom he would have wished it least" (516c). Socrates concludes from this argument that Pericles made the Athenians more unjust and worse—and hence that he was "not good in political affairs" (516d).

Other scholars have noted that Socrates' description of events here is hardly fair to Pericles.[61] We might also find the analogy between the politician and the "caretaker of asses, horses, or oxen" (516a)—the basis for Socrates' claim that a good politician will make those in his care gentler—an inappropriate way to model democratic politics. Yet even if we reject the comparison, and are hesitant to accept Socrates' standards for what counts as successful political activity, Socrates' argument suggests that the relationship between Athenian leaders and the demos poses problems for both parties.

Most obviously, Socrates has reminded Callicles that advising the demos can be a dangerous practice and may not benefit the adviser. Pericles has failed at the basic task of Gorgias' conception of rhetoric—manipulating his audience for his own (perceived) advantage. Gorgias' manipulative conception of rhetoric proves an inadequate description of actual politics. Nor is Pericles' failure unique; Socrates notes that all the politicians Callicles had praised were ultimately called to account by the Athenian demos (516d–e). Cimon was ostracized "so that they would not hear his voice for ten years," Themistocles forced into exile, Miltiades almost killed. Politicians at Athens, far from being master manipulators of the demos, cannot even avoid harsh punishment at the hands of their supposed subjects.[62]

If Athenian politicians are unable to avoid being held to account for their leadership and the advice they give, Socrates nonetheless does not claim that this accountability relationship redounds to the benefit of the Athenians. The

Athenians are unable to exercise their accountability functions to their own advantage. When contemporary Athenians praise Pericles and other past leaders, "they say that those men made the city great; but that it is swollen and festering with sores underneath on account of those ancient men, they do not perceive. For without moderation and justice they have filled up the city with harbors, dockyards, walls, tribute, and such drivel; so then when that access of weakness comes, they will charge the counselors then present, but will extol Themistocles, Cimon, and Pericles, the ones responsible for the evils" (518e–19a). Socrates' argument here is complex. In part he relies on a claim that the Athenians are unable to recognize what is actually good for them—the "drivel" of dockyards and tribute covers up the reality that the city is "festering with sores." This critique of Athenian accountability relies on a Socratic conception of the good, one that his interlocutors (and fellow democratic citizens) may not have access to and that they may therefore find difficult to assess. Yet Socrates also argues that the Athenians are ignorant of who is responsible for the evils that are going to befall them. Importantly, these are evils that the Athenians themselves could recognize, associated with the fall of the empire and the tyranny of the Thirty. To emphasize the point, Plato employs a narrative trick: the rot at the heart of the empire may not be visible to Socrates' interlocutors in the *Gorgias*, who are in the midst of the Peloponnesian War.[63] But the ultimate collapse of the Athenian empire would be at the forefront of Plato's audience's mind when reading these passages: the relevant context, as Dodds notes, is the "disaster which overwhelmed Athens in 404": "It was the creators of the Athenian [*archē*] who set their country on the wrong course, and thus made its ruin inevitable."[64] Other commentators have explicated the critique of Athenian democratic imperialism that Plato develops here.[65] Yet Plato also offers a broad challenge to the basis of a democratic politics of accountability, on grounds that anyone can access. Like Diodotus in his critique of Cleon, Socrates raises the possibility that assessments of responsibility in politics may be more difficult than citizens would like to believe. This threatens to undermine the efficacy of the Athenian politics of accountability so central to the city's practice of democracy.[66] Athenian accountability practices undermine the Gorgianic myth of rhetorical impunity. But that does not mean that they serve the interests of the demos in any straightforward way. Orators and the demos both fail to live up to Socratic standards of good politics—but they also fail to achieve their own standards for success.

The *Gorgias* thus offers a political argument that takes into account the limits of the Socratic analysis of power and meets partisans of both the enabling and the usurping conceptions of demagoguery on their terms. The dialogue challenges the usurping conception of demagoguery by showing that the accountability relationship between the demos and orators and the frequency with which orators were punished undermines the claim that orators were able to use the demos straightforwardly as instruments of their will. As I have now begun to show, Socrates in turn undermines the enabling conception of demagoguery, stressing the difficulties the demos faces in using the machinery of democratic politics, including institutions of accountability, to achieve their chosen ends. I continue this line of argument in the following section.

IV. Socrates and the Ideological Power of the Demos

If we take the fact of oratorical accountability seriously, what picture of rhetoric are we left with? Socrates offers something of an answer in developing his contrasting model of rhetoric in the second part of the dialogue, which holds rhetoric to be a "part of flattery." In so identifying rhetoric, Socrates makes two key claims. First, rhetoric is not a *technē*: "And I assert that it is not art but experience [*empeiria*] because it has no reasoned account, in regard to the thing to which it administers or the things it administers, of what sort of things they are in their nature; and so it cannot state the cause of each thing" (465a). As such, rhetoric lacks a foundation in real knowledge—in particular, in real knowledge of human goods. This claim is closely linked to the second key feature of Socrates' definition of rhetoric: it aims at gratifying humans (a matter for experience) rather than improving them (the task of an art, based on knowledge of human goods). As Socrates claims, flattery "gives no heed to the best but hunts after folly with what is ever most pleasant, and deceives, so as to seem to be worth very much" (464d).

Socrates' definition of rhetoric as (a part of) flattery complements the diagnosis of the central flaw in Gorgias' model of rhetoric. Given the fact of oratorical accountability, we can see flattery as the default strategy of an orator facing the demos. The demos can reward and punish the rhetor at will and with impunity. The incentive to flatter is therefore built into the orator-demos relationship, insofar as a gratified audience is more likely to reward than punish its gratifier. Yet the diagnosis of rhetoric as flattery does not in itself answer our questions concerning the balance of power between orator and demos. After all, in the excerpt from Aristotle's *Politics* with which we opened this chapter, flattery is the tool with which orators come to rule over the opinions of the people. It is undeniable that there was a structural power asymmetry between orator and demos. But did that asymmetry decisively limit the orator's ability to deploy speech as an instrument of power?

On Josiah Ober's reading of the *Gorgias*, Plato acknowledges severe limits to the power of speech:

> The reader learns that public speech caters indiscriminately to the desires of the many (thereby corrupting them) while *simultaneously serving to corrupt the speaker and enslave him to the multitude*. This is because it was not actually the speaker who controlled the rhetorical process and its outcome by shaping mass opinion to conform to his own wishes; rather, the mass audience controlled the speaker, whose desire for honor and power led him first to imitate his audience and finally to become identical to the mob. Along the way, the dialogue once again exposes the reality that lies at the heart of the democracy: that in Athens, the demos really does rule. It reveals that the instrument of demotic rule is an ideological hegemony over each citizen, and especially over would-be leaders.[67]

Ober thus reads Socrates' interventions in the dialogue as adding up to a compelling picture of "demotic rule" through ideological hegemony.

Ober's account also flags a strange feature of Socrates' analysis, although Ober himself does not make much of it: Socrates' portrayal of the relationship between orator and demos is inconsistent. The orator is said both to imitate his audience and to become identical to them (see 481 and 510, as discussed below). Ober interprets the inconsistency temporally and thereby salvages a coherent picture: the orator first imitates the demos, and when that fails, he strives to really become identical to the people. In what follows, I take a different approach. Rather than finding in Socrates' discussion with Callicles a unified account, I read Socrates as offering several discrete pictures of the orator-demos relationship in which the orator comes to light as an increasingly subservient, marginal, and even pitiable figure. On the first model, the orator retains some control over his audience. On the second model, although extremely constrained in what he can argue and the effects he can obtain, the orator remains a free agent. On the third model, he is radically subservient to the demos and must alter his very being just to escape his interactions with the demos unscathed. In the following pages, I elaborate on these three models. In doing so, I stress the ways in which aspects of the last two models depart from the realities of Athenian politics.

The first model can be inferred from Socrates' comments about the power of rhetoric as he introduces his conception of it as flattery. It is clear that at this point in the dialogue, he has some respect for the effects rhetoric can accomplish. As he tells Gorgias, "In my opinion, then, Gorgias, [rhetoric] is a certain pursuit that is not artful but belongs to a soul that is skilled at guessing, courageous, and terribly clever at associating with human beings;

and I call its chief point flattery" (463a). Socrates has denied that rhetoric is a *technē*, but he does not thereby declare that it is altogether powerless.[68] The orator is skilled at guessing and willing to take risks to achieve his own ends. In stressing the orator's cleverness at associating with human beings, Socrates leaves open the possibility of the orator being able to manipulate his audience. Indeed, the power of rhetoric is reaffirmed just below. Having established an analogy between cookery and rhetoric, with both identified as forms of flattery, Socrates sets up a competition between a cook and a doctor: "If the cook and the doctor had to contest among children or among men as thoughtless as children which of the two, the doctor or the cook, has understanding about useful and bad foods, the doctor would die of hunger" (464d–e). This analysis of rhetoric's power is close to Gorgias' own; the return of the contest between orator and doctor in the guise of a contest between a cook and a doctor underscores this point.

Socrates' second model presents the orator as operating under significantly stricter constraints. This model is on display early in Socrates' discussion with Callicles, where Socrates analyzes Callicles' relationships to his two loves: the Athenian demos and a young man of the same name (Demos). As Socrates tells him, "I perceive you on each occasion unable, terribly clever though you are, to contradict what your boyfriends say and how they say things are, but you turn yourself around up and down. In the assembly, if, as you are saying something, the Athenian people denies that it is so, you turn around and say what it wishes . . . for you are not able to oppose either the proposals or the speeches of your boyfriends" (481d–e). On the previous model, there seemed to be space for the orator to pursue his own line of thought and plan of action. On this second view, the orator is so attuned to the nuances of the demos' desires, and so driven to please his audience, that he is unable to put forward a consistent plan of his own. The "cleverness" highlighted in the first model is longer of any use to him. The orator, unwilling to contradict the demos, finds himself significantly constrained by the demos' desires.

For Socrates' second model to be sound, the orator must have significant access to those desires. Accordingly, Socrates offers a picture of assembly debate in which that access is immediate and detailed. Reactions occur in real time: "If you are saying something, [and] the Athenian people denies that it is so, you turn around and say what it wishes." Reactions are also content rich: the orator can observe the audience's wishes, and the demos is said to give "speeches" and "proposals." Although this helps establish Socrates' argument, it does so by exaggerating the degree to which communication in the assembly was a reciprocal activity. Formally, audience communication to speakers was supposed to be nonexistent: while any citizen attending an assembly meeting could speak if he so desired, the audience was expected to listen quietly to the speeches.[69] In practice this norm of silence was violated, and scholars such as Josiah Ober have persuasively argued for the many ways in which the audience could communicate with the orator. In real time, these ranged from nonverbal cues to heckling; the audience could also signal their desires after the speech through voting and through "their subsequent behavior toward the speaker."[70] Yet to see the limitations of the verbal communication that the audience could deploy, we need only turn to the most well-known example of such a display, the *thorubos*. The *thorubos*—the disruptive clamor with which the demos could express its disapproval of a speaker and force him from the rostrum—is, significantly, primarily a vehicle for expressing *disapproval* (although it could also be used to express approval or praise of a speaker's point). Here is how Socrates elsewhere depicts the nature of mass audience communication: "[They sit] together in great numbers, in the *ekklēsia* or the courts or the theater or encamped or in some other common assembly of the masses. With a great *thorubos* they censure and praise the things done and said, each exceedingly, shouting and applauding. In addition, the rocks and the place where they are, re-echoing twofold the *thorubos*, furnish censure and praise."[71] To be sure, Socrates thinks that the *thorubos* is an awesome display that can have a powerful effect on the speakers it is directed at as well as on those who hear its roar. Yet it is not clear how the *thorubos*—or any other form of collective display—could signify in detail the content of the audience's wishes, let alone how it could rise to the level of "speeches" and "proposals," as Socrates' model of demos-orator interaction here seems to require.

As the discussion with Callicles progresses, Socrates offers a more radical view of the dependence of the orator on his audience. This third model has two relevant features. First, Socrates gets Callicles to agree to limit their analysis of power to "the art for the preparation of suffering no injustice or as little as possible" (510a). In doing so, the range of rhetoric's effects is implicitly reduced: we are now in a world where the most rhetoric can aspire to be is a kind of master defensive activity. Second, and more centrally, Socrates argues that where a "savage and uneducated tyrant" is ruler, only those "being of the same character and praising and blaming the same things" will have great power (510b–c). He who wishes to acquire power, then, must "immediately from youth . . . accustom himself to rejoice and to be distressed at the same things as the master and to make preparations so as to be as much as possible like that man" (510d). To acquire power, it is not enough to say what the tyrant finds agreeable and refrain from contradicting his desires; rather, one must actually become like the tyrant. Successful persuasion requires one not only to know[72] one's audience well enough to appeal to them but also to become like them oneself. Deploying the demos-tyrant analogy, Socrates warns Callicles that in Athens you must "become as much as possible like the Athenian people, if you are to be a dear friend to it and to have great power in the city" (513a).

Socrates' final model of the orator-demos relationship thus amounts to a denial of the very possibility of oratorical manipulation, but it only reaches this conclusion by effacing the difference between the orator and the demos altogether. Socrates explicitly denies that one could succeed at convincing one's audience without becoming like them: "If you think any human being at all will impart to you a certain art such as to make you have great power in this city while being unlike the regime, whether for better or for worse, as it seems to me, you are not taking counsel correctly, Callicles. For you must be not an imitator but like these men in your very own nature, if you are to achieve something genuine in friendship with the Athenian people" (513a–b). It is worth reflecting on just how odd Socrates' assertion is here. His focus on the character of the speaker being crucial to efforts at persuasion is not in itself noteworthy. Aristotle develops this idea at length in his *Rhetoric*. Yet Aristotle does not arrive at Socrates' extreme conclusion. Rather, in Aristotle's view, "since all people receive favorably speeches spoken in their own character [*ēthei*] and by persons like themselves, it is not unclear how both speakers and speeches may *seem to be of this sort through use of words*."[73] Aristotle thinks that accommodating one's character to one's audience is relatively easy and can be accomplished at the level of language and appearance. Socrates, in utterly denying this, places himself outside the rhetorical tradition and, indeed, outside the realm of the plausible.[74]

Nonetheless, it is crucial to note that the argument, if sound, would serve to disqualify Callicles from a position of leadership in a democratic city. While some commentators read Callicles as a committed democrat—a true lover of the demos and thoroughly indoctrinated into democratic ideology—such a picture is difficult to sustain given Callicles' infamous critique of egalitarian politics that he develops in his opening speech (e.g., 483).[75] Kahn therefore concludes that there is an "underlying conflict" between Callicles' "elitist convictions" and "popular aspirations."[76] But this conflict is only insurmountable politically if it is true, as Socrates claims, that one must be thoroughly like the demos to lead a democratic city. If contempt for ordinary citizens and even democracy is compatible with advising the demos, then a path to leadership for Callicles remains open. At stake in whether Callicles accepts Socrates' arguments here may be the willingness of men like him to engage in democratic politics. If Socrates must exaggerate the power of the demos to make democratic politics thoroughly unattractive to a Callicles, then the image of the slavish orator will have served its purpose.

Within the dramatic context of the dialogue, Socrates' exaggerated portrayal of the demos' control over the orators thus serves to emphasize to would-be democratic leaders such as Callicles and their potential teachers such as Gorgias that orators are not as powerful as they might like to believe. Yet as readers of the dialogue, I do not believe that we are meant to take Socrates' final images of the relationship between orator and demos entirely seriously. Rather than offering evidence for the thoroughgoing domination of the orators by the demos, they point to the limitations of that domination.

These limitations are highlighted again in yet another metaphor for the rhetor-demos relationship that Socrates provides, this one in the *Republic*. There, Socrates likens the sophists who claim to teach wisdom to

> [someone] learning the moods and appetites of a huge, strong beast that he's rearing—how to approach and handle it, when it is most difficult to deal with or most gentle and what makes it so, what sounds it utters in either condition, and what sounds soothe or anger it. Having learned all this through tending the beast over a period of time, he calls this knack wisdom, gathers his information together as if it were a craft, and starts to teach it.[77]

Here is Josiah Ober's reading of this passage:

> The keeper is quickly trained to cater to the beast's needs by its infernal bellowing and its response to different sorts of speech. In the end, through a sort of Pavlovian behavioral conditioning, he will learn to provide the beast with whatever it wants. Having been well trained in this fashion, the keeper, although self-evidently the beast's servant, then claims to have mastered (and to be able to teach others) the secrets of beast-management.[78]

In spite of Ober's confidence, it is not "self-evident" to me that the keeper is the beast's servant. That judgment hinges on a number of factors. Above all, it requires downplaying the significance of the keeper's ability to soothe and infuriate the beast, to approach it and handle it, all of which imply that he might be able to direct it. It also requires abstracting away from the deeply insulting and dehumanizing portrayal of the demos as a beast. Ober reads the *Gorgias* and the *Republic* as being in broad agreement with one another and as jointly supporting his thesis that Plato recognized and criticized absolute popular control over public speech. In contrast, I think that Socrates in the *Gorgias* has offered a portrait of *what would need to be true* for that domination to be fully effective: either the demos would have to be able to communicate perfectly with the orators, or the orators themselves would have to become exactly like the demos. Absent these conditions, we are left with a much weaker claim for the demos' power: orators are accountable to the demos, which engenders flattery and requires them to stay on the good side of the people. But that structural relationship does not preclude the possibility of oratorical manipulation.[79]

V. Conclusion: Beyond Socrates' Political Aporia

As I have argued, Socrates in the *Gorgias* runs two arguments on parallel tracks. On the first, "philosophical," argument, neither those exercising coercive decision-making power in the city, whether tyrant or demos, nor those orators who may seek to persuade and manipulate them, can be said to exercise power in the city insofar as they lack a true understanding of their own good. Without such an understanding, attempts to achieve what seems good to an agent are ultimately fruitless (section I). This is a radical critique of politics as ordinarily practiced, and it is clear from the action of the dialogue that it receives little uptake from the interlocutors. Whatever the philosophical merits of the argument, it remains politically inert. Yet Socrates also seems willing to confront his interlocutors on their own terms. Socrates tries to show that participating in democratic politics—whether as an ordinary member of the demos or as an orator-adviser—is unlikely to satisfy political actors even within the horizons of their own conception of the good. Orators must always be keenly aware of their vulnerability to punishment, revealing their aspirations to domination as a fantasy. And the demos, for all its power, may not be able to utilize the politics of accountability consistently to their own advantage (as they understand it). Both sets of arguments, we might think, are negative, underscoring the limits of what politics can achieve. The *Gorgias* might therefore seem like a fundamentally pessimistic dialogue.

I want to conclude by suggesting that there may be something more constructive to be gleaned from it. Taking the two lines of argument together, the *Gorgias* can be read as working through a particular problem: Is it possible to succeed at offering good advice if you and your audience disagree fundamentally about the good? Callicles poses this problem particularly sharply toward the end of the dialogue, when he presses Socrates on how he would fare before an Athenian jury if he refused to practice rhetoric and flattery. Socrates recognizes that his prospects would be grim:

> I will be tried as a doctor accused by a cook would be tried among children. For consider what such a human being, caught in these circumstances, would say in defense, if someone accused him and said, "Boys, this man here has

done many bad things to you yourselves; and he corrupts the youngest of you by cutting and burning; and he causes you to be at a loss by reducing and choking you, giving the most bitter draughts and compelling you to be hungry and thirsty—unlike me, who regale you sumptuously with many pleasant things of all sorts." What do you think a doctor, caught up in this bad situation, would have to say? Or if he told the truth, that "I did all these things, boys, in the interest of health," how great a clamor, do you think, would rise up from such judges? Wouldn't it be great? (521e–22a)

Here, of course, Socrates foreshadows his own trial, and the dialogue can be read as offering an explanation for Socrates' inability to win his acquittal. He was faced with just the problem I am identifying: How can one persuade an audience ignorant of their own good and unable to identify a false adviser from a true one that you mean to help, not to harm, them? The *Apology* can be read as a good-faith effort to make such an argument, but Socrates in that dialogue is not surprised that he is unable to win his acquittal.[80]

As the *Gorgias* implicitly acknowledges, the *historical* Socrates failed to solve this problem. And so we might think that the dialogue offers little more politically than a counsel of despair. There seem to be only two options: either a wholesale reconstitution of the political, so that those with a true understanding of the good would replace the ignorant as wielders of political power (the ostensible solution of the *Republic*), or if that proves impossible or undesirable, a retreat from politics and an embrace of political quietism on the part of the philosopher.

On my reading of the *Gorgias*, the dialogue presents arguments that might point to a third option. What can be done to persuade an audience, like the doctor's jury of children, that is radically ignorant of their own good? Direct appeal to the good—in this case, the doctor's claim to be working in the interest of health—is unlikely to persuade.[81] This is precisely the strategy that fails with Polus and Callicles in the *Gorgias*. Yet if Polus does not come to agree with Socrates that it is better to suffer injustice than to be unjust, Polus or someone like him might come to see through arguing with Socrates that orators and even tyrants are considerably more constrained in their actions and power than is usually understood to be the case.

The dialogue also holds out the possibility of a kind of learning on the part of the demos. In setting the dialogue during the Peloponnesian War but explicitly foreshadowing the fall of the Athenian empire, Plato suggests that the demos of the fifth century—puffed up on dockyards, tribute, and a vision of empire—was unable to recognize these seeming goods as actually bad. But his own audience—including, perhaps, ordinary Athenians of the fourth century—might better be able to see the consequences of such a policy, consequences they, too, if only in retrospect, could recognize as bad.[82] Throughout, then, Plato portrays Socrates as engaged in an attempt to limit the expression of the desire for power, ordinarily understood, even among those who do not share Socrates' basic philosophical commitments. The dialogue at the very least leaves open whether such a strategy can be successful. I am inclined to read Plato as himself attempting just such a strategy in part through his dramatization of Socrates' inability completely to realize it. While Socrates himself did not have a solution to his political aporia, future actors may yet learn from past failures.

Conclusion

On June 12, 2017, President Trump convened his first full cabinet meeting. The president wasted little time in touting the record of his nascent administration: "I will say that never has there been a president—with few exceptions; in the case of FDR, he had a major depression to handle—who's passed more legislation, who's done more things than what we've done . . . we've achieved tremendous success." After his opening remarks, he asked the members of his cabinet to introduce themselves. Vice President Pence set the tone for what would follow: "Thank you, Mr. President. And just the greatest privilege of my life is to serve as the—as vice president to the president who's keeping his word to the American people and assembling a team that's bringing real change, real prosperity, real strength back to our nation." One by one, the members of the cabinet took their turns to praise the leader and acknowledge his great popularity: "The response is fabulous around the country"; "I want to thank you for getting this country moving again, and also working again"; "On behalf of the entire senior staff around you, Mr. President, we thank you for the opportunity and the blessing that you've given us to serve your agenda and the American people." Only a few declined the opportunity directly to praise their new boss; James Mattis, the secretary of defense, said only, "It's an honor to represent the men and women of the Department of Defense. And we are grateful for the sacrifices our people are making in order to strengthen our military so our diplomats always negotiate from a position of strength. Thank you."[1] In the context of the new administration, the expression of these anodyne sentiments amounted to a frank statement of (relative) independence—an act of courage.

If Trump's cabinet meetings recall the classical Greek image of the tyrant surrounded by obsequious advisers, then during his 2016 campaign, he played the role of demagogue, willing and able to deploy flattering rhetoric of his own. As he told an audience of supporters in Iowa in September of that year, "People don't know how great you are. People don't know how smart you are. These are the smart people . . . These are really the smart people."[2] Trump combined such appeals with a purported willingness to speak "plainly and honestly," offering a "straightforward assessment" of an America in crisis and his own prospective role in saving it.[3] Such scenes from the 2016 presidential campaign and the Trump administration vividly illustrate how the ancient Greek analysis of power's ability to warp and inflect political discourse continues to resonate today. As I have shown, that analysis unfolded through reflection on and dramatization of the idea that the demos, with respect to its advisers, is much like a tyrant.

I have argued that the demos-tyrant analogy was more than mere polemic. Of course, ancient Greek political actors and theorists deployed the analogy rhetorically. When Cleon reminds the demos that their empire is like a tyranny, he means to shock them out of their complacency and strengthen their resolve to treat the Mytileneans harshly (not to say unjustly). When Xenophon, in depicting the Arginusae trial, has the assembled citizens cry out that nothing and no one should be able to stop them from doing what they please, he means to criticize the demos by invoking the arbitrariness of tyrannical rule. But as the individual chapters of this book show, the analogy was also deployed in fifth- and fourth-century sources to gain analytical leverage in thinking through a cluster of political concepts—accountability, advice, responsibility, control. Reflecting on these concepts across political contexts allowed Greek thinkers to articulate a set of fundamental political questions and confront a set of difficult trade-offs and tensions political actors may face. The demos-tyrant analogy was deployed to formulate questions concerning the effects of unaccountable power, develop a normative critique of its exercise, and consider the conditions for its possible justification. And a consideration of the politics of advice across regime types allowed ancient Greek theorists to explore the tension between the control exercised by powerful decision-makers on the one hand (including through the exercise of democratic accountability) and their reliance on competent, independent advice on the other.

One effect of this discourse was to call into question one of the signal achievements of Athenian democracy. Recognition of the value of accountability in politics—that power should be checked, interrogated, controlled, and made to answer for its exercise—was not a uniquely democratic commitment. The democratic achievement was rather the assertion of the principle—and the creation of institutions to give it life—that accountability processes should be under the supervision and control of the collective body of citizens, judging and deciding together (the demos). We should not underplay the scope of the achievement here: it reflects a commitment to (relative) inclusion and instantiates a claim about whose interests the city's politics should reflect. While Athenian democracy's exclusions of slaves, women, and metics cannot be discounted, the extension of participatory rights far down the socioeconomic scale—including in accountability procedures such as the *dokimasia, euthunai, eisangelia,* and the *graphē paranomōn*—was a democratic achievement. Placing these institutions in the hands of the demos was part of an effort to make politics responsive to the needs and interests of ordinary citizens.

This *aim* was not, by and large, the central target of criticism. Rather, philosophers, historians, and dramatists all illuminated the ways in which the exercise of accountability powers, seemingly so straightforward, is in fact extraordinarily difficult. Establishing some degree of trust between decision-makers and accountable subordinates is of paramount importance (regardless of regime type) but is not easy to do given the threat the former pose to the latter. Such relationships pose for decision-makers worries about manipulation and the usurpation of power—worries that are themselves vulnerable to being manipulated and abused. The overarching sense one gets from the sources is recognition of the serious difficulties political actors face in getting things to go *right*: knowing whom to trust; incentivizing subordinates to act in one's interest while avoiding perverse incentives; making correct—or even just useful—ascriptions of responsibility and blame; and coping with the informational and knowledge burdens attendant on the exercise of accountability powers.

In confronting these problems, the Greek discursive tradition I have analyzed worked out the logic of accountability and laid bare its assumptions. This enterprise was in part critical, highlighting the limits of what a politics of accountability might achieve, but it also worked constructively, exploring what it would take to make accountability institutions and practices serve their professed purposes. Investigations across different political contexts were at the heart of this project. Of course, this required attention to the differences between regime types. But in playing with the image of the demos-as-tyrant, fifth- and fourth-century authors were able to attend to the ways in which the political logics of different regime types might converge. Herodotus' exploration of the role of trust in mediating accountability relationships between tyrants and their courtier-advisers could be applied to and extended through reflection on democratic politics. Ideas traveled from autocratic to democratic contexts and back out again. The danger posed by powerful unaccountable decision-makers, and the strategies other political actors might use in serving (and at times confronting) them, were paradigmatically articulated through the language of tyranny. But writers as diverse as Thucydides, Aristophanes, Plato, Isocrates, and Aristotle all appreciated the relevance of such analyses to democratic politics, and each in turn contributed to the Greek tradition of reflecting on accountability politics across regime types.

The key insight driving this cross-regime analysis, and the portability of the Greek theory of the politics of accountability and advice, is that democratic inclusion—revolutionary as it was—did not fundamentally alter the structure of the problems these authors sought to explore. These problems—of trust, manipulation, incentives, and the knowledge burdens attendant on exercising accountability functions well—are neither uniquely democratic nor uniquely autocratic. They follow from the structure of asymmetric accountability and power relationships. And in spite of the emphasis much recent scholarship has placed on a generalized culture of mutual accountability at work in democratic Athens, the central political institutions were highly discretionary and fundamentally asymmetrical. For these reasons, they could helpfully be modeled through comparisons with the tyrant. Athens' democratic achievement was a system that aimed at popular control and accountability to the demos—not an idealized system of reciprocal or mutual accountability as imagined by philosophers and deliberative democrats. Both that achievement and the problems it engendered are obscured by attempts to downplay the fundamental fact of popular unaccountability and the role unaccountable ordinary citizens played in Athenian politics.

The worries about the politics of accountability articulated in the ancient Greek sources have their counterparts in contemporary political scientists' concerns about the efficacy of electoral accountability. In *Democracy for Realists*, Christopher Achen and Larry Bartels argue that even minimalist accounts of electoral accountability through retrospective evaluations of incumbent performance are hopelessly optimistic. In retrospective voting, voters assess whether incumbents have performed well or not and then vote to retain high performers and replace the miscreants. Achen and Bartels explicate and model the "fundamental difficulty of the voters' task" given uncertainty and lack of information (to say nothing of misinformation).[4] They argue that voters' retrospective judgments are often "myopic" (overweighting short-term assessments compared with longer-term considerations) or even "blind": "When [voters] are in pain they are likely to kick the government . . . whether or not objective observers can find a rational basis for blame."[5] Alexander Guerrero similarly doubts that citizens are "capable of engaging in informed monitoring and evaluation of the decisions of their representatives" given widespread ignorance of the conduct of officials and the difficulty of informing oneself about and evaluating complex policies.[6]

Just as with Plato's assessment of the failures of Athenian accountability in the *Gorgias*, such pessimistic interpretations of the evidence are highly contestable.[7] The point of drawing the comparison between ancient and modern democratic accountability is not to suggest that the skeptics of democratic accountability are right, nor merely to show that their worries have an extremely long pedigree. I want to emphasize instead the self-consciously *general* and *comparative* approach central to ancient Greek reflection and theorizing on this topic. The contemporary political science literature on accountability focuses overwhelmingly on electoral institutions and representative democracy. Turning to ancient Greek sources and evidence yields the (perhaps surprising) conclusion that the same problems we associate with accountability in the representative democratic regimes of complex twenty-first-century societies also arose in the highly participatory "direct" democracy of ancient Athens. Ancient Greek theorizing on the topic also situated the problems democratic regimes faced within a broader discourse about the difficulties of monitoring and control applicable across political contexts.

If the Greek theoretical tradition took accountability quite generally to raise a host of difficult problems, it also explored the particular problems attendant on holding counselors accountable for their advice. As I showed throughout the preceding chapters, Greek political theory was alive to the many ways in which accountability relationships could condition and inflect political discourse. While they illuminate deep problems, the texts do not support a general claim that the power of a decision-maker like a tyrant or collective demos, with the ability to reward and punish advice, makes good political discourse impossible. This is not the conclusion to draw from those texts that focus on the autocratic case, such as Herodotus' *Histories* and Isocrates' letters, which both explicitly consider ways in which autocrats can succeed in securing counsel. Nor, turning to democracy, is that conclusion to be drawn from Thucydides' depiction and analysis of assembly debate. As the evidence discussed in chapter 5 suggests, the Athenians recognized the value of frank advice and were often able to secure it (even if their institutions did not always encourage its expression). Only Socrates in the *Gorgias* goes so far as to suggest that advice may be of no use at all for those who do not have knowledge of the good (whether individual rulers or collective actors like the demos). Yet as I argued in chapter 6, even that radically pessimistic view is qualified by other arguments Plato offers in the dialogue. In any event, we should not let Plato's acerbic judgments stand as the last word on Athenian democracy.

On the contrary, Athenian democracy was committed to mediating political decision-making through reason and speech. Ancient democrats accepted Diodotus' claim that words are necessary guides to action, the only means available to us to "explore the future in all its uncertainty."[8] Speech was an unavoidable structural component of mass decision-making. The demos was a collective agent given life in and through the democratic institutions of the polis. Structurally, it could only act by considering and deciding on the basis of the logos of others: a recommendation of the *boulē*; a suggestion put forth in the assembly by *ho boulomenos*; a defendant's exculpatory pleas; a penalty proposed by a prosecutor. That Athenian assembly debate consisted of more than *mere* proposals—that courses of action were debated, challenged, criticized, and revised—strongly suggests that ordinary citizens recognized the provision of advice as a prerequisite to sound political decision-making.

The ancient Greek experience with the politics of accountability and advice and the literature that arose reflecting directly on that experience are valuable precisely because neither posits a deep, eternal, and insurmountable clash between reason on the one hand and politics or the exercise of power on the other. The attention to institutional detail that runs throughout all of the texts I analyze in this book serves as an intrinsic rebuke to such a sweeping claim. The problems that the participants in this discourse discover and investigate arise within the context of institutions created by human beings through politics; they may admit of amelioration by the same means.

At the same time, the tradition I have analyzed here identifies what we can take to be a constitutive tension at the heart of democratic politics and perennial threats to democratic discourse when conditions are structured such that unaccountable decision-makers are able to hold advice-givers accountable. Athenian democratic decision-making attempted to bring together two fundamental political desiderata. On the one hand, democracy meant that political outcomes ought to be subject to the control of the demos—a politics directly responsive to the interests of the many. On the other hand, there was broad recognition that political decisions should be taken in light of and with the aid of good advice and frank discussion. Yet a commitment to both values does not guarantee that they will always fit neatly together or that institutions can be easily designed to facilitate both.

In explicating that trade-off and dramatizing its stakes, the Greek authors I took up in this book were engaged in a particular form of democratic theory (and political theory more broadly). They were not rejectionist critics of democracy and partisan foes of the demos. But neither was theirs an entirely sympathetic engagement that would aim to call Athenian democracy back to its own best self. What comes out clearest is the insistence on a kind of political realism. Not all good things will always go together: democratic accountability may undermine democratic political discourse. This is not a criticism of democracy per se; it equally applies to any regime in which those in power both seek to control subordinates through accountability procedures and rely on them for independent exercises of judgment. But authors as diverse as Aristophanes, Thucydides, Plato, and Aristotle all suggest, at various points, that it is precisely the wide latitude given to the collective judgments of the demos—unaccountable ordinary citizens—that exacerbates Athens' problems. Insofar as these authors implicitly or explicitly advocate a form of politics where the collective judgments of citizens are displaced from the center of politics to its margins—Aristophanes' Demos made beautiful, Diodotus' moderate city, the accountability regime of Plato's *Laws*, Aristotle's democracies where participation is controlled and curtailed—they were offering fundamental challenges to democracy as the Athenians would have understood it.

Modern representative democracies have implicitly followed their advice, displacing popular collective judgment from the center of our politics. Yet in doing so, we have not escaped these Greek problems altogether. Robust accountability to the people has been replaced with the dubious control afforded by elections. And electoral processes—where individual politicians compete through speech for the favor of the citizens—themselves give rise to the forms of political discourse the Greek tradition concerned itself with. The potential trade-off between holding political elites accountable and encouraging sound political discourse continues to hold today; learning to navigate that trade-off is crucial in an era when both accountability and good advice are seemingly in short supply.

Notes

Introduction

1. Well, "raptly" for the most part. Some seem to be paying little attention at all, as Quentin Skinner has noted; see his *Hobbes and Republican Liberty*, 11.

2. This remains true even in light of the arguments put forth by Josiah Ober and others suggesting that the audience in an Athenian assembly was more communicative than many scholars have assumed (and than the laws of Athens strictly allowed for). See Ober, *Athenian Revolution*, chap. 8, a reprint of his review of M. H. Hansen's *The Athenian Assembly in the Age of Demosthenes*. The primary means of audience communication to an orator was the *thorubos*, a mass cheer or jeer that could either affirm what the speaker said or signify disapproval, even to the point of driving him from the speaker's platform. On the *thorubos*, see especially Bers, "Dikastic thorubos"; and Tacon, "Ecclesiastic 'Thorubos.'"

3. As Hobbes well knew, Sparta, while distinctive among Greek city-states for preserving the archaic institution of monarchy, was not ruled by its kings. Thucydides' depiction of Archidamus in book 1 is illustrative: the king believes that war with Athens would be unwise, but the decision is not his to make. Instead, he must attempt to persuade an assembly of Spartans—which he is unable to do successfully (1.80–85). Cf. Skinner, *Hobbes and Republican Liberty*, 11: "Below the figure of Archidamus we see the Spartan *Aristoi* actively deliberating with their king." On the frontispiece's depiction of Sparta, see also Pope, "Thucydides and Democracy," 282.

4. The earliest reference to the three kinds of regime is Pindar, *Pyth.* 2.86–88 (ca. 477 BCE); see also Herodotus 3.80; and Aristotle, *Pol.* 1279a.

5. Oligarchic regimes, too, made use of unaccountable magistracies, such as the ephorate in Sparta. And even in oligarchic regimes less idiosyncratic than Sparta's, decisions might be made by large groups of unaccountable citizens in councils and assemblies. The citizens and magistrates of an oligarchy, then, would also rely on speeches and advice to aid them in decision-making. Nonetheless, as best as we can tell from the evidence, the politics of advice in oligarchic regimes did not regularly display the dynamics I explicate in this book. For further discussion, see chapter 1 below.

6. For the context, see Harvey Yunis' introduction to Demosthenes, *Speeches 18 and 19*, 23–31. Demosthenes' associate, Ctesiphon, was being prosecuted for honoring Demosthenes with

a crown before he had undergone his *euthunai* (the mandatory accountability procedure after a term of office)—illegally, or so argued Aeschines.

7. Demosthenes 18.172–73. The translation is Yunis', from *Speeches 18 and 19*.

8. See Usher, "Symbouleutic Oratory."

9. See, for example, Demosthenes 18.1 ("*ton antidikon sumboulon*," referring to his opponent in a trial), and Aeschines 1.29, 2.65, 3.2. Dinarchus 1.31 has "*tōi demōi sumbouleuein ērxato*" (he began to advise the demos), speaking of Demosthenes' career as an orator.

10. See, for example, Schofield, *Plato*, 24, on Socrates' use of *sumbouleuein* to describe his own private activity in the *Apology*. Schofield notes that *sumbouleuin* is "the term standardly used . . . for political advice and in particular for contributions to debate in the assembly." For uses of *sumbouleuein* in Plato's *Gorgias*, see chapter 6 below. Thucydides uses an older Attic form of the root, *xumboul-*, in reference to democratic discursive practices at 1.140, 3.42.

11. Perlman, "Politicians"; and Finley, "Athenian Demagogues." Finley begins his essay with a quotation from George Grote, who also had much to say about Athenian orators as advisers; see below, chapter 2, for discussion.

12. Hansen, "Athenian 'Politicians,'" 46. Cf. Ober's discussion of the positive valence of the term at *Mass and Elite*, 107. See also Ober, *Democracy and Knowledge*, 32: "Democratic leadership was built on a model of the volunteer expert adviser constantly seeking public attention and approval through direct communication with the citizenship."

13. Yunis, *Taming Democracy*, 273.

14. Kallet-Marx, "Money Talks," 193–94.

15. Elster, introduction to *Deliberative Democracy*, 1. See also Gutmann and Thompson, *Why Deliberative Democracy?*, 8, which traces deliberative democracy's "roots" back to Athens. James Fishkin often cites what he takes to be the deliberative elements of Athenian democracy: see, for example, his remarks on "The Athenian Solution" in his essay "Deliberative Democracy." More recently, Mirko Canevaro has offered a detailed interpretation of Athenian assembly procedure through the lens of deliberative democracy. See Canevaro, "Majority Rule vs. Consensus."

16. Those living closer to the city center presumably were better represented than those living farther out. On attendance, see Hansen, *Athenian Democracy*, 125–27; and Sinclair, *Democracy and Participation in Athens*, 114–23. Sinclair argues that while the assembly may have been dominated by poorer citizens, we should not assume that some more well-off Athenians did not also attend and play a "passive" role (i.e., listening to speeches and voting).

17. For an overview of the functions of the assembly, see Hansen, *Athenian Democracy*, chap. 6.

18. On *isēgoria*, see Raaflaub, "Democracy, Oligarchy"; and Lewis, "*Isēgoria* at Athens."

19. Yack, "Rhetoric and Public Reasoning," 419.

20. For example, unlike many contemporary theorists, Yack argues that impartiality is an inappropriate deliberative ideal, at least from the Aristotelian perspective. He also explicitly leaves room for appeals to emotions and to the character of the speaker, persuasive strategies detailed in Aristotle's *Rhetoric* but viewed with suspicion by some contemporary theorists. See "Rhetoric and Public Reasoning," 418, 426–27.

21. Yack, 420.

22. See Landauer, "*Parrhesia* and the *Demos Tyrannos*"; Daniela Cammack argues persuasively for this claim in "Deliberation in Ancient Greek Assemblies."

23. Aristotle, *EN* 1112a30–31. Unless otherwise noted, translations from the *Nicomachean Ethics* are from Aristotle, *Complete Works*.

24. *EN* 1112a28–29.

25. *Pol.* 1284a28–34. Unless otherwise noted, translations of the *Politics* are from Aristotle, *Complete Works*.

26. See Aristotle, *Rhet.* 1355b, on seeing and choosing the correct means of persuasion.

27. See *EN* 1112b25–30.

28. *EN* 1112b10–11, translation mine.

29. On this interpretation of Demosthenes' role in the assembly, we might think that the natural question he should pose to himself and his audience is "What should we Athenians do?" But it is worth emphasizing that this is not the question he usually poses in his speeches; instead, he frequently draws a sharp distinction between himself and the Athenians (whom he addresses in the second person). See, for example, 23.211 and *Exordium* 18. Demosthenes frequently contrasts *sumbouleuein* with *bouleuesthai*, with the former activity assigned to speakers and the latter to the audience.

30. Here is another way of thinking about it: to claim to be a *sumboulos* is both to make a kind of claim of superiority and also to acknowledge one's subordinate role in the decision-making process. Not all speakers in the assembly would have sought to portray themselves so self-consciously as an adviser distinct from the demos. As P. J. Rhodes has recently stressed, Athenian assembly debate would have "included contributions from occasional speakers as well as from the regulars" ("Demagogues and *Demos*," 250). For an ordinary citizen, making occasional contributions to assembly debate may not have felt like a radically distinct activity from listening, thinking, and voting. As I argue in the coming chapters, matters would have been very different for Demosthenes and others who sought to play a leadership role in the city through giving advice—and who took on distinctive risks in doing so.

31. Plato, *Seventh Letter* 330d–31a, translation and emphasis mine. See also Yunis, *Taming Democracy*, 161–64. Debates over the authenticity of the letter continue. See Myles Burnyeat and Michael Frede's *The Pseudo-Platonic "Seventh Letter"* for a powerful set of arguments against Plato's authorship and against using the letter as good evidence regarding Plato's time in Syracuse. For my purposes here, the authenticity and reliability of the letter is relatively unimportant—what I want to emphasize is the way that the terms for advice-giving are used across regime types.

32. From comedy, see, for example, Aristophanes' *Knights* 1111–14; from history, Thucydides 2.63; and from philosophy, Aristotle, *Pol.* 1292a. All of these texts are discussed further below.

33. Roberts, *Marx's Inferno*, 3.

34. For example, as I take up in later chapters, both individual tyrants and collective agents, like peoples, are frequently described in our texts as "changing their mind." While this is a feature of discussions of both autocratic and democratic decision-making, an analysis must attend to the differences between individual and collective political actors here and elsewhere.

35. Aristotle, *Pol.* 1292a11–12, 20–23, translations modified.

36. Anderson, "Personality of the Greek State," 15. See also Glowacki, "Personification of Demos," for an overview of the surviving depictions of the demos personified in Athenian official inscriptions. Notably, many of the examples place Demos in an active role, crowning individual honorands (a typical function of the Athenian assembly).

37. Hobbes, *Elements of Law*, chap. 21.5. Skinner quotes the passage at *Hobbes and Republican Liberty*, 11–13.

38. *Elements of Law*, chap. 21.5.

39. *Knights* 752–55. The translation is Jeffrey Henderson's, from the Loeb *Aristophanes*, vol. 1.

40. Herodotus 5.97.2. Unless otherwise noted, quotations of Herodotus in this chapter are from Andrea Purvis' translation in *The Landmark Herodotus*.

41. Again, the authenticity of the letter is not important for my claim here; I cite this not as Platonic political philosophy but as expressing a view in common currency in Greek antiquity.

42. *Seventh Letter* 328b–c, emphasis mine. The translation is from Plato, *Complete Works*.

43. Strauss, *On Tyranny*, 75.

44. See, for example, Ober, *Political Dissent*; and Roberts, *Athens on Trial*. Roberts traces both the development of antidemocratic critical traditions at Athens and their afterlife in the history of political thought.

45. This objection differs from the first insofar as many scholars take rhetorical persuasion to be outside the bounds of democratic deliberation. For a critique of this view, see Garsten, *Saving Persuasion*.

46. *Gorgias* 452e. Unless otherwise noted, quotations from the *Gorgias* are from James H. Nichols' translation of the dialogue.

47. For example, *Rhet.* 1357a–58b. Unless otherwise noted, quotations from Aristotle's *Rhetoric* are from George Kennedy's translation in *On "Rhetoric": A Theory of Civic Discourse*.

48. Hesk, "Types of Oratory," 45.

49. *Gorgias* 456b. I discuss this passage further in chapter 6.

50. *Rhet.* 1358b. The glosses in brackets are Kennedy's, not mine.

51. *Rhetoric to Alexander* 1421b. The translation is from Aristotle, *Complete Works*.

52. See, for example, the introduction to George Kennedy's *A New History of Classical Rhetoric*: the Greek *rhētorikē* "specifically denotes the civic art of public speaking as it developed in deliberative assemblies, law courts and other formal occasions under constitutional government in the Greek cities, especially the Athenian democracy" (3). See also Worthington, "Rhetoric and Politics," 255–57, on "Democracy and the Rise of Rhetoric."

53. See also Michael Gagarin's account in "Background and Origins," 30. Intriguingly, Thomas Cole has noted that some ancient sources also link Corax "explicitly to the Sicilian tyrants." See Cole, *Origins of Rhetoric*, 53. Cole also points there to possible connections between persuasive speech in democratic and autocratic contexts, focusing on Pindar.

54. Yunis, "Constraints of Democracy," 224–25.

55. The story about advice that I tell here thus cuts across the history of rhetoric in interesting ways. *Sumboulia*—advice—is a much older term than *rhētorikē*. Histories of rhetoric usually move from the sophists' teachings through Plato's polemics to Aristotle's and Isocrates' reaffirmations and (re-)constructions of the discipline, along with an examination of its actual deployment in Attic oratory. They rarely focus much on the language of advice that I make central to this project. And where they do so, they rarely look at it across time and across political contexts. For example, David Timmerman and Edward Schiappa explore Aristotle's use of *sumboul-* words as "terms of art" in *Classical Greek Rhetorical Theory*. But they do not consider whether Aristotle, in deploying this vocabulary, is drawing on a longer tradition; indeed, they specifically rule that possibility out (see chapter 4). Aristotle's use of *sumboul-* words of course reflects his distinctive and novel theory of rhetoric. But we should not rule out of bounds the possibility that in describing and analyzing sumbouleutic rhetoric, Aristotle is consciously engaging with the prerhetorical tradition of reflecting on the problem of advice.

56. This view is often associated with Mogens Herman Hansen. For a concise statement of Hansen's view, see his *Athenian Democracy*, 151. See also Ostwald, *From Popular Sovereignty*, for an extended argument stressing the rise of the rule of law. For the view that the institutional

reforms after the Peloponnesian War did not profoundly affect the character of Athenian democracy, see Ober, *Athenian Revolution*, chap. 8. Much of the debate hinges on the relationship between the courts and the assembly. Hansen interprets the role of the courts as a check on the power of the demos. Others see both the courts and the assembly as manifestations or instantiations of the demos' power. See Ober, *Athenian Revolution*, 118; and Sinclair, *Democracy and Participation in Athens*, 70–71, on this. Sinclair offers what I take to be convincing evidence that the courts could be considered "a cross-section of the Demos at large or virtually the same as the Demos." See further in the literature cited by Sinclair at footnote 105.

57. See Ostwald, *From Popular Sovereignty*; and Harris, *Democracy and Rule of Law*.

58. I discuss these issues in more detail in chapter 1.

59. See the analysis of Aristophanes' *Wasps* and of Diodotus' speech in Thucydides in chapters 2 and 4 below.

60. I elaborate on and defend this approach in my essay "Democratic Theory and the Athenian Public Sphere."

61. Ober introduces this method in chapter 1 of *Mass and Elite*; see especially 43–45.

62. See Jones, "Athenian Democracy and Its Critics," 1.

63. Harvey Yunis also draws attention to the value of Demosthenes' perspective in *Taming Democracy*.

64. On the periodization of Greek tyranny, see Lewis, *Greek Tyranny*, introduction and chaps. 1–3. Autocratic rule was an outlier in the Greek world during the period I am interested in, although it never disappeared entirely and was beginning to come back into prominence with the rise of Macedon. Recent scholarship has fruitfully engaged with the practice of autocratic rule in fourth-century Sicily and tyrants' propaganda and self-presentation: see Kathryn Bosher's introduction to *Theater outside Athens* and related contributions in that volume. See also Morgan, *Pindar and Syracusan Monarchy*, which uses Pindar's poetry to address, in the context of fifth-century Sicilian autocratic politics, some of the same questions and themes surrounding the politics of advice that I take up in this book.

Chapter One

1. Aeschines 3.6. Translations of Aeschines are mostly my own; some are modifications of Charles Darwin Adams' translations in the Loeb edition of Aeschines' speeches.

2. Aeschines 3.22.

3. Aeschines 3.17.

4. Cf. how Lynette Mitchell traces the way in which tyranny becomes a point of "critical analysis" in both popular and philosophic constitutional thinking in her "Tyrannical Oligarchs at Athens."

5. Euben, *Corrupting Youth*, 97n21. Note that Euben's definition does not include the power to sanction. On the relationship between sanctioning and accountability see Philp, "Delimiting Democratic Accountability." Philp argues that accountability need not include the power to sanction; on his definition, "A is accountable with respect to M when some individual, body or institution, Y, can require A to inform and explain/justify his or her conduct with respect to M" (32). On this definition, "the power to sanction for failing to give an account . . . is a necessary condition" for accountability; "the power to sanction for the content of that account" is not (30).

6. Manin, Przeworski, and Stokes, introduction to *Democracy, Accountability and Representation*, 10, quoted in Philp, "Delimiting Democratic Accountability," 29.

7. Most books on Athenian institutions contain at least some discussion of accountability procedures. A focused treatment is given by Jennifer Tolbert Roberts in *Accountability in Athenian Government*. Contemporary scholarly work on institutions of accountability and Athenian constitutional structure more generally owe much to Mogens Herman Hansen's work in the 1970s. See especially *The Sovereignty of the People's Court in Athens in the Fourth Century B.C. and the Impeachment of Generals and Politicians* and *Eisangelia*. Hansen's *Athenian Democracy in the Age of Demosthenes* is an indispensable synthesis and summary of the earlier research, and Sinclair's *Democracy and Participation* offers a helpful overview in chapter 6.

8. Rhodes, "Nothing to Do with Democracy," 116.

9. In addition to my own work on this question, there are two important recent exceptions: Farid Abdel-Nour and Brad Cook's "As If They Could Be Brought to Account" and Kinch Hoekstra's "Athenian Democracy and Popular Tyranny." I discuss Hoekstra's and Abdel-Nour and Cook's arguments at various points below, in this chapter and the next, as they bear on my own reconstruction of Athenian unaccountability and its relation to tyranny.

10. Elster, "Accountability in Athenian Politics," 277.

11. Roberts, *Accountability*, 7.

12. Euben, *Corrupting Youth*, 97–99.

13. Markovits, *Politics of Sincerity*. Markovits points to the *dokimasia* all citizens undertook when they came of age; the Athenian "spirit of civic-mindedness"; ostracism; oaths taken by jurors and others; and the Athenian network of gossip as factors that contributed to generalized accountability (54–55, 60–61).

14. Borowiak, *Accountability and Democracy*, 88. See also Christ, "Evolution of the *Eisphora*," for a discussion of the role of mutual scrutiny among wealthy elites in administering the *eisphora* (a direct tax) in Athens.

15. I discuss arguments for Athens' culture of accountability and attempts to link Socratic philosophical practice to Athenian accountability discourse in "Democratic Theory and the Athenian Public Sphere." This paragraph draws on the argument there.

16. In what follows, I use *popular unaccountability* as a shorthand for "the unaccountability of jurors and assemblymen."

17. Jones, *Athenian Democracy*, 61.

18. The rise of popular institutions of accountability was an important aspect of the development of popular sovereignty at Athens throughout the fifth century. Many of the accountability institutions discussed in this section had predemocratic, nonpopular precursors. As noted in Aristotle, *Ath. Pol.* 3, "[Under the first constitution of Athens], the Council of the Areopagus had the duty of watching over the laws, and had wide-ranging and important powers in the city since it punished and fined all offenders without appeal." The translation is John M. Moore's, from Aristotle, *Politics and Constitution of Athens*; unless otherwise noted, translations from the *Constitution of Athens* are from this edition. Scholars doubt whether Aristotle himself wrote the *Constitution of Athens*, but it is generally taken as a work by him or his school. I follow the practice of attributing it nominally to Aristotle. Scholars have interpreted the passage under consideration as describing the Areopagus' role in holding the predemocratic archons to account. The Areopagus' powers probably included the administration of versions of *dokimasia*, *euthunai*, and *eisangelia*. For an attempt at reconstructing the historical development of institutions of accountability in the fifth century from their predemocratic precursors to their democratic forms, see Ostwald, *From Popular Sovereignty*, 40–77. See also Wallace, "Greek Oligarchy." I discuss the role of the Areopagus further, below.

19. Estimates of the number of magistrates in democratic Athens vary. For discussion, see Allen, *World of Prometheus*, appendix A.

20. See Hansen, *Athenian Democracy*, 218–20.

21. Lysias 16.9, translation mine; see Balot, "Democracy and Political Philosophy," 188–89, for further discussion and an argument linking *dokimasia* to Socratic philosophical practice. See also Schlosser, *What Would Socrates Do?*, chap. 2, on the possible relationship between Socratic and democratic accountability.

22. Hansen, *Athenian Democracy*, 223.

23. Hansen, *Athenian Democracy*, 223.

24. Melissa Lane has recently argued that elections played an important role in Athenian politics as a mechanism of popular control. She reads Aristotle (in *Pol.* 3.11) as arguing that "the popular multitude might justifiably be *kurios* in controlling the office holders" through a combination of election and inspection (the *euthunai*). Yet even on this Aristotelian account, elections are not sufficient for accountability. See her "Popular Sovereignty as Control," 57–60. The quoted text is at 60; see also her citation of *Pol.* 1281b31–34 as a "full-blown account of the control thesis" (61).

25. Thucydides 2.65.3–4.

26. Robinson, *Democracy beyond Athens*.

27. *Pol.* 1317b25–30.

28. Robinson, *Democracy beyond Athens*, 226.

29. Aristotle, *Ath. Pol.* 3. See note 18 above for the text and discussion.

30. See Aristotle, *Pol.* 1271a.

31. On the absence of popular participation in the judiciary at Sparta, see de Ste. Croix, *Origins of the Peloponnesian War*, 131–38; and Cartledge, *Spartan Reflections*, 52.

32. *Pol.* 1282a25.

33. Thucydides 4.74. Unless otherwise noted, translations from Thucydides are Jeremy Mynott's, from *The War of the Peloponnesians and the Athenians*. For further discussion of this passage, see Simonton, *Classical Greek Oligarchy*, 128.

34. I am less sure than Hansen that the *euthunai* were relatively unimportant (as argued at *Athenian Democracy*, 223–24). Particularly in the fifth century, from our sketchy evidence, it seems likely that they were important instruments of democratic control. See the attention given to them in the Aristotelian *Constitution of Athens* (e.g., sections 38–39, 48) and a suggestive comment of Plutarch's regarding the murder of Ephialtes: that he was feared by the oligarchs for he was "inexorable in exacting accounts [*peri tas euthunas*] from those who wronged the people, and in prosecuting them" (Plutarch, *Life of Pericles* 10.8, quoted in Loraux, *Divided City*, 74).

35. The Athenian political year was divided into ten prytanies. During each prytany, fifty of the five hundred members of the *boulē* would serve as a kind of executive committee for the state. One assembly meeting each prytany was designated the *ekklēsia kuria*, or "chief meeting."

36. Hyperides 4.7–8. Unless otherwise noted, translations from Hyperides are Craig R. Cooper's, from *Dinarchus, Hyperides, and Lycurgus*. Here the translation is slightly modified.

37. Hansen, *Eisangelia*, 60–61.

38. See Hansen, *Eisangelia*, 58–59; and Roberts, *Accountability*, for the (relatively few) extant cases of *eisangelia* against orators.

39. See Bers, "Dikastic thorubos"; and Tacon, "Ecclesiastic 'Thorubos,'" for full discussions. See also Robert Wallace's discussion of the *thorubos* in "Power to Speak."

40. The rise of the *graphē paranomōn* at some point in the late fifth century has been linked

to the decline of ostracism, which, some argue, could likewise be used to hold nonmagistrates accountable. See Roberts, *Accountability*, 153–58. Cf. Forsdyke, *Exile, Ostracism, and Democracy*, chap. 4, which stresses ostracism's symbolic role in the polis rather than its function as a kind of all-purpose accountability mechanism.

41. On the *graphē paranomōn* in general, see Hansen, *Sovereignty of the People's Court*; Hansen, *Athenian Democracy*, 205–12; Sinclair, *Democracy and Participation in Athens*, 152–56; Roberts, *Accountability*, 153–60; and Yunis, "Law, Politics, and *Graphē Paranomōn*."

42. While attempts to reconstruct Spartan assembly procedure are speculative and controversial, the features I identify in this paragraph are reasonably secure. See Cartledge, *Spartan Reflections*, chap. 3. For Aristotle's analysis of oligarchic manipulation of the agenda and other attempts to control assemblies of citizens, see *Pol.* 1298b.

43. See also Wallace, "Greek Oligarchy," on this point.

44. Cook, "Ancient Political Factions," 88.

45. [Anaximenes?], *Rhetoric to Alexander* 1423a14–15; 1424b.

46. *Rhet.* 1366a12–13, translation Kennedy's.

47. *Hell. Oxyr.* 18.2. Translations and text are from *Hellenica Oxyrhynchia*, edited and translated by McKechnie and Kern.

48. *Hell. Oxyr.* 18.4.

49. *Hell. Oxyr.* 7.2.

50. Xenophon, *Hell.* 5.2.35, translation mine: "*hoti tēs en tēi Helladi tarachēs pasēs ekeinos te kai Androkleidas aitiōtatoi eien.*"

51. On the democratic context of this trial, see Cook, "Ancient Political Factions"; and Emily Mackil, *Creating a Common Polity*, 338.

52. Plutarch, *Life of Pelopidas* 25.6, translation mine: "*hōs amaurōsōn tēn Pelopidou kai Epameinōndou doxan.*"

53. Plutarch, *Life of Pelopidas* 25.7: "*touto to psēphisma graphetai Pelopidas paranomōn.*" On the *graphē paranomōn* at Thebes, see also Robinson, *Democracy beyond Athens*, 59–61.

54. Robinson, *Democracy beyond Athens*, 61n182.

55. Simonton, *Classical Greek Oligarchy*, 7.

56. Simonton, 77.

57. Plutarch, *Moralia* 805c. Translations from Plutarch's *Moralia* are Harold Fowler's, from the Loeb edition.

58. Robinson, *Democracy beyond Athens*, 226.

59. Canevaro, "Twilight of *Nomothesia*," 67; see also Simonton, *Classical Greek Oligarchy*, chap. 2.

60. For a concise overview of the Athenian system of prosecution and its implications, see Allen, *World of Prometheus*, 45–49.

61. See Harris, "The Penalty for Frivolous Prosecution in Athenian Law," chap. 4.3, in *Democracy and Rule of Law*, 405–22, for an overview of the evidence and relevant procedures, as well as an argument that the Athenians took these rules very seriously.

62. On sycophancy in Greece, see especially Christ, *Litigious Athenian*.

63. On the age for assembly attendance, see Sinclair, *Democracy and Participation in Athens*, 31; for jury service, see Aristotle, *Ath. Pol.* 63.3. Hansen interprets the higher age for jury service as an attempt to "put the power of judging into the hands of the eldest and most experienced" (*Athenian Democracy*, 181).

64. Waldron, *Political Political Theory*, 168.

65. Waldron, 168.

66. See Edward Harris' and Lene Rubinstein's introduction to *The Law and the Courts in Ancient Greece* for a forceful argument that jurors were subordinated to the rule of law in Athens.

67. Hansen, *Athenian Democracy*, 182, citing Max Fränkel. I have added the numbers to the clauses for ease of reference. They correspond substantively (but not numerically) to the clauses outlined by Edward M. Harris in "Rule of Law," 57. Harris argues there for the importance of the oath as evidence for the reality of the rule of law.

68. Cf. Rhodes, "Keeping to the Point," and Lanni, *Law and Justice*, chap. 3, esp. 43n16, 41–46. Rhodes argues for Athenian adherence to broad standards of relevance; Lanni argues (correctly, in my view) that jurors as a matter of course considered extralegal factors when reaching their verdicts.

69. Demosthenes 21.47; unless otherwise noted, translations from Demosthenes in this chapter are my own. Some are modified from the Loeb edition of Demosthenes' speeches.

70. Demosthenes 21 (*Against Meidias*) is the classic prosecution of hubris. See Yunis, "Law, Politics, and *Graphē Paranomōn*," 362; and Lanni, *Law and Justice*, 68, for discussions of the law. See Wilson, "Demosthenes 21," 164–66, for a discussion of its place in democratic ideology. David Cohen (*Law, Violence, and Community*, 189–90) makes a similar point about the vagueness of the laws with respect to prosecutions of impiety (*asebeia*).

71. As Matthew Christ argues, "Jurors' understanding of community norms and ultimately their sense of what was right (*to dikaion*) determined how and even whether they applied laws" (*Litigious Athenian*, 41).

72. This process is known as "incubation." See Harris, *Dreams and Experience*, for a discussion of the practice (at 157, he takes up this case in particular). Harris is doubtful that Athenians in general trusted in dreams as evidence of much.

73. Hyperides 4.4, translation mine.

74. See further the discussion in Ober, *Mass and Elite*, 111–12: "Hyperides was exploiting the ambiguity between the old legal meaning of the term rhetor—which in the mid-fifth century had apparently been 'decree-proposer'—and the everyday meaning of the term as it was used in oratory and would be understood by the jurors." I doubt that we need to posit an older, stricter usage of the word *rhētōr* to understand what is going on here; as I have been arguing, the Athenian judicial system was rife with such ambiguities that allowed juries (and also prosecutors and defendants) considerable leeway in judging (and constructing) cases.

75. As Adriaan Lanni argues in *Law and Justice*, chap. 3.

76. See Yunis, "Law, Politics, and *Graphē Paranomōn*," 361.

77. Yunis, 369–70.

78. Lanni, *Law and Justice*, 72.

79. Hansen, *Athenian Democracy*, 182.

80. Lycurgus 1.79. Translations of Lycurgus are by Edward Harris, from *Dinarchus, Hyperides, and Lycurgus*. On the importance of oaths in the democracy, see Cole, "Oath Ritual."

81. Hansen, *Athenian Democracy*, 183.

82. Although Hansen makes much of the difference between an oath and a curse, based on a reading of Demosthenes 24.78. Cf. Loraux's argument for the importance of the oath in *The Divided City*, chap. 5.

83. *Ath. Pol.* 64–66. E. S. Staveley offers a helpful reconstruction of the system for randomizing jurors in *Greek and Roman Voting and Elections*, 112.

84. Hansen, *Athenian Democracy*, 197; see also Staveley, *Greek and Roman Voting and Elec-*

tions, 111–12; and on bribery, see MacDowell, *Law in Classical Athens*, 72–73. Cf. Bers, "Just Rituals," for another interpretation of the procedures surrounding the courts—one that fits well with my overarching point in this chapter. Bers considers the complex machinery to be primarily of symbolic importance, a "ceremony aimed at alleviating the Athenians' anxiety about the democratic jurors—their general quality, number, and probity" (553).

85. Aeschines 1.87.

86. See Hansen, *Athenian Democracy*, 197, for a list of references.

87. Lanni, "Spectator Sport," 183.

88. Lanni, 187–88.

89. Markovits, *Politics of Sincerity*, 59–60.

90. Demosthenes 25.98, quoted in Lanni, "Spectator Sport," 188.

91. Aeschines 3.247, quoted in Lanni, "Spectator Sport," 188.

92. On this point, see also Abdel-Nour and Cook, "As If They Could," 447.

93. Lysias 12.91. Unless otherwise noted, translations of Lysias are W. R. M. Lamb's, from the Loeb edition.

94. Demosthenes 20.165: "*Kai gar hekastos humōn idiai methexei tēs doxēs tōn koinēi gnōsthentōn.*"

95. Aeschines 3.233.

96. On the distinction between laws and decrees, see Hansen, *Athenian Democracy*, chap. 7.

97. Of course, it is unlikely that Plato would have viewed this as a cost.

98. *Laws* 945c, translation mine.

99. *Laws* 946d–e.

100. *Laws* 947e, translation mine.

101. *Laws* 947e–48b.

102. *Laws* 761e, translation mine.

103. Morrow, *Plato's Cretan City*, 550. I follow Morrow's analysis of the system of accountability in Magnesia in much of this section.

104. See Morrow, 265–67, 269, on the role of what he calls "the court of the demos" in Magnesian politics. Morrow argues persuasively that Plato may have intended decisions of the "court of the demos," at least in capital cases, to be subject to appeal to a court consisting of higher magistrates, who would themselves be accountable (269).

105. On the election of the *euthunoi* by the citizens at large, see *Laws* 945e–46a. Loraux notes, *a propos* of *Laws* 767–68, that regular citizens continue to play a role in the court system of Magnesia (*Divided City*, 230–31). As Morrow correctly stresses, however, such courts are not courts of final appeal: Plato denies "to his popular courts the judicial supremacy which was such an important factor in the power of the demos at Athens" (*Plato's Cretan City*, 261).

106. See Hoekstra, "Athenian Democracy and Popular Tyranny"; and Lane, "Popular Sovereignty as Control." Hoekstra in particular recognizes the importance of the demos-tyrant analogy for understanding popular sovereignty at Athens.

107. See, for example, Ober, *Mass and Elite*, 163–65, for a discussion of "the wisdom of the masses"; see also Waldron, "Wisdom of the Multitude," for an influential reconstruction of Aristotle's arguments related to collective judgment.

108. Hansen, *Athenian Democracy*, 207.

109. Demosthenes, *Exordium* 44.1, quoted in Ober, *Mass and Elite*, 164.

110. Aristotle, *Pol.* 1281a–b. See Lane, "Popular Sovereignty as Control," section III, for the claim that Aristotle has elections and accountability mechanisms in particular in mind here.

111. Demosthenes 23.97, cited by Hansen in *Athenian Democracy*, 207n311, along with a passage from Diodotus' speech in Thucydides (3.43.4–5). The Thucydides citation does not seem to me to offer any more support to Hansen's view than the Demosthenes passage does.

112. Thucydides 2.40.2. It is noteworthy that Pericles does not use the word *idiōtēs* here: the target of his ire is the *apragmōn*. L. B. Carter has interpreted the passage as directed against peasants and "rich quietists." See his *Quiet Athenian*, 27–28, 50–51. He notes that others have taken the passage as directed against intellectuals such as Thucydides himself (40–41). I think Pericles may have had in mind ordinary citizens who refused to play their part in upholding the "amateur ideal" of Athenian politics; see Hansen, *Athenian Democracy*, 308–9. Peter Wilson offers another example of *apragmōn* being used to signify a person playing no role at all in politics at Demosthenes 21.83. Here the status of being *apragmōn* is linked to being poor. See Wilson, "Demosthenes 21," 180.

113. Demosthenes 23.62, 18.78.

114. Demosthenes 22.37.

115. Demosthenes 24.112.

116. For example, Demosthenes 25.97, 52.28; and Aeschines 3.252–53. In this respect, the *idiōtēs* discourse also contextualizes my discussion of the *sumboulos* in the introduction. In one sense, anyone who got up to speak in the assembly was advising (*sumbouleuein*). Yet to claim for oneself the status of a *sumboulos* was to claim to be doing something different from your average speaker (who might consider himself, and be plausibly considered by his audience, to be a mere *idiōtēs*). Cf. the discussion in Rhodes, "Demagogues and *Demos*," 250–56.

117. Aeschines 2.181, cited by Ober, *Mass and Elite*, 282.

118. Demosthenes 22.37.

119. *Republic* 521b.

120. See, for example, Demosthenes 44.4, 34.1; see also Socrates' self-representation as a stranger to the courts in the opening passages of the *Apology*.

121. Demosthenes 24.66. On this form of legal procedure, see Hansen, *Athenian Democracy*, 166.

122. Demosthenes 19.182. Note here that one could, at least in principle, retain one's status as an *idiōtēs* even while speaking in the assembly. The quote also suggests one drawback of participation by *idiōtai*—they are unskilled. But unskilled yet well-meaning amateurs are preferable, on the Athenian view, to skilled but seditious political experts.

123. See Demosthenes' juror who simply fails to understand the arguments presented to him, discussed above.

124. For example, Aeschines accuses Demosthenes of "taking vengeance on private citizens" (Aeschines 1.173). See also Demosthenes 25.38 for the view that charging private citizens instead of public men is a bad thing. Demosthenes 24.112–13, cited earlier, makes a similar point. The context for considering holders of small-time magistracies *idiōtai* is that holding them too strictly accountable for their small errors constitutes an abuse. To be clear, the small-time magistrate *idiōtēs* is still subject to *euthunai*, as all magistrates are, and Demosthenes does not suggest that there is anything improper about that. The idea, though, is that to prosecute him to the full extent of the law is an abuse.

125. Demosthenes 25.40, emphasis mine.

126. Aeschines 1.195.

127. Demosthenes 10.70. This speech is not always accepted as a work of Demosthenes, but for our purposes here, the attribution is unimportant.

128. Demosthenes 26.3.

129. Demosthenes 26.4. Cf. Allen, *World of Prometheus*, 193: "Demosthenes uses the distinction between what was private and what public to express the idea that those who rise to prominence through politics must take especial care to recognize that they have entered the realm where they will be directly impacting the shared life of the city" (with reference to Demosthenes 24.192). This is right, I think, but only gets at half of what is going on with references to the *idiōtēs* in Athenian judicial and deliberative oratory. Orators such as Demosthenes also use the distinction between public and private to attempt to establish who should be immune from the high degree of scrutiny that falls upon those who enter "the realm where they will be directly impacting the shared life of the city." Nor is the division absolute: as I have been arguing throughout this chapter, jurors and assemblymen straddle the divide between *idiōtai* and *politeuomenoi*. Matthew Christ has also emphasized the way in which a claim to *idiōtēs* status could also serve to limit a litigant in an Athenian court—after all, an *idiōtēs* should not appear too knowledgeable about legal matters (Christ, *Litigious Athenian*, 203–6). All this was, as Christ recognizes, in the service of giving "the impression that [the litigant] was, like the average juror, an *idiōtēs*, and therefore deserved indulgence when presenting his case and dealing with legal questions" (203).

130. Hyperides 4.27, translation mine.

131. For attempts at calculating how frequently the courts would have met and how often individual jurors might have succeeded at getting themselves impaneled, see Hansen, *Athenian Democracy*, 186; and Sinclair, *Democracy and Participation in Athens*, 128–31, 225–26.

132. Lycurgus 1.79. Lene Rubinstein takes Lycurgus here to be using *idiōtēs* only in the sense of *ho boulomenos* ("Political Perception of the *Idiōtēs*," 126). Ober interprets it in a looser sense: "All Athenian citizens who were not serving in magistracies or on juries were *idiōtai*, if we are to accept Lycurgus" (*Mass and Elite*, 111).

133. *Pol.* 1275a, translation mine. On the strength of this passage and others, some scholars have been tempted to argue that perhaps the jurors were, after all, magistrates. Yet this view quickly runs into the central problem we are dealing with: accountability. Jurors did not undergo *dokimasia* at the beginning of their tenure nor *euthuna* at the end of it, procedures all (other) magistrates underwent. Plato also recognizes that it is difficult to say whether popular jurors should be thought of as magistrates (see *Laws* 768c). These considerations also suggest the limits of the agent-accountability framework I have been using to analyze the role of the demos in this chapter. It is noteworthy that neither Plato nor Aristotle makes the modern move in assessing the role of juries and the assembly—that is, to consider them as principals in a principal-agent model.

134. Aeschines 3.232–33, emphasis and translation mine but following the Loeb edition in parts.

Chapter Two

1. Plutarch, *Life of Solon* 31.1–2, translation mine.

2. Plutarch tells the story in the context of Solon, late in life, taking on an advisory role for Peisistratus. Perhaps Plutarch thought (rightly) that the Aristotelian version of the story undermines our perception of Peisistratus' gentle rule and hence would call into doubt the propriety of Solon serving him.

3. *Ath. Pol.* 16.8, emphasis and translation mine. James McGlew, in his *Tyranny and Political Culture*, cites this passage as an example of Aristotle praising Peisistratus for "answering a

summons" but does not note the way in which the summoner's fear might undermine that praise (79).

4. On Peisistratus' use of club bearers as his bodyguard, see Aristotle, *Ath. Pol.* 14.

5. Diodorus Siculus 11.26.4, translation mine.

6. Diodorus Siculus 11.26.5–6.

7. Note also the echo of Lysias' speech for Mantitheus, discussed in chapter 1 above. Mantitheus uses the occasion of his *dokimasia* to give an account of his whole life ("*pantos tou biou logon didonai*," Lysias 16.9).

8. On the ideological uses of this story by the rulers of Syracuse, see Sian Lewis, *Greek Tyranny*, 118–21. Ancient sources relay other cases where tyrants made use of assemblies of citizens to solidify and legitimize their rule, as when Peisistratus uses an opportunity to address the assembled citizens of Athens to trick them into disarming (Aristotle, *Ath. Pol.* 15.4). For discussion of this and other similar cases, see Luraghi, "Anatomy," 72–74; and Hammer, "Plebiscitary Politics."

9. Herodotus 3.142. Unless otherwise noted, translations from Herodotus in this chapter are Andrea Purvis', from *The Landmark Herodotus.*

10. Herodotus 3.142.

11. Kurt Raaflaub also notes the resonances between this scene and the constitutional debate in *Discovery of Freedom* (110), as does Christopher Pelling in "Herodotus and Samos" (8–9). Raaflaub also notes the anachronisms inherent to the story: Maiandrius' offer to found a temple dedicated to Zeus Eleutherius as part of his abdication is in keeping with a protocol established long after his historical rule.

12. Herodotus 3.143.

13. The imprisoned Samians come to a bad end. Shortly after these events, Maiandrius falls ill. His brother, Lycaretus, expecting that Maiandrius will die, kills all the prisoners. Herodotus' judgment of the story—"and so it seems the Samians did not want to be free" (3.143)—strikes me as an unfair one. Rather, I think that Samians did not *know how* to become free. Cf. McGlew, *Tyranny and Political Culture*, 130: the Samians should have "come together to the Acropolis as soldiers determined to expel Maeandrius or kill him, not singly, like accountants intending to liberate Samos with ledgers and pens." This misses the connection between accountability and democracy, but I agree with the spirit of it. The Maiandrius story is usually discussed in the context of the difficulty of giving up tyranny. See, for example, Saxonhouse, *Athenian Democracy*, 35; and Raaflaub, "Philosophy, Science, Politics," 165–66.

14. Luraghi, "To Die like a Tyrant," 64. The two cases are Miltiades of Athens, tried in Athens for acting as tyrant of the Chersonesus (Herodotus 6.104), and Thrasydaeus, tried and executed in Megara for acting as tyrant of Agrigentum (Diodorus Siculus 11.53.5).

15. As Luraghi puts it, "Tyranny was an offense that provoked essentially summary justice" ("To Die like a Tyrant," 64, and throughout for the colorful stories of tyrants' deaths).

16. Luraghi, "Anatomy," 72; and "To Die like a Tyrant," 49.

17. The *Persians* was first performed in Athens in 472 BCE. Kathryn Bosher, in "Hieron's Aeschylus," argues that it may have first been staged in Syracuse, at the court of Hieron, circa 475/4. She offers a tentative reading of the play as in part a meditation on the difference between good (Darius) and bad (Xerxes) autocratic rulers. This would give the play's presentation of tyranny and unaccountability a somewhat different resonance, but the theme would still be apt for the audience.

18. *Persians*, 209–14. The quotation is from Aeschylus, *Persians*, ed. and trans. Hall.

19. Aeschylus, *Prometheus Bound*, 9–11, 324, translations mine.

20. The quotation is from Kantzios, "Politics of Fear in *Persians*," 11. See also Edith Hall's notes to lines 209–14 accompanying her translation of the *Persians*.

21. See Forsdyke, "Athenian Democratic Ideology," for a persuasive argument linking strands of Athenian democratic ideology, exemplified in Aeschylus' *Persians*, with central arguments and themes in Herodotus' *Histories*. In this section, I concentrate only on Otanes' speech. For a reading of the entire constitutional debate, with copious citations to the large secondary literature, see Pelling, "Speech and Action," 123–58.

22. Herodotus 3.80, translation mine.

23. Herodotus 3.80.

24. Herodotus 3.80.

25. Wohl, *Love among the Ruins*, 220, referencing Herodotus 1.96.2, 5.32, 3.53. The erotic desires of kings and tyrants frequently help drive Herodotus' plots: for example, Gyges' rise to become king of the Lydians begins with Candaules' erotic obsession with his wife's beauty (1.8.1). Wohl notes too that the earliest attested use of the word *tyranny* (Archilochus, frag. 19 W) links it to *erōs*, "even if only in the form of a (suspiciously) vehement denial: 'I do not love great tyranny'" (*Love among the Ruins*, 220).

26. Wohl, *Love among the Ruins*, 220.

27. While her focus is on psychology, fantasy, and imagination—the "psychic life of ideology"—Wohl is also well aware of the role of institutions in the discourse: "The lust and sexual license of tyrants were a common trope in the Athenian imagination of tyranny: absolute political power was thought to have its natural end in unbridled sexual aggression" (*Love among the Ruins*, 9). Cf. Dewald, "Form and Content," 30. Dewald argues that Herodotus sets up a "despotic template" in the *Histories*, which he explores and plays with throughout the narrative ("Form and Content," 27). See also Forsdyke, "Uses and Abuses of Tyranny," 238–39.

28. Herodotus 3.31.

29. McGlew cites this story, as well as Periander's sexual relations with his wife's corpse, as perhaps representing "the extension of this freedom [i.e., the tyrant's sexual freedom] to the grotesque" (*Tyranny and Political Culture*, 26). Wohl notes a similar dynamic at play on the psychological level. Ordinary citizens might "look to tyrants to imagine 'what exceeds the ordinary.' But the tyrant has no tyrant to look to, no imagined excess to serve as *a limit on his pleasure* or a spur toward desire" (*Love among the Ruins*, 243–44, emphasis mine).

30. See Allen, "Speech of Glaucon," 5: "The main point of the Ring of Gyges is that all penalties have been removed."

31. *Republic* 359a. Translations from the Platonic dialogues in this section are from Plato, *Complete Works*. On Socrates' rejection of the supposed goodness of being able to act unjustly without paying the penalty, see also chapter 6 below.

32. *Republic* 359e–360d.

33. *Republic* 359e–60a.

34. *Republic* 360b.

35. See McGlew, *Tyranny and Political Culture*, 26–27n23.

36. *Gorgias* 469d.

37. *Gorgias* 470a.

38. The Platonic treatment of these issues also reflects fifth-century sophistic debates about the benefits of transgressing the laws if one can escape punishment. In Antiphon's framing, there is a conflict between *nomos* (convention) and *phusis* (nature): "So if one transgresses against

legal institutions without being noticed by those who agreed upon them, he escapes shame and punishment; but if they notice, he does not. But if, contravening what is possible, he does violence to anything produced by nature, the harm is not less if no man notices him, and it is not greater if all men see him. For it is not because of opinion that he is harmed, but because of the truth" (B 44). Cf. the position of the Anonymous of Iamblichus, who denies that even someone by nature "immune to illness and suffering, extraordinarily large, and indestructible in body and soul" could "live in impunity without submitting to the law" (6.2–5). The translations of both texts are from Laks and Most, *Sophists, Part 2*.

39. *Republic* 571b–d.

40. *Republic* 573c–d. See also Wohl, *Love among the Ruins*, 221: "For Plato Eros is both the origin and the essence of tyranny," citing *Republic* 573b.

41. Forsdyke, "Uses and Abuses of Tyranny," 243.

42. Although if we look beyond the constitutional debate and take Herodotus' depictions of the lives and actions of his kings—in particular Cambyses—as, among other things, rich commentary on tyrannical souls, we might have to revise even this claim.

43. Nino Luraghi argues that "until the fourth century it seems to have been unimportant to determine precisely whether it was monarchic power that woke up by itself such features in potentially any man, or whether the potential tyrant needed to possess the necessary vices before reaching for monarchy" ("Anatomy," 77). Yet the thesis propounded by Otanes seems to complicate that claim. It is not, perhaps, a thoroughgoing effort to determine which comes first, lawless desire or unaccountable power. But it is a clear recognition of the important relationship between the two and a hypothesis about the relationship's structure.

44. *Laws* 875b.

45. Even if Herodotus recognizes that aspiring tyrants are also driven by *erōs*.

46. Robin Osborne has argued that there were a number of important differences between the discourse surrounding tyranny in Athens in the fifth and fourth centuries. I accept the general point, but I believe the discourse surrounding the question of accountability, in particular, spans the two time periods. See Osborne, "Changing the Discourse."

47. *Pol.* 1295a19–22, translation mine.

48. For tyranny as the *antistrophos* to *pambasilea*, see *Pol.* 1295a18. The specification of *pambasilea* as absolute rule in accordance with the king's will is at 1287a8–10 (translation mine): "*archei panta kata tēn heautou boulēsin ho basileus.*"

49. Luraghi, "Ruling Alone," 19.

50. Luraghi, "Anatomy," 78.

51. Plutarch, *Life of Lysander* 19, translation mine.

52. As Josiah Ober notes ("Tyrant Killing as Therapeutic *Stasis*," 215). While both democrats and philosophical critics of democracy attacked tyranny as a bad regime, democrats tended to collapse the distinction between tyranny and monarchy (witness Aeschines' insistence on only *three* kinds of rule, making no allowance for any difference between varieties of autocracy), while philosophers such as Aristotle, as we've just seen, left some room in their theories for the possibility of a good single ruler.

53. Aeschines 3.6. Translations of Aeschines in this chapter are my own, with some modified from Adams' translation in the Loeb edition.

54. Aeschines 3.22.

55. Athenian A: "Tell me again, why don't we hold jurors accountable?" Athenian B: "That's easy. They are *idiōtai*, just like us!" Athenian A: "Ah. I see. But tell me, how do we know they are

idiōtai? I mean, they do wield a lot of power around here. And I see them lining up for jury service almost every morning. So what is it that makes them *idiōtai*, exactly?" Athenian B: (*Pauses. Thinks.*) ". . . erm. Well . . . they *are* unaccountable. What else could they be?"

56. *Knights*, 1111–14. The translation is slightly modified from Jeffrey Henderson's in the Loeb *Aristophanes*. Other translations from the *Knights* in this chapter are Henderson's.

57. I return to the *Knights* at the end of this section.

58. *Wasps*, 88–90. Translations from the *Wasps* are from Aristophanes, *Wasps*, trans. Sommerstein, although I have modified them slightly in places.

59. *Wasps*, 103–5.

60. *Wasps*, 106.

61. *Wasps*, 223–27: "If anyone angers that tribe of old men, it's just like a nest of wasps. They've even got a very sharp sting sticking out from their rumps, which they stab with, and they shout and jump about and strike you like sparks of fire." See Konstan, *Greek Comedy*, 19, for a discussion of the jurors' anger. The jurors' democratic ferocity finds echoes in other plays by Aristophanes: Pericles' fear of the demos at *Peace* 606–608; *Acharnians* 375–76, where the older citizens are said to look forward to "biting with their ballots"; and *Knights* 1126–30, where old man Demos claims to treat the city's politicians with calculated ferocity, raising them up and knocking them down. I return to this passage from the *Knights* below.

62. For example, at *Wasps*, 240, 287ff.

63. *Wasps*, 158–60.

64. *Wasps*, 278–80.

65. *Wasps*, 320–22.

66. *Wasps*, 515–18.

67. *Wasps*, 548–51.

68. *Wasps*, 555.

69. Indeed, when pressed by his son to recall "the benefits you get from your so-called dominion over Greece" (576–77), Philokleon offers rather few material benefits. I discuss this further below.

70. *Wasps*, 619–30.

71. *Wasps*, 560f.

72. *Wasps*, 583–86.

73. *Wasps*, 587, translation modified.

74. As Lisa Kallet has noted; Kallet sees this as a symbol of the demos as rich tyrant, stressing the importance of the demos' wealth to the demos-tyrant analogy ("*Demos tyrannos*," 139–40). In my view, Kallet's emphasis on wealth obscures what I take to be a more important point about the institutional position of the jurors within the city. I engage with Kallet's argument further below.

75. Perhaps because tyranny is never mentioned in the passage, it is not often read as a satire of the tyrant. See Henderson, "Demos, Demagogue, Tyrant," 160: "It is noteworthy that in comedy this rulership [of the demos] is typically characterized as 'rule' (*archē*), 'monarchy' or the like rather than as 'tyranny.'" David Konstan reads the passage as involving a "childish" (rather than tyrannical) "desire for flattery that transparently betrays the pathetic self-importance of the weak and helpless" (*Greek Comedy and Ideology*, 18).

76. Compare the portrayal of Zeus in Aeschylus' *Prometheus Bound* with *Wasps*, 620–30 and 518, quoted above.

77. Henderson, "Demos, Demagogue, Tyrant," 167.

78. Excerpted from *Wasps*, 605–20.

79. *Wasps*, 417, translation mine.

80. *Wasps*, 463–70, translation modified to reflect Aristophanes' use of the language of tyranny.

81. *Wasps*, 488–95, translation modified (see note directly above).

82. Henderson, "Demos, Demagogue, Tyrant," 163–64. See also Konstan, *Greek Comedy*, 173 and 173n32 for more citations.

83. See John Zumbrunnen's discussion of the susceptibility of Aristophanes' plays to multiple interpretations in "Fantasy, Irony." See also S. Douglas Olson's "Politics and Poetry in Aristophanes' *Wasps*," for further discussion of the role of tyranny in the play.

84. *Knights*, 1321, modifying Henderson's "handsome" to "beautiful."

85. *Knights*, 1330. Demos is hailed as "king of the Greeks" by the chorus a few lines later, at 1333.

86. Wohl, *Love among the Ruins*, 112–15.

87. *Knights*, 1316–18.

88. *Knights*, 1332, as noted in Wohl, *Love among the Ruins*, 110–11.

89. *Knights*, 1115–20.

90. *Knights*, 1121–30.

91. See the back and forth between Demos and the chorus at 1110–50.

92. Wohl notes that "however we read the end, it is flattering to its audience: those leaving the theater go either as sovereign Demos (if they buy the transformation) or as clever Demos (if they don't)" (*Love among the Ruins*, 120).

93. *Wasps*, 588–89.

94. Kallet, "*Demos tyrannos*," 142; see also 139.

95. Cf. Kallet's claim that this institutional role is itself tied closely to their wealth. I see wealth and power as operating relatively independently in the play, as suggested in part through the depiction of Philokleon's character; he is not particularly interested in money or in offering combined displays of power and wealth. Rather, it is the institutional power of the courts that attracts him to the role of juror.

96. The description of the events at Arginusae here is based on Xenophon, *Hell.* 1.6–1.7. Unless otherwise noted, translations from the *Hellenica* in this section are John Marincola's, from *The Landmark Xenophon's Hellenika*. Diodorus Siculus also recounts the events, with a number of discrepancies. I take Xenophon as my chief source because his account, unlike Diodorus', focuses at length on the trial of the generals itself, which is my primary interest.

97. For detailed historical reconstructions of the events surrounding the episode, see Andrewes, "Arginousai Trial"; and Hamel, *Battle of Arginusae*. On the possible importance of the promise to free the slave-rowers, which may have contributed to popular hostility toward the generals, see Hunt, "Slaves and Generals."

98. Plato, *Apology* 32b–c; see also Xenophon, *Hell.* 1.7.15.

99. *Hell.* 1.7.4.

100. *Hell.* 1.7.6, translation mine.

101. *Hell.* 1.7.8.

102. Hamel, *Battle of Arginusae*, 81.

103. *Hell.* 1.7.12.

104. *Hell.* 1.7.19.

105. *Hell.* 1.7.35, translation mine.

106. Sara Forsdyke discusses Callixeinus' death in the context of popular justice in *Slaves Tell Tales*, chap. 5.

107. Forsdyke, "Uses and Abuses of Tyranny," 240. See also Forsdyke on Arginusae in *Exile, Ostracism, and Democracy*: "Xenophon makes a great deal out of the fact that these latter generals were not given a regular trial, and on this basis suggests that the Athenian democracy abused its judicial power to the detriment of those elites who undertook to serve the polis as leaders" (180).

108. Grote, *History of Greece*, 916.

109. Grote, 916. See also Forsdyke, *Exile, Ostracism, and Democracy*, 195: "Although egregious, the execution of six of the generals without proper trial was a single instance of injustice, not a regular practice."

110. Johnstone, *History of Trust*, 131.

111. Johnstone, 134–35.

112. Johnstone, 135.

113. *Hell.* 1.7.16.

114. *Hell.* 1.7.19.

115. Yunis, "Law, Politics, and *Graphē Paranomōn*," 378–79.

116. Grote, *History of Greece*, 915.

117. Johnstone argues that members of the *boulē* were in some cases subject to a collective liability regime in the distribution of rewards and punishment (*History of Trust*, 132).

118. See Hamel, *Battle of Arginusae*, 90.

119. On Xenophon's narrative, Euryptolemus himself is nearly held to account merely for arguing against trying the generals. After Euryptolemus and a few other men argue against trying the generals collectively, one Lyciscus suggests that Euryptolemus and his supporters be tried by the same trial as the generals if they do not withdraw their proposal (*Hell.* 1.7.13).

120. Thucydides 1.122.3. See generally Wohl, *Love among the Ruins*, for discussion of the relationship between tyrannical *erōs* and Athenian imperialism in the ancient sources.

121. See Connor, "*Tyrannis polis*"; and Morgan, introduction to *Popular Tyranny*.

Chapter Three

1. "Difficult circumstances" translates Heinrich Bischoff's "*schwierigen Lagen*" in his *Der Warner bei Herodot*.

2. For example, Amasis writes an advisory letter to Polycrates at 3.40; Mardonius turns to an oracle for advice in dealing with the Athenians (8.133), and the Cymeans do the same in Brachidae to deal with the Persians (1.157–60); daughters advise fathers at 5.51 (where Gorgo advises Cleomenes to end his conversation with Aristagoras) and at 3.124 (where Polycrates' daughter advises him not to make the journey to Magnesia); the wife of the Egyptian king Sesostris suggests to him a particularly gruesome way to build a bridge at 2.107; Masistes seeks advice from his sons in 9.113; and Darius' trick to ensure his rise to the Persian throne is devised by his groom, Oebares (3.85). See Vivienne Gray, "Short Stories in Herodotus' *Histories*," on variations in the patterns of advice stories in the *Histories*.

3. Bischoff, *Der Warner*, 307, translation mine.

4. The quotation is from Lattimore, "Wise Adviser," 34. Lattimore's essay is an early influential work on advisers in Herodotus, itself influenced deeply by Bischoff's analysis of the "tragic warner."

5. As Bischoff and Lattimore tended to do.

6. In the scenes of counsel I analyze in this chapter, *sumboul-* words make frequent appearance. But they are not the only words Herodotus uses for advice—he also uses *gnōmē, noutheteō, paraineō,* and *hupotithēmi.* While Herodotus does not use *sumboul-* words *exclusively* in political contexts, there are only a few exceptions (two or three in some forty-four uses).

7. *Sumboul-* words appear in Aesop's fables (ca. sixth century BCE): for example, Fable 236 in Ben Perry's compilation *Aesopica.* The moral of Fable 236 reads, "Those thoughtless in their own affairs are also not suitable to give advice to their neighbors [*eis tas tōn pelas sumboulias adokimoi*]." Words with the *sumboul-*root also appear in some of the sayings of the seven wise men (sixth/seventh century BCE): for example, "Give the best advice to the citizens" (*Politais ta beltista sumbouleuein*), attributed by Diels and Kranz (*Die Fragmente der Vorsokratiker,* 1:63) to Kleoboulos. There are also scattered uses in fifth-century Athenian tragedy predating Herodotus; for example, Aeschylus, *Persians,* 175.

8. Redfield, "Herodotus the Tourist," 116. See also Lombardini, "*Isonomia* and the Public Sphere," 408–12, for a discussion of Herodotus' use of *es meson.* I engage with Lombardini's argument further below.

9. See, for example, Harrison, "Persian Invasions," 569–70; and Forsdyke, "Herodotus, Political History," 234. See also Hohti, "Freedom of Speech," 24: "Constraint is a characteristic of a *tyrannis,* while in a democracy one is free either to speak or keep quiet."

10. Pelling has written a series of articles since the 1990s on these issues. They include "Thucydides' Archidamus and Herodotus' Artabanus," "Educating Croesus: Talking and Learning in Herodotus' Lydian Logos," and "Speech and Narrative in the *Histories.*" All three of these articles were helpful in thinking through the issues in this chapter.

11. See, for example, Pelling, "Speech and Narrative," 108; and Forsdyke, "Herodotus, Political History," 234.

12. Unless otherwise noted, translations from Herodotus in this chapter are Andrea Purvis', from *The Landmark Herodotus.*

13. Translation mine.

14. Richmond Lattimore, citing Bischoff, claims that the only example of a king physically attacking an adviser is Cambyses' assault on Croesus at 3.36 ("Wise Adviser," 26n5), but that is not the only time a king has an adviser physically punished, as this story attests.

15. Translation mine. See also Herodotus' claim that Cyrus "appointed" them (*dietaxe*) to different offices, setting up some as house builders and others as guards.

16. The language of command runs through this passage as well: when Cyrus "ordered" (*ekeleue*) the other boys to seize the spoilsport, the other boys obeyed (*peithomenōn de tōn paidōn*).

17. In order to help Darius conquer Babylon, Zopyrus disfigures himself and appears before the Babylonian council, blaming Darius for his injuries to earn their trust.

18. See section III below for discussion.

19. I discuss these two cases in more detail in section IV below.

20. See Arlene Saxonhouse's discussion of the Babylonians' custom as one that seeks to draw on natural equality rather than undermine it at *Athenian Democracy,* 42.

21. Xerxes here is made to utter a Persian version of a very old Greek idea, traceable to *Iliad* 1.79. Calchas, the priest of Apollo, is unwilling to tell the assembled Greeks that Agamemnon is at fault for their failure in battle. The difference is that in that case, Achilles is around to stand as surety for his safety. In the Persian courts, there is no one filling Achilles' role.

22. One possible exception is the discussion between Cambyses and the Magi over the status

of Persian law, discussed in chapter 1 above. For interactions confirming Cambyses' need for flattery, see 3.34–35.

23. See, for example, Croesus' cryptic remark to Cambyses at 3.34: "In my opinion, son of Cyrus, you do not seem to be like to your father, for he, you know, had sired a son such as you to leave behind." Whether this is praise or veiled criticism, it is certainly oblique.

24. I briefly discuss the substance of Cambyses' reply below, in note 57.

25. Pelling, "Speech and Narrative," 106. (Pelling is here analyzing a different court scene, but the lesson applies equally well to Herodotus' depiction of Cambyses.) See also Pelling, "Educating Croesus," 168–72, for further reflections on speaking at court.

26. At 1.208, Cyrus transfers Croesus to Cambyses, presumably in part to give his son access to Croesus' counsel.

27. Translation mine.

28. Stahl, "Learning through Suffering?," argues that Croesus' bad advice here means that he has forgotten the wisdom he gained on the pyre. Cf. Shapiro, "Learning through Suffering," for a persuasive response.

29. See Lombardini, "*Isonomia* and the Public Sphere," 412, discussed in more detail below.

30. The verb *sunageirein*, "to gather or assemble," is the same verb used in book 3 for convening an assembly of citizens in Samos. *Sugkalein* is used by Aristophanes in the *Lysistrata* for Lysistrata's convening of the women of Athens for an assembly (see also Herodotus 2.160 for convening a council of wise men).

31. See Pelling, "Educating Croesus," 167–68.

32. As Susan Shapiro notes in "Learning through Suffering."

33. The Greek (*para tou boulomenou apodeiknusthai*) implies a suggestive parallel with the Athenian principle that *ho boulomenos* ("whoever wishes") may speak in the assembly. Of course, *ho boulomenos'* privilege to speak to Darius cannot be assumed, as Coës' maneuvers show.

34. Not all such attempts at negotiating an alignment of interests are so successful (for either king or adviser). When Histiaeus, one of the agitators behind the Ionian revolt (5.35), is confronted by the king, his denials of complicity are accompanied by elaborate claims to share in Darius' interests (5.106). These are, of course, lies. Histiaeus is eventually captured and executed (6.30).

35. Hohti, "Freedom of Speech," 20–22.

36. Translation mine: "*Sullogon epiklēton Perseōn tōn aristōn epoieeto, hina gnōmas te puthētai spheōn kai autos en pasi eipēi ta thelei.*"

37. Translation mine. Compare Xerxes' *idiobouleuein* with Artabanus' "I advise" at 7.10.

38. Pelling, "Speech and Narrative," 108. He also emphasizes the request for "whoever wishes among you to give an opinion" and notes the similarity between Xerxes' request and the Athenian herald's call to open assembly debate ("Who wishes to speak?").

39. Lombardini, "*Isonomia* and the Public Sphere," 411.

40. Lombardini, 412.

41. Cf. Lombardini, 410, which to my mind runs together questions of contestation and control.

42. See also 1.56, where Croesus considers which of the Greeks to ally himself with and comes to see that the relevant choice is between Sparta and Athens, as well as 5.24, where Darius writes to Histiaeus, whom he does not trust, that he has thought hard and realized that Histiaeus is his most loyal subject. Here Darius uses the phrase as part of a plan to deceive his listener, but

the claim to have considered a course of action and discovered a plan does describe what Darius has done—he is just lying about the particular plan.

43. Translation mine. Rosalind Thomas notes the connection between this passage and the Sophistic movement and Protagoras (*Herodotus in Context*, 266).

44. Translation mine.

45. This is more than simply a recognition that the process of listening to counsel must have an end and that eventually Xerxes will have to decide for himself. Rather, Artabanus appears to suggest that Xerxes should consider the issues on his own (*proskepsamenos epi seōutou*).

46. Pelling reads Artabanus as arguing strongly against Mardonius and only obliquely against Xerxes (see below). But Artabanus' discussion of slander includes a plain accusation that Xerxes has "done wrong." It is perhaps this element of Artabanus' speech that most justifies Herodotus' judgment at 7.46 that Artabanus spoke freely in this instance. See section IV below for further discussion.

47. See Pelling, "Thucydides' Archidamus and Herodotus' Artabanus," 135: Xerxes "is learning from his wise adviser, but learning the wrong lesson."

48. See Hohti, "Freedom of Speech," 25, for a discussion of Xerxes' lack of anger. Donald Lateiner has argued that laughter is rarely a good thing in the *Histories*; Xerxes' laughter signals his failure to understand Demaratus' advice and to take it seriously ("No Laughing Matter," 179). Lateiner notes that laughter functions as a "narrational indication of a character's disdain and as an authorial intimation of disaster in store for the laugher" (174). Yet Xerxes' later defense and praise of Demaratus complicates this reading (7.237; see discussion below).

49. Artabanus at 7.10, Demaratus at 7.234–35.

50. Translation mine.

51. Translation mine.

52. See also Darius' critique of competitiveness in oligarchy in the constitutional debate (3.82).

53. See also 7.99, where she is described as offering the best advice to Xerxes among all his allies.

54. Pelling sees all this as exemplifying "the sly maneuverings which typify a court" ("Speech and Narrative," 111). Rosaria Munson has argued that Artemisia's "very role as wise adviser [here at 8.68 and at 8.101–3] depends on her not being subject to the overbearing pressures that the Persian system imposes upon the other deliberators—deference to a royal tradition and fear for personal safety" ("Artemisia in Herodotus," 96–97). This overstates her independence—as 8.68–9 clearly indicates, at least in the eyes of others at the Persian court, she was not immune to royal punishment.

55. Pelling, "Speech and Narrative," 111.

56. See Harrison, "Persian Invasions," 569–70.

57. It is actually Cambyses, interestingly enough, who poses this problem most sharply. In response to Croesus' admonishments at 3.36, Cambyses claims that it is Croesus' fault that Cyrus died: "You brought ruin to Cyrus, who trusted you." In Cambyses' view, this disqualifies Croesus from giving advice in the future. This is presumably the wrong conclusion for Cambyses to draw, but it is a tempting one. See Peter Stahl, who takes Cambyses' objection quite seriously: "Is there no certain basis at all for well-meaning human advice and no chance of avoiding calamity by good counsel in history?" ("Learning through Suffering," 25–26). Pelling, too, is sensitive to the limits of advice's efficacy in all his essays on counsel in Herodotus.

58. Pelling, "Thucydides' Archidamus and Herodotus' Artabanus," 132; see also his "Speech and Narrative," 109: "Artabanus has to be more indirect still."

59. On Socleës, see Gray, "Herodotus and Images of Tyranny"; and Johnson, "Herodotus' Storytelling Speeches." Gray notes that Herodotus adapts "the stock situation in which a proposal provokes a dissatisfied silence from the general audience in Homer, but is broken by a lone voice whose opposition wins their acclaim" (383; 383n53 for citations from the *Iliad*). Johnson recognizes some parallels between Artabanus and Socleës (7) but does not note that the two men are the only ones specifically recognized as speaking "freely" (*eleutherōs*) in the *Histories*. He also stresses a feature of the Greek debate notably absent in Persia. After Socleës' speech, the rest of the Greeks "break into speech"; after Artabanus' speech, Xerxes cuts off all debate (7–8). The Greek debate, a meeting between the Spartan allies and thus between equals or near equals, has no Xerxes to dominate it (although the initial reticence of the other allies before Socleës' speech may hint at a fear of the Spartans).

60. Pelling, "Speech and Narrative," 111–12.

61. See the treatment of Leonidas after Thermopylae at 7.238.

62. Pelling, "Speech and Narrative," 114. Peter Derow links the stoning of Lycides and his family to the Athenian execution of Artayktes, whose son is stoned to death before his eyes (9.120), comparing both incidents with Persian atrocities ("Herodotus Readings," 37–38). Similarly, the stoning of Lycides echoes Herodotus' portrayal of some autocrats' treatment of unwanted and/or unsuccessful advice (as I argue below).

63. Forsdyke, *Slaves Tell Tales*, 152. Forsdyke argues that popular, participatory justice often played out alongside formal processes; popular elements could even be integrated into the "formal" institutions of justice, as in the case of adultery (154–55).

64. Forsdyke, 159.

65. Forsdyke, 153.

66. See the discussion above, in chapters 1 and 2.

67. Pelling, "Thucydides' Archidamus and Herodotus' Artabanus," 132, apropos of the Athenian treatment of Alexander, who bore the initial peace offering from Mardonius, at 8.140.

68. Hohti, "Freedom of Speech," 19.

69. Lombardini, "*Isonomia* and the Public Sphere," 418.

Chapter Four

1. The view that Herodotus and Thucydides share certain substantive commitments, literary techniques, and even methodological concerns is increasingly accepted by classicists, political theorists, and Ancient historians. See, for example, Rood, "Thucydides' Persian Wars"; and Rogkotis, "Thucydides and Herodotus." See also Hornblower, *Commentary on Thucydides*, 2:122–45, for a list and discussion of parallel passages in the texts.

2. Unless otherwise noted, translations of Thucydides in this chapter are Jeremy Mynott's, from *The War of the Peloponnesians and the Athenians*.

3. Diodotus is otherwise unattested in our sources. But most commentators doubt that Thucydides would have made him up entirely, and so he is usually accepted as a historical figure. Nonetheless, as Hornblower notes, "it is artistically satisfying to have the famous and raucous Kleon opposed and defeated on his own terms by an utterly obscure figure who then retires into the shadows from which he came" (*Commentary on Thucydides*, 1:432).

4. Mario Vegetti has argued that fifth-century writers, including Thucydides, tend to blur

questions of causality and responsibility together: "Explicit theoretical reflection on causal connections and forms of explanation based upon them emerged only gradually and with considerable uncertainty from the fuzziness of moral, political, and judicial language to do with
culpability, responsibility, and imputability of facts and actions" ("Culpability, Responsibility,
Cause," 271). So we might think that in using *aitia* somewhat loosely and tracking actors' invocations of it, Thucydides strays from an "objective" historical account centered on real causes. But
I don't think Thucydides is engaged in fuzzy thinking here: rather, he is explicitly interested in
how actors assess responsibility and culpability because such assessments play a crucial role in
the political events he is interested in narrating and explaining. For a recent examination of *aitia*
and causality in the text with a focus on Thucydides' treatment of human nature, see also Jaffe,
Thucydides on the Outbreak of War.

5. There is a considerable literature on Thucydides' vocabulary for assessing causation and
responsibility—words including *aitia*, *prophasis*, the adjective *aitios*, and the substantive *to ai-
tion*. Much of it is focused on what Thucydides might have meant in his famous distinction at
1.23 between *tas aitias* for the war—usually translated as "grievances" or "reasons"—and *tēn
alēthestatēn prophasin*, or the "truest cause" of the conflict. See, for example, Sealey, "Thucydides,
Herodotos"; Kirkwood, "Thucydides' Words for 'Cause'"; and Rhodes, "Thucydides on the
Causes." Rhodes cautions readers not to place too much weight on Thucydides' particular choice
of words—his vocabulary in this domain may not be precise.

6. As Rhodes and others note, *aitiai* are invoked and assessed by the actors in Thucydides'
narrative "to explain an actor's reason for acting" or a "ground for complaint" (Rhodes,
"Thucydides on the Causes," 161, 159); *aitia* "expresses a reaction to another's conduct" (Kirkwood, "Thucydides' Words for 'Cause,'" 58).

7. Edward Harris' "How to Address the Athenian Assembly" analyzes Cleon's speech as an
inappropriate deployment of judicial tactics and rhetoric in the deliberative venue of the assembly. I engage further with Harris' argument below.

8. Gomme, *Historical Commentary on Thucydides*, 2:315, quoted in Harris, "How to Address
the Athenian Assembly," 94-95.

9. As Clifford Orwin has noted, "Oddly, Thucydides himself nowhere passes judgment on
the degree of its [the Mytilenean demos'] complicity in the revolt" (*Humanity of Thucydides*,
142). See also Westlake, "Commons at Mytilene," for the judgment that canvassing the available
evidence from Thucydides' narrative and Cleon and Diodotus' speeches as to the complicity of
the Mytilenean demos is "disappointingly inconclusive" (434).

10. Thucydides does frame the *timing* of the revolt as a matter of necessity: "Now, however,
they were forced [*anagkasthentes*] to stage their revolt before they intended" (3.2). Framing the
revolt as a matter of "necessity" sharply poses the question of responsibility for action. But it
need not determine the answer. See Hoekstra and Fisher, "Thucydides and Politics of Necessity,"
on Thucydides' interest in cases of "intentional action constrained in some significant way by
powers over which one has little or no control" (3). These are cases of what they call "practical
necessity"—and Thucydides' speeches and narrative pose the question of whether practical necessity exculpates without offering a clear answer.

11. See Pope, "Thucydides and Democracy," on this point.

12. See Westlake, "Commons," 431-32, for a detailed discussion.

13. Orwin, *Humanity of Thucydides*, 143. See also Westlake, "Commons," 436-37: "The guilt
or innocence of the commons must have appeared to him to be an issue of hardly any relevance
to the climax of his account."

14. Hornblower, *Commentary on Thucydides*, 1:383.

15. *Pol.* 1304a5–10.

16. Pope, "Thucydides and Democracy," 284–85.

17. Pope argues that Thucydides takes all Greek cities to be systems of "collective responsibility," in contrast to non-Greek cities "under arbitrary personal rule" (281); in part for this reason, "the holistic view of the *polis* is the one that Thucydides himself finds congenial" (285). One of the main claims I have been advancing in this book is that rather than positing a sharp contrast between systems of arbitrary rule and systems of collective responsibility, our Greek sources explore the ways in which arbitrariness and accountability may coexist in one and the same political structure. The Mytilenean debate is in part about just this problem.

18. Harris, "How to Address the Athenian Assembly."

19. See Harris, 101, for a fuller discussion of excusing conditions in judicial rhetoric and Cleon's deployment of these tropes.

20. See Lebow, "Thucydides and Deterrence," 164: "Cleon sounds surprisingly like Thomas Schelling when he argues that the Athenian empire depends not only on superior strength, but on a demonstrable willingness to use that strength to punish those who rebel or resist."

21. On Cleon's populism and anti-intellectualism, see especially Orwin, "Democracy and Distrust," 315: "Particularly suspect are fancy words and big thoughts." On Cleon as a critic of logos in politics, see, for example, Saxonhouse, *Free Speech and Democracy*, 162: "The demagogue Cleon brashly . . . condemns the exercise of speech as a hindrance to action." For the claim that Cleon "radically undercuts the value of democratic deliberation" see, for example, Burian, "Athenian Tragedy as Democratic Discourse," 107.

22. See, for example, Hesk, *Deception and Democracy*, 248–58.

23. Both Thucydides (5.16.1) and Aristophanes (*Knights*, 801–9) also suggest that Cleon profited directly from allied bribes during the war; an Athenian policy of ferocious retribution might raise the value of being on Cleon's good side.

24. For the comparison between Sthenelaidas and Cleon, see, for example, Cartwright, *Historical Commentary on Thucydides*.

25. For example, "They are wronging [*adikousi*] our allies and the people of the Peloponnese. They may have been good against the Persians in the past but now they are bad as far as we are concerned, so they deserve a double dose of punishment for changing from good to bad" (1.86.1).

26. Translation mine.

27. Note that Sthenelaidas here takes the identification of *aitia* to be unproblematic, an assumption he shares with Cleon.

28. Edward Harris reads Cleon as accusing his fellow orators of deploying epideictic rhetoric rather than deliberative rhetoric in their speeches and the demos as behaving like an audience "of spectators who are concerned with the speaker's ability" ("How to Address the Athenian Assembly," 95, citing Aristotle's *Rhetoric* 1358b). Harris locates the central irony of Cleon's speech in his attack on "his opponents for making the wrong kind of speech in the Assembly" (97), followed by his deployment of a judicial speech instead of a deliberative one. Harris helpfully illuminates Cleon's dependence on judicial rhetoric and tropes. Nonetheless, I think he underplays the extent to which Cleon's speech actually is forward-looking and the role of assessing *aitia* in making forward-looking judgments.

29. Villacèque, *Spectateurs de paroles!*, 253, translation mine. Villacèque sees in Cleon's rejection of a model of spectator-citizenship an attack on Athenian democracy. Crucial to her argument is the claim that in castigating the assemblymen for acting like *theatai*, he is criticizing a

model of boisterous, active citizenship (on display in the assembly and also at theatrical contests) that was a crucial component of democratic sovereignty. I agree with Villacèque that democratic sovereignty at Athens was premised on a model of active citizenship, including forms of active participation for the democratic "audience"—jurors and assemblymen. And I also agree that spectatorship and theater were important venues for democratic political activity and education. Yet I think the distinction Cleon draws here, between spectatorship and deliberation, is an important one. There is a difference between actively attending a political speech when one is fully aware that one must make decisions based on it and listening to a piece of political rhetoric when one is free of the burden (and privilege!) of deliberation and decision. See Heath, "Response to Burian, Hesk, Barker," for a persuasive argument for this claim.

30. See Wohl, *Love among the Ruins*, 95: "Cleon proposes the model of an active listener who is . . . strong, resistant, and authoritative."

31. Saxonhouse, *Free Speech and Democracy*, 154.

32. See MacLeod, "Reason and Necessity," 69, for a discussion of Cleon's conflation of an assembly decree (*psēphisma*) with a law (*nomos*).

33. Here I think Cleon's argument echoes Thucydides' own attempt to distinguish his text from "the writings of the chroniclers, which are composed more to make good listening than to represent the truth" (1.21).

34. Cartwright, *Historical Commentary on Thucydides*, 49, in comparing Sthenelaidas to Cleon.

35. See Allen, *World of Prometheus*, 151, on competing claims to anger and pity in judicial rhetoric: "Each contender had to use his speech to define the pitiable and that which was worthy of anger in order to make a claim on his jurors' votes." See also Villacèque, who sees Cleon as arguing that the assemblymen should be wary of the emotional appeals of orators and should trust their own instincts instead (*Spectateurs de paroles!*, 252–53).

36. Cleon claims further that this relaxed attitude is a function of living in a democracy: "Just because you enjoy an absence of fear and intrigue in your everyday relations with each other you assume the same applies to your relation with your allies" (3.37.2).

37. Harris, in keeping with his argument that Cleon is using forensic rhetoric against the Mytileneans, translates *aitia* at 3.39.6 as a claim that the Mytileneans are "guilty" but *aitioi* at 3.38.4 to suggest that Cleon "blames" the Athenians ("How to Address the Athenian Assembly," 97). I think Cleon is using the terms similarly in each case: he is interested in responsibility more broadly, not just legal culpability. Arlene Saxonhouse also notes parallels between Cleon's ascriptions of responsibility to the Mytilenean demos and his Athenian audience ("Deciding to Go to War," 176–77). I encountered this article too late to engage with it fully in writing this chapter, but her interpretation of the debate there shares much with my own.

38. For example, Wohl, *Love among the Ruins*, 95; and Villacèque, *Spectateurs de paroles!*, 251–52.

39. Thus, for all of Cleon's attacks on orators who speak to please, he may himself be no different. Cleon's speech is a piece of rhetoric, and the arguments he marshals are not primarily abstract claims about deliberation but rather intended to persuade the Athenian audience before him.

40. See for example the Old Oligarch's claim that in a democracy citizens can always claim to have been absent during a vote or otherwise to disagree with the demos' decision in the assembly ([Xen.] *Ath. Pol.* 2.17, in Moore, *Aristotle and Xenophon on Democracy and Oligarchy*).

41. See also Hoekstra and Fisher, "Thucydides and Politics of Necessity."

42. Here then is another way in which the rhetorical situation Cleon is faced with shapes his arguments.

43. Wohl, *Love among the Ruins*, 106–7.

44. Translation mine. Harris also notes this wonderful start to the speech, arguing that the twin disclaimers serve to separate Diodotus' rhetoric from dicastic and epideictic oratory.

45. Translation mine.

46. Orwin, "Democracy and Distrust," 319–20.

47. Cf. Jaffe, *Thucydides on the Outbreak of War*: "At the highest level of abstraction, . . . it is human nature that bears [*aitia*] for the Peloponnesian War" (16n36).

48. Scholars debate what exactly Diodotus has in mind here in characterizing the demos' advisers as *hupeuthunoi*. It is possible that he has the *graphē paranomōn* in mind, although it is unclear whether the institution was in place at this early date. See Gomme, *Historical Commentary on Thucydides*, 2:316: "Not especially 'liable to the graphe paranomon,' the action of which is doubtful at this date; but, generally, 'held responsible for the advice we give.'"

49. Colin MacLeod sees a tension between the two parts of Diodotus' argument ("Reason and Necessity," 73). As I argue here, the tension is actually in Athenian practice, and Diodotus' argument exposes it. MacLeod rightly notes that Diodotus' arguments "make plain the unconditioned power of the *demos*" and draws the analogy to the tyrant, "accountable to no-one" (74).

50. As I will suggest in the conclusion to this chapter, the demos' insulation from the consequences of their decisions may be illusory.

51. Here I disagree with Saxonhouse's claim that both Diodotus and Cleon blame the demos for the problems they see with Athenian assembly debate (*Free Speech and Democracy*, 157).

52. See Schlosser, "'Hope, Danger's Comforter.'"

53. As Arlene Saxonhouse points out, "gift of Zeus" is a plausible gloss on Diodotus' name (*Free Speech and Democracy*, 156).

54. See Hornblower, *Commentary on Thucydides*, 1:439: "The *gnōmē* or motion of Diodotus . . . prevailed in the sense that it won more votes. Thucydides is not necessarily saying that people were convinced by his particular arguments."

55. Although Thucydides also notes here that the inhabitants are nearly massacred: the Athenians "plundered the city as if they had taken it by storm, and the generals were scarcely able to stop them destroying the inhabitants as well."

56. See, for example, Cornford, *Thucydides Mythistoricus*, 206–10.

57. Rood, "Thucydides' Persian Wars," 166.

58. Rood, 161–62; see also Rogkotis, "Thucydides and Herodotus," 65–66.

59. As it is called by John Holton in "*Philanthropia*, Athens, and Democracy."

60. Diodorus 13.31, translation mine.

61. Hobbes, *Leviathan* 31.

Chapter Five

1. Thucydides 3.42.6; translations of Thucydides in this chapter are Mynott's.

2. Thucydides 3.43.2.

3. Thucydides 6.9.2. Of course, Nicias' advice is not heeded (and even as he gives it, he is clear-eyed about the prospects for its success). Nicias abandons his straight talk in his second speech, where he tries to manipulate the Athenians into renouncing the voyage by stressing the immensity of the undertaking; as we saw last chapter, this backfires spectacularly. See also

Saxonhouse, *Free Speech and Democracy*, 165–71, who stresses that Alcibiades' success lies in part in his "ability to understand the people to whom he speaks"; by contrast, Nicias so badly misunderstands the Athenian character that he "fails to recognize" that detailing the "enormous resources" required for the invasion "will incite rather than deter" (171).

4. The Greek roots are *pan* ("all") and *rhēsis* or *rhēma* ("speech").

5. Isocrates 7.20. Unless otherwise noted, translations of Isocrates in this chapter come from *Isocrates I* (translated by David Mirhady and Yun Lee Too) and *Isocrates II* (translated by Terry Papillon), with some translations modified.

6. Plato, *Republic* 557b. Translations of Plato in this chapter are from John M. Cooper's edition of his *Complete Works*. Euripides' *Phoenician Women* 390–91 also offers a window into the importance of *parrhēsia* in the Athenian mind. Jocasta asks Polyneices, "What is most difficult for exiles?" Polyneices replies, "One thing is greatest—not having *parrhēsia*" (translation mine).

7. Scholarly work has linked *parrhēsia* with various facets of democratic life. For *parrhēsia*'s relationship to comedy, see Halliwell, "Comic Satire"; and Henderson, "Attic Old Comedy." For *parrhēsia*'s relationship to virtues such as courage see Monoson, *Plato's Democratic Entanglements*, 52–53; and Balot, "Free Speech, Courage, Democratic Deliberation." On its relationship to shame, see Tarnopolsky, *Prudes, Perverts, and Tyrants*, chap. 3; and Saxonhouse, *Free Speech and Democracy*, esp. chap. 2. See Monoson's *Plato's Democratic Entanglements*, Saxonhouse's *Free Speech and Democracy*, and Markovits' *Politics of Sincerity* for discussions of *parrhēsia*'s place in democratic ideology more broadly.

8. Saxonhouse, *Free Speech and Democracy*, 209.

9. Saxonhouse, 214.

10. Plato, *Republic* 567b.

11. Monoson, *Plato's Democratic Entanglements*, 55. For a discussion of the "Athenians' official views and self-representation" as pertaining to tyranny, see also Raaflaub, "Stick and Glue."

12. Aeschines 3.220, translation and emphasis mine.

13. See Simonton, *Classical Greek Oligarchy*, 241–43. My discussion of the oligarchs' response to the unnamed citizen's frankness immediately below is indebted to Simonton's analysis.

14. The events recounted here immediately precede the Athenian recapture of the city, discussed above in chapter 4, section III.

15. Thucydides 4.130.4.

16. Saxonhouse, *Free Speech and Democracy*, 1–2.

17. Nicostratus, frag. 29 K, in Kock's *Comicorum atticorum fragmenta*, 2:227, translation mine. I thank Matthew Simonton for drawing my attention to this passage.

18. There were certain things one could not accuse a fellow citizen of without being liable legal action: for example, being a shield-thrower or parent-beater (Lysias 10.6–9). It was also against the law (at least in the fourth century) to verbally abuse magistrates, at least while they were performing their public duties (see Lysias 9.6). See Halliwell, "Comic Satire," for an overview of restrictions on speech and an attempt to reconstruct the chronology of their adoption.

19. See especially Henderson, "Attic Old Comedy," for the political role of comic *parrhēsia*. Henderson is particularly attentive to the ways in which the comic stage was freed from some of the limitations of political discourse in other formal political settings, such as the assembly and courts: it could give voice to a wider range of views, address a wider audience more representative of the polis, and engage experimentally with political ideas outside of the "practical constraints of deliberative debate" (272). How far comic *parrhēsia* was directly protected by law

is unclear: scholars disagree whether the comic theater enjoyed special legal exemption from other restrictions on speech and whether, conversely, specific laws and decrees were ever passed expressly limiting what could be said on the comic stage. See Halliwell, "Comic Satire," for a careful examination and weighing of the evidence and arguments.

20. Monoson, *Plato's Democratic Entanglements*, 60–62; see also Saxonhouse, *Free Speech and Democracy*, 92–93, on the contrast between *parrhēsia* and rhetoric.

21. Examples of uses of *parrhēsia* in the assembly are discussed in detail below. For appeals to *parrhēsia* in judicial contexts, see, for example, Demosthenes 23.204, 37.55.

22. Monoson, *Plato's Democratic Entanglements*, 62, emphasis mine.

23. On preferences versus judgments in deliberative democratic theory, see, for example, Elster, "Market and Forum," 10–11.

24. Markovits, introduction to *Politics of Sincerity*.

25. But see London, "How to Do Things," for a treatment of a kind of *parrhēsia* in an autocratic (but non-Greek) context. Konstan, *Friendship in the Classical World*, offers a discussion of *parrhēsia*'s function in Hellenistic courts (see below). See also Kathryn Morgan's recent *Pindar and the Construction of Syracusan Monarchy in the Fifth Century BC*. Morgan analyzes the tyrant Hieron's efforts to represent himself as "allowing frank advice and comic mockery" (16) and how Pindar in his poems helps construct a positive vision of monarchy in which a king like Hieron acknowledges that he requires "prudent counsel." This in turn provides the poet with the "freedom to speak 'honestly'" (2–3).

26. See also my discussion of deliberation and advice in the introduction.

27. Here I depart somewhat from D. M. Carter's claim that *parrhēsia* was merely an "attribute, . . . something that the citizen of one city was more likely to display than that of another," and a characteristic that Athenians displayed merely as "a sort of side effect of their political enfranchisement" ("Citizen Attribute, Negative Right," 198–99). I agree with Carter that it would be wrong to conceive of *parrhēsia* as a "right," given that it was not absolutely protected by law. Yet *parrhēsia* was also more than just a citizen attribute, since it was conceived of not merely as a "side effect" of political enfranchisement but as something that could be granted and encouraged (or forbidden and discouraged) by the regime. Moreover, as I explore below, many Athenians expected that granting and encouraging *parrhēsia* would have positive effects. As I argue throughout this chapter, the word *parrhēsia* could refer both to a privilege of free speech that could be promoted or restricted by the regime and also to a practice or attribute that could be exercised by citizens, whether or not the privilege of *parrhēsia* was well protected (although, to be sure, where it was not well protected, one might expect to find less of it).

28. Isocrates 2.53. I discuss this passage further below.

29. *Ath. Pol.* 16.6, translation from *Politics and the Constitution of Athens*.

30. Monoson, *Plato's Democratic Entanglements*, 55; and Saxonhouse, *Free Speech and Democracy*, 90.

31. The letter to Antipater dates most likely from 340, the letter to Nicocles perhaps from the 360s. On dating Isocrates' letters, see Terry Papillon's brief discussion accompanying his translation of the letters in *Isocrates II*.

32. Isocrates, *Ep.* 4.6.

33. Isocrates, *Ep.* 4.7.

34. Isocrates 2.4.

35. Herodotus 7.39; see above, chapter 3. Translation from Purvis' *Landmark Herodotus*.

36. Herodotus 1.207; see above, chapter 3.

37. See the examples of Demaratus (Herodotus 7.101) and Coës (4.97), both discussed in chapter 3 above.

38. Isocrates, *Ep.* 4.6.

39. Isocrates 2.28, translation mine. Cf. Carter, "Citizen Attribute, Negative Right," 211: "I am not aware of any accounts of *historical* tyrants restricting free speech . . . a tyrant sees little need actively to discourage free speech when his very person is discouraging enough. . . . Because *parrhēsia* is only an attribute, and not anyone's right, it is not so much something a tyrant actively restricts, as something his subjects are indisposed to exercise." That Isocrates attempts to get Nicocles and Antipater to "grant *parrhēsia*" to their advisers suggests that even if we accept Carter's distinction between a tyrant's "actively" restricting free speech versus discouraging it (passively?) through his "very person," *parrhēsia* was still seen as something an autocrat or tyrant could *promote*—for example, by attempting to establish it as a privilege.

40. Demosthenes 4.51, quoted in Monoson, *Plato's Democratic Entanglements*, 61 (the translation comes from there).

41. See also (Thucydides') Diodotus' claim in the Mytilenean debate (chapter 4, above).

42. Konstan, *Friendship*, 94, 97, 102.

43. Isocrates 2.48. See also 12.1, where Isocrates claims "mythic" discourse has popular appeal.

44. Isocrates 2.49.

45. Isocrates 2.50.

46. Isocrates 2.53. I have modified the translation in the final clause. That clause reads in Greek as follows: "*hoti sumboulos agathos chrēsimōtaton kai turannikōtaton hapantōn tōn ktēmatōn estin.*"

47. Isocrates 3.21.

48. As Kathryn Morgan claims in her "Tyranny of the Audience," 186.

49. On Timotheus, see Isocrates 15.130–33.

50. Cf. Morgan, "Tyranny of the Audience," 186–87. Morgan sees that Isocrates taught his audience to flatter the demos but does not recognize that Isocrates' analysis implies the same need for flattery in autocratic contexts—and for precisely the same reasons.

51. Isocrates, *Ep.* 4.5.

52. The language here recalls the stock tyrannical phrase "do what he wishes" (see discussion of the constitutional debate and the trial of the Arginusae generals in chap. 2 above). Is this perhaps why Isocrates believes the *sumboulos* to be the most tyrannical or kingly of all possessions?

53. Although, as I argue below, the issue is not clear-cut—the Attic orators often claim that they and speakers like them are not granted *parrhēsia* either.

54. See Too, *Rhetoric of Identity in Isocrates.*

55. On Isocrates' constitutional pluralism, see Morgan, "Tyranny of the Audience," 182, 188–91.

56. Isocrates 8.14.

57. Isocrates 8.3.

58. Isocrates 8.4.

59. Isocrates 8.5.

60. Isocrates 8.72–73, emphasis mine.

61. Foucault, *Fearless Speech*, 77, 82–83.

62. See Monoson, *Plato's Democratic Entanglements*, 55; and Markovits, *Politics of Sincerity*, chap. 2.

63. Grote, *History of Greece*, 812. The excerpt from Thucydides' text is from 8.1.2, discussed in the conclusion of chapter 4, above. Grote's modern editors (Mitchell and Caspari) respond to his endorsement of accountability for orators with a trenchant presentation of the opposing view, linking it to the problem of *parrhēsia*: "It would have been more just and more expedient to give the speakers the fullest benefit of the boasted Athenian [*parrhēsia*]. Provided that the assembly was really competent to weigh evidence, it should have encouraged a free expression of opinion on all sides. We may admire the institution of [*euthuna*] for executive magistrates; to apply it to debates on difficult questions of policy was a course of doubtful advantage" (812n4).

64. Monoson, *Plato's Democratic Entanglements*, 55. Cf. Balot, "Free Speech, Courage, Democratic Deliberation," 244–46, arguing that the *thorubos*, viewed positively by a number of scholars, could have detrimental effects on democratic debate for reasons similar to those I discuss here in reference to the asymmetrical accountability relationship between the orators and the demos.

65. Monoson, *Plato's Democratic Entanglements*, 55.

66. Demosthenes 9.3–9.4. The translation is modified from the Loeb edition of Demosthenes' *Works*; unless otherwise noted, translations of Demosthenes in this chapter are from the Loeb edition. Cf. D. M. Carter's discussion of this passage in "Citizen Attribute, Negative Right," 208–9.

67. Demosthenes 15.1, translation mine.

68. See page 136 above.

69. Isocrates 12.10, translation mine.

70. Isocrates 5.81, translation mine: "*egō gar pros men to politeuesthai pantōn aphuestatos egenomēn tōn politōn.*" Isocrates' presentation of these natural disadvantages also suggests how they may nonetheless work in his favor: he has developed a mode of counsel that leaves him relatively unconstrained by the strictures of accountability Demosthenes and other public orators must confront.

71. Demosthenes 8.34.

72. Demosthenes 3.3.

73. Demosthenes 3.22.

74. Demosthenes 3.30–31. See also Demosthenes 23.209–10: Demosthenes makes the same claim that the demos, once the master of the politically active citizens (*despotēs tōn politeuomenōn*), is now their servant (*hupēretēs*). Here too Demosthenes blames the proposers of decrees (*aitioi d' hoi ta toiauta graphontes*) rather than the demos.

75. It is tempting to speculate that the disagreement between Demosthenes and Isocrates over who is really to blame could be related to the different relationships they have with the demos. Does Isocrates' relative independence allow for a freer (not to say more accurate) assessment?

76. Aristotle, *Pol.* 1292a5, translation from Aristotle, *Complete Works*.

77. Aristotle, *Pol.* 1292a26–28, translation mine.

78. Aeschines 3.6. The translation is from the Loeb edition.

79. What I have been calling flattery in this essay shares a number of features with what Simone Chambers calls "plebiscitary rhetoric" in her "Rhetoric and the Public Sphere." Chambers, drawing on a reading of the *Gorgias*, argues that plebiscitary rhetoric is engendered by the lack of "dialogic accountability" between orator and demos. Yet the absence of dialogic accountability does not mean that the relationship was characterized by a total lack of accountability; instead, the accountability relationship ran only one way, with the assembled citizens able to hold the

orators accountable but not vice versa. On my analysis, it is not so much a lack of accountability as a particular form of asymmetric accountability that helped to encourage the practice of plebiscitary rhetoric in the Athenian assembly.

Chapter Six

1. *Pol.* 1292a7–11. Unless otherwise noted, translations from Aristotle's *Politics* in this chapter are my own, following in places Reeve's translation in Aristotle, *Politics*.

2. *Pol.* 1292a11–13.

3. *Pol.* 1292a20–23.

4. *Pol.* 1292a26–28.

5. *Pol.* 1312b11–13.

6. See, for example, Aristotle, *Pol.* 1305b, 1308a.

7. Lane, "Origins of Statesman-Demagogue Distinction."

8. Lane, 189.

9. Lane, 190; see also Aristotle, *Pol.* 1292a, 1304b20–21.

10. *Pol.* 1305b24–27.

11. *Ath. Pol.* 28.4. Translations of the *Ath. Pol.* in this chapter are from Aristotle, *Politics and the Constitution of Athens*.

12. Finley, "Athenian Demagogues," 4. The quoted passage is Thucydides 2.65, which I discuss below.

13. Finley, 17.

14. Thucydides 2.65, Hobbes' translation.

15. Aristotle, *Ath. Pol.* 27. Finley discusses the competing accounts of Pericles' rule in "Athenian Demagogues," 4–5.

16. Hobbes, *Elements of Law*, 21.5. See also my discussion in the introduction. Hobbes' judgment was echoed by Rousseau in the *Discourse on Political Economy*: "Athens was in fact not a Democracy, but a very tyrannical Aristocracy, governed by philosophers [savants] and orators" (*Social Contract and Discourses*, 254).

17. Thucydides 2.65.10, Mynott's translation.

18. The phrase is John Zumbrunnen's (*Silence and Democracy*, 2).

19. Ober, *Mass and Elite*, 43–44. The consequences in fact could be more severe than Ober indicates in this passage, given the liability of Athenian orators to severe sanctions.

20. Ober, 336–39.

21. Ober, 43: "As Aristotle clearly recognized, an orator who wishes to persuade a mass audience must accommodate himself to the ethos—the ideology—of his audience." Ober offers a slew of citations from Aristotle's rhetoric in support of this claim (43n101). Note, though, that there is already something strange about Ober's claim, insofar as it conflates ethos and ideology.

22. Ober, *Athenian Revolution*, 20.

23. See, for example, Ober, *Political Dissent*, discussed further below.

24. This is a sketch of the protreptic structure of the *Alcibiades I*.

25. As Charles Kahn argues ("Drama and Dialectic," 116). I engage further with Kahn's argument below.

26. Note that Polus' interest in both the tyrant and the orator nicely reflects the basic confusion I am exploring in this chapter. Viewed from one perspective, it seems obvious that the tyrant has power in the city. But from another perspective, it might be the tyrant's persuasive

adviser who seems truly to rule. Polus' argument seems to assume that depending on the circumstances either could be true—although perhaps not both simultaneously.

27. Unless otherwise noted, translations of the *Gorgias* in this chapter are from Nichols' edition. See also 466c, which ascribes these powers to the orator as well as the tyrant. Here Polus is accepting Gorgias' account of the power of rhetoric to manipulate and control; I discuss this position at length in section II.

28. Kurt Raaflaub's "Stick and Glue" argues by contrast that Athenian democrats had a mostly negative view of tyrants and tyranny. See Connor, "*Tyrannis polis*"; Tarnopolsky, *Prudes, Perverts, and Tyrants*; and Wohl, *Love among the Ruins*, chap. 4, for arguments that Athenian attitudes toward tyranny were deeply ambivalent. Wohl notes that Raaflaub's earlier work also allowed for a more positive identification of the demos and the tyrant (184n32), quoting Raaflaub: "Sure, we rule like a tyrant, but just consider how marvelous and enviable the rule of a tyrant is!" (Raaflaub, "*Polis tyrannos*," 76, translation mine).

29. McKim, "Shame and Truth," 35.

30. See Doyle, "Desire, Power and the Good"; and Penner, "Desire and Power in Socrates," for reflections on and defenses of this line of argument.

31. See, for example, Wallach, "Platonic Power and Political Realism," 43–44.

32. Socrates sometimes seems to be making the former argument. But even when he claims that orators and tyrants do not do what they wish, even when they do what seems best to them, he is relying on an account of voluntary action that takes acting "under the guise of the (real) good" as a condition of voluntariness.

33. Contra Richard McKim, who reads this section of the dialogue as implying that Polus— and indeed everyone else in the world, as Socrates paradoxically maintains—really believes the Socratic axiom deep down ("Shame and Truth," 47). Christina Tarnopolsky stresses by contrast that Polus' inability to escape Socratic refutation is best explained by a deep ambivalence in his views (*Prudes, Perverts, and Tyrants*, chap. 2).

34. As Kahn notes, Socrates' argument for this claim "relies directly and repeatedly" on the logic of the argument for the claim that it is better to suffer than to commit injustice ("Drama and Dialectic," 86).

35. See Wallach, "Platonic Power and Political Realism," 44: "Socrates' presuppositions about the nature of reality sound goofy to Callicles, and, in the *Republic*, Thrasymachus, Glaucon and Adeimantus."

36. Kahn, "Drama and Dialectic," 115.

37. Devin Stauffer's *The Unity of Plato's "Gorgias"* identifies this inability as the "deepest limitation of Socrates' argument": it "could never be persuasive to someone who thinks that there is rarely a significant gap between what seems best to people—that is, the objects of the most manifest human desires—and the true good that people wish for" (53).

38. Tarnopolsky, *Prudes, Perverts, and Tyrants*, neatly describes the elenchus as "insufficiently therapeutic": "It can diagnose and lay bare the contradictions in a person's way of life and the norms that he uses to guide him in this life, but it cannot show this person how to change this life in accordance with the new insights gleaned from his interaction with Socrates" (125).

39. See Tarnopolsky, *Prudes, Perverts, and Tyrants*, chap. 4, for an argument about the political efficacy of the myth. Stauffer, *Unity of Plato's "Gorgias,"* sees Socrates' aim in the dialogue as convincing Gorgias of the deep attachments humans have to justice, even if their views are incoherent and false. This is the first step toward developing a new kind of rhetoric that might protect philosophy from the city. On Stauffer's view, the ultimate failure of the protreptic

is unsurprising, since Socrates himself is not committed to the moral principles he espouses in the dialogue. See Kahn, "Drama and Dialectic," 115–16, for an argument that the elenchus might fail to convert the interlocutors but that Plato's dramatization of it in the *Gorgias* might nonetheless succeed at converting his readers.

40. See Kahn, who notes the "intense pressure" Socrates brings to bear on Gorgias "to answer as he does" ("Drama and Dialectic," 79). Kahn's emphasis on the *ad hominem* nature of Socrates' refutation of Gorgias is echoed by Stauffer, *Unity of Plato's "Gorgias"*; and Tarnopolsky, *Prudes, Perverts, and Tyrants*; my interpretation of Socrates' confrontation with Gorgias shares much with theirs.

41. From 449c, where Gorgias promises to speak briefly and boasts of his prowess at doing so, through 452e, which I discuss below, Gorgias primarily limits himself to very short answers—so short that they are hard to make much sense of.

42. See also Aristotle's claim that slaves are animate tools: "*ho gar doulos empsuchon organon*" (*EN* 1161b4).

43. Barney, "Gorgias' Defense," 101.

44. As Dodds points out with reference to 455c5: "Socrates lures Gorgias on with a discreet hint at the advantages of a free advertisement." See Dodds, "Commentary," 208–9; see also Stauffer, *Unity of Plato's "Gorgias,"* 27.

45. Dodds, "Commentary," 210, on 455b4. Dodds also cites Hippocrates, *de Arte* 7, "where we are told that ignorance and fear often lead patients to resist treatment" (210–11).

46. I make this distinction here because it marks a crucial difference between this case and the later competition between a doctor and a pastry chef before a jury of children (464e). Gorgias is able to succeed at persuading patients to undergo painful treatment because they recognize that health is a good and that health is not always promoted by the most pleasurable treatment. The jury of children, by contrast, may not be able to recognize any good other than pleasure at all.

47. *Encomium of Helen* 13, translation mine. For discussion of the relevance of this passage to the *Gorgias* see also Wallach, *Platonic Political Art*, 183.

48. Dodds, "Commentary," 216. Dodds offers one possibility for justifying the seeming conflation between the size of the audience and their status as knowledgeable or ignorant, appealing to "crowd psychology" (209).

49. This may leave open the possibility of manipulation by orators—but that manipulation would have to be for the audience's own good.

50. There is a considerable literature on why Gorgias accedes to these Socratic premises and whether his decision to do so is well motivated or not. See Barney, "Gorgias' Defense," 105 and accompanying footnotes, for relevant citations and discussion.

51. Tarnopolsky, *Prudes, Perverts, and Tyrants*, 90. Tarnopolsky argues that Socrates' manipulations may ultimately be for Gorgias' own good insofar as they aim at opening Gorgias to the experience of "learning something new" (64). Tarnopolsky's view and my own clash with Josiah Ober's claim that "in the *Gorgias*, Socrates works hard to prevent the conversation from devolving into competitive rhetorical performances" (*Political Dissent in Democratic Athens*, 192), Ober correctly cites passages from Socrates' discussion with Polus in which Socrates "resists" Polus' use of rhetoric (e.g., 447b–c, 461e–62a). Yet Ober overlooks the ways in which Socrates *elicits* rhetorical displays from Gorgias, in part, as I argue, to show him the limitations of those displays and the dependence of the orator on his audience. On the role of the audience in the *Gorgias* as part of a philosophical community, see also Keum, "Why Did Socrates?"

52. Johnstone, *History of Trust*, 150.

53. Stauffer, *Unity of Plato's "Gorgias,"* 33, comes to a similar conclusion, although emphasizing reputational concerns rather than political risk: "Perhaps if his art were indeed all-powerful, he would have no need to worry about its public reputation."

54. See Tarnopolsky, *Prudes, Perverts, and Tyrants*, 113.

55. See Ober, *Political Dissent*, 202.

56. Moss, "Doctor and Pastry Chef," 244.

57. Moss, 244.

58. See Wallach, *Platonic Political Art*, 178–211, for an analysis of the political art and its relationship to rhetoric in the *Gorgias*. Wallach's argues that Plato's aim is "to shift the ultimate context for evaluating political success from the acquisition of wealth and strength to the care of the soul" (195). By contrast, I see one task of the *Gorgias* as identifying alternative lines of political and moral argument that might be politically efficacious when that ultimate goal seems out of reach.

59. Nichols notes that the translation here is Dodds' (the Greek has "*tōn ta ōta kateagotōn*"—literally, "those broken in respect to their ears"). As Nichols explains, "Certain aristocratic or oligarchic Athenians affected a pro-Spartan taste, which included fondness for boxing and the like" (115n154).

60. See, for example, Ryan Balot's *Courage in the Democratic Polis* on Athenian democratic conceptions of courage.

61. See, for example, James Nichols' footnotes in his translation, 115–16.

62. Cf. Stauffer, *Unity of Plato's "Gorgias,"* who sees Socrates' critique of Pericles as unfair and unrealistic and hence (intentionally) unpersuasive (153–54). This is only half right: the argument that Athenian politicians are bad because they failed to make the citizens better by Socrates' lights may be unpersuasive to those who do not share Socrates' account of the virtues and the good. But the argument that neither the demos nor the orators achieve their own posited ends is potentially more persuasive. My focus on punishment and accountability here shares much with Bickford, "This Way of Life": "When Socrates talks about the 'failures' of Pericles and other admired statesmen, he does so by changing the terms of what politicians should be aiming at. But he also draws attention to the fact that rhetoric offered them no protection from the ire of the many" (135).

63. The dramatic date of the *Gorgias* is a matter of dispute. The reference at 503c to Pericles' recent death would suggest a date in the 420s; Socrates' reference at 473c to his service on the *boulē* the previous year would seem to date the conversation to 405.

64. Dodds, "Commentary," 364. Of course, we need not concur in Plato's judgment that the destruction of the Athenian empire was inevitable. But the basic logic of Plato's claim—that political events might unfold over a timeline that renders attempts to hold political actors accountable otiose—is compelling.

65. See especially Tarnopolsky, *Prudes, Perverts, and Tyrants*.

66. Socrates' claims about the difficulties of assigning responsibility to politicians resonate with contemporary democratic concerns about the ability of voters to engage successfully in "retrospective voting." See, for example, Achen and Bartels, *Democracy for Realists*. For further discussion, see the conclusion to the book below. For arguments that ancient Athens overcame the informational challenges of direct democratic decision-making through mechanisms of knowledge aggregation and institutional design and that contemporary democracies might follow suit, see Ober, *Democracy and Knowledge*, and Ober, *Demopolis*.

67. Ober, *Political Dissent*, 190, emphasis mine.

68. Except in the strictest Socratic sense of "power."

69. See Hansen, *Athenian Democracy*, 146.

70. See Ober, *Mass and Elite*, 104.

71. Plato, *Republic* 492b–c, translation mine. Compare this account with Xenophon, *Hell.* 6.5.36, where the *thorubos* suggests that the Athenians are divided in response to a proposal; here the demos has no single corporate will, no unified proposal for the orator to parrot.

72. Or, perhaps, to be skilled at guessing their nature, if we adopt Socrates' *atechnic* vocabulary for discussing rhetoric.

73. Aristotle, *Rhet.* 1390a32–35, George Kennedy's translation, emphasis mine.

74. Ober reads these claims for the impossibility of adapting one's speech to one's audience as part of an argument in the dialogue demonstrating the degree to which Callicles has been thoroughly ideologically dominated by the demos. I do not think Ober recognizes the degree to which Socrates' arguments here are, on their face, implausible and what that suggests about how we are to interpret the dialogue. See Ober, *Political Dissent*, 202.

75. See Euben, "Democracy and Political Theory": Callicles counts among those critics of democracy that "present themselves as lovers of the demos" (203)—even if they are something else altogether.

76. Kahn, "Drama and Dialectic," 100.

77. Plato, *Republic* 493a–b, translation from Plato, *Complete Works*.

78. Ober, *Political Dissent*, 236.

79. Put another way, I think the model of ideological hegemony and its effects that Ober reads into the *Gorgias* is implausible. However, it is important to note that this is not the only model of the workings of ideological hegemony that Ober offers. In *Mass and Elite*, Ober offers one that actually seems to rely on the *uncertainty* that characterizes orator-demos interaction: "Politicians competed for popular favor in public contests which were played according to certain conventions, but the details of the rules remained vague: when was *charis* good and when was it bad? . . . *None of the answers were spelled out, and so politicians always operated from a position of uncertainty*. . . . The vague and internally contradictory rules they devised for those who would play the game of political influence allowed the demos to reserve for itself the right to cast its own judgments according to its own lights—and hence to keep control of the state" (335–36, emphasis mine). This is clearly a different model of ideological hegemony than the one on display in Ober's reading of the *Gorgias*, in which it is the transparency of the demos' desires that allows it to maintain its control over the orators.

Ober carries over the assumption of transparency into his later work. See, for example, the civic dignity game in *Demopolis* (115–22), in which all of the actors, including the demos, are aware of the payoffs each player assigns to the various moves and outcomes in the game. It is only because of this transparency that "each individual predictably acts in ways that sustain the regime" and that attempts to usurp democratic power will be few and far between (114). I think the model stressing uncertainty more accurately captures the relationship between orator and demos. What Ober does not emphasize enough, however, is the degree to which this uncertainty not only keeps the orators on their toes but also leaves open the possibility of manipulation.

80. Plato, *Apology* 36a, 38d.

81. Indeed, it is not even clear that deploying Gorgianic rhetoric might have saved Socrates here. This is, again, the difference between the jury of children and Gorgias' successful attempts to persuade his brother's patients to undergo painful treatments. Gorgias could succeed because,

in principle, his audience accepted that painful treatments might be conducive to a good they recognized: health. In the "jury of children" case, it is not clear that the children recognize the good of health at all and so are unwilling to undergo painful treatment to promote it.

82. My reading of the dialogue differs from Stauffer's (*Unity of Plato's "Gorgias"*) insofar as I think that for Plato, internalizing this lesson would count as real progress on the part of ordinary citizens. Plato's goal is not to make politics safe for philosophy by developing deceptive and misleading accounts of justice suitable for the masses. On the contrary, to the extent that citizens and orators come to appreciate the limits of their own power, they will have understood something ethically valuable and true. On the other hand, I read Plato as less friendly to democracy than Tarnopolsky does in *Prudes, Perverts, and Tyrants*. For the lesson Plato wants the demos to learn, fundamentally, is their own inability to manage directly the city's affairs. While Plato wants democratic citizens to embrace this lesson, I have my doubts about its democratic effects.

Conclusion

1. The transcript and video of the cabinet meeting can be found at https://factba.se/transcript/donald-trump-remarks-cabinet-meeting-june-12-2017 (accessed January 8, 2019).

2. Donald Trump, campaign rally speech, Council Bluffs, Iowa, September 28, 2016. The speech can be watched at https://www.c-span.org/video/?415991-1/donald-trump-campaigns-ottumwa-iowa (accessed January 8, 2019).

3. Donald Trump, speech at the Republican National Convention, Cleveland, OH, July 21, 2016, https://assets.donaldjtrump.com/DJT_Acceptance_Speech.pdf (accessed January 8, 2019).

4. Achen and Bartels, *Democracy for Realists*, 164; see also their discussion of the challenges facing retrospective voters in their chapter 4.

5. Achen and Bartels, 118; see also their chapter 6 for evidence on myopic economic voting.

6. Guerrero, "Against Elections," 140.

7. Other political scientists have vigorously challenged Achen and Bartels' pessimistic interpretations of the evidence on voting behavior. See Susan Stokes' "Accountability for Realists," for an argument that even myopic voter judgments can lead to effective accountability. See also Fowler and Hall, "Do Shark Attacks Influence Elections?," for a response to Achen and Bartel's most famous example of blind retrospection: their claim that shark attacks have influenced presidential elections.

8. Thucydides 3.42.2, Mynott's translation.

Bibliography

Abdel-Nour, Farid, and Brad Cook. "As If They Could Be Brought to Account: How Athenians Managed the Political Unaccountability of Citizens." *History of Political Thought* 35, no. 3 (2014): 436–57.

Achen, Christopher, and Larry Bartels. *Democracy for Realists: Why Elections Do Not Produce Representative Government*. Princeton, NJ: Princeton University Press, 2016.

Aeschines. *Speeches*. Translated by Charles Darwin Adams. Loeb Classical Library. Cambridge, MA: Harvard University Press, 1948.

Aeschylus. *Persians*. Edited and translated by Edith Hall. Warminster, UK: Aris and Phillips, 1996.

———. *Persians. Seven against Thebes. Suppliants. Prometheus Bound*. Translated by Alan Sommerstein. Loeb Classical Library. Cambridge, MA: Harvard University Press, 2009.

Allen, Danielle. *The World of Prometheus*. Princeton, NJ: Princeton University Press, 2000.

Allen, R. E. "The Speech of Glaucon in Plato's *Republic*." *Journal of the History of Philosophy* 25, no. 1 (1987): 3–11.

[Anaximenes?]. *Rhetoric to Alexander*. Vol. 2 of *The Complete Works of Aristotle*, edited by Jonathan Barnes. Princeton, NJ: Princeton University Press, 1984.

Anderson, Greg. "The Personality of the Greek State." *Journal of Hellenic Studies* 129 (2009): 1–22.

Andrewes, Antony. "The Arginousai Trial." *Phoenix* 28 (1974): 112–22.

Aristophanes. *Aristophanes*. Translated by Jeffrey Henderson. Loeb Classical Library. 4 vols. Cambridge, MA: Harvard University Press, 1998–2002.

———. *Wasps*. Translated by Alan Sommerstein. Wilts., UK: Aris and Phillips, 1983.

Aristotle. *The Complete Works of Aristotle*. Edited by Jonathan Barnes. 2 vols. Princeton, NJ: Princeton University Press, 1984.

———. *On "Rhetoric": A Theory of Civic Discourse*. Translated by George A. Kennedy. Oxford: Oxford University Press, 2007.

———. *Politics: A New Translation*. Translated by C. D. C. Reeve. Indianapolis: Hackett, 2017.

———. *Politics and the Constitution of Athens*. Edited by Stephen Everson. Cambridge: Cambridge University Press, 1996.

Balot, Ryan. *Courage in the Democratic Polis*. New York: Oxford University Press, 2014.

———. "Democracy and Political Philosophy: Influences, Tensions, Rapprochement." In *The Greek Polis and the Invention of Democracy*, edited by Johann Arnason, Kurt Raaflaub, and Peter Wagner, 181–204. Oxford: Wiley-Blackwell, 2013.

———. "Free Speech, Courage, and Democratic Deliberation." In *Free Speech in Classical Antiquity*, edited by Ineke Sluiter and Ralph M. Rosen, 233–60. Leiden, Netherlands: Brill, 2004.

Barney, Rachel. "Gorgias' Defense: Plato and His Opponents on Rhetoric and the Good." *Southern Journal of Philosophy* 48, no. 1 (2010): 95–121.

Bers, Victor. "Dikastic thorubos." In *Crux: Essays Presented to G. E. M. de Ste. Croix on His 75th Birthday*, edited by Paul Cartledge and F. David Harvey, 1–15. London: Imprint Academic, 1985.

———. "Just Rituals. Why the Rigmarole of Fourth-Century Athenian Lawcourts?" In *Polis & Politics: Studies in Ancient Greek History*, edited by Pernille Flensted-Jensen, Thomas Heine Nielsen, and Lene Rubinstein, 553–62. Copenhagen: Museum Tusculanum Press, 2000.

Bickford, Susan. "This Way of Life, This Contest: Rethinking Socratic Citizenship." In *The Cambridge Companion to Ancient Greek Political Thought*, edited by Stephen Salkever, 126–55. Cambridge: Cambridge University Press, 2009.

Bischoff, Heinrich. *Der Warner bei Herodot*. In *Herodot: Eine Auswahl aus der Neueren Forschung*, edited by Walter Marg, 302–19. Munich: C. H. Beck, 1962.

Blanshard, Alastair. "What Counts as the Demos? Some Notes on the Relationship between the Jury and 'the People' in Classical Athens." *Phoenix* 58 (2004): 28–48.

Borowiak, Craig. *Accountability and Democracy*. Oxford: Oxford University Press, 2011.

Bosher, Kathryn. "Hieron's Aeschylus." In *Theater outside Athens: Drama in Greek Sicily and South Italy*, edited by Kathryn Bosher, 97–111. Cambridge: Cambridge University Press, 2012.

———. Introduction to *Theater outside Athens: Drama in Greek Sicily and South Italy*, edited by Kathryn Bosher, 1–16. Cambridge: Cambridge University Press, 2012.

Bourke, Richard, and Quentin Skinner, eds. *Popular Sovereignty in Historical Perspective*. Cambridge: Cambridge University Press, 2016.

Burian, Peter. "Athenian Tragedy as Democratic Discourse." In *Why Athens? A Reappraisal of Tragic Politics*, edited by D. M. Carter, 95–118. Oxford: Oxford University Press, 2011.

Burnyeat, Miles, and Michael Frede. *The Pseudo-Platonic "Seventh Letter."* Edited by Dominic Scott. Oxford: Oxford University Press, 2015.

Cammack, Daniela. "Deliberation in Ancient Greek Assemblies." *Classical Philology*, forthcoming.

Canevaro, Mirko. "Majority Rule vs. Consensus: The Practice of Democratic Deliberation in the Greek *Poleis*." In *Ancient Greek History and Contemporary Social Science*, edited by Mirko Canevaro, Andrew Erskine, Benjamin Gray, and Josiah Ober, 101–56. Edinburgh: Edinburgh University Press, 2018.

———. "The Twilight of *Nomothesia*: Legislation in Early-Hellenistic Athens." *Dike* 14 (2011): 55–85.

Carter, D. M. "Citizen Attribute, Negative Right: A Conceptual Difference between Ancient and Modern Ideas of Freedom of Speech." In *Free Speech in Classical Antiquity*, edited by Ineke Sluiter and Ralph M. Rosen, 197–220. Leiden, Netherlands: Brill, 2004.

Carter, L. B. *The Quiet Athenian*. Oxford: Oxford University Press, 1986.

Cartledge, Paul. *Spartan Reflections*. Berkeley: University of California Press, 2001.

Cartwright, David. *A Historical Commentary on Thucydides*. Ann Arbor: University of Michigan Press, 1997.

Chambers, Simone. "Rhetoric and the Public Sphere: Has Deliberative Democracy Abandoned Mass Democracy?" *Political Theory* 37 (2009): 323–51.

Christ, Matthew. "The Evolution of the *Eisphora* in Classical Athens." *Classical Quarterly* 57 (2007): 53–69.

———. *The Litigious Athenian*. Baltimore: Johns Hopkins University Press, 1998.

Cohen, David. *Law, Violence, and Community in Classical Athens*. Cambridge: Cambridge University Press, 1995.

Cole, Susan Guettel. "Oath Ritual and the Male Community at Athens." In *Dēmokratia: A Conversation on Democracies, Ancient and Modern*, edited by Josiah Ober and Charles Hedrick, 227–48. Princeton, NJ: Princeton University Press, 1996.

Cole, Thomas. *The Origins of Rhetoric in Ancient Greece*. Baltimore: Johns Hopkins University Press, 1991.

Connor, W. R. "*Tyrannis polis*." In *Ancient and Modern: Essays in Honor of Gerald F. Else*, edited by John D'Arms and John Eadie, 95–109. Ann Arbor, MI: Center for Coordination of Ancient and Modern Studies, 1977.

Cook, Margaret. "Ancient Political Factions: Boiotia 404 to 395." *Transactions of the American Philological Association* 118 (1988): 57–85.

Cornford, Francis. *Thucydides Mythistoricus*. London: Edward Arnold, 1907.

Demosthenes. *Speeches 18 and 19*. Translated by Harvey Yunis. Austin: University of Texas Press, 2005.

———. *Works*. Translated by J. H. Vince, A. T. Murray, and N. J. DeWitt. Loeb Classical Library. 7 vols. London: Heinemann, 1926–49.

Derow, Peter. "Herodotus Readings." *Classics Ireland* 2 (1995): 29–51.

Dewald, Carolyn. "Form and Content: The Question of Tyranny in Herodotus." In *Popular Tyranny: Sovereignty and Its Discontents in Ancient Greece*, edited by Kathryn Morgan, 25–58. Austin: University of Texas Press, 2003.

Diels, Hermann, and Walther Kranz. *Die Fragmente der Vorsokratiker*. Vol. 1. Zurich: Weidmann, 1992.

Dinarchus, Hyperides, and Lycurgus. Translated by Ian Worthington, Craig R. Cooper, and Edward M. Harris. Austin: University of Texas Press, 2001.

Diodorus Siculus. *Bibliotheca Historica*. Edited by K. T. Fischer and F. Vogel. 5 vols. Leipzig, Germany: Teubner, 1888–1906.

Dodds, E. R. "Commentary on Plato's *Gorgias*." In *Gorgias*, by Plato. Edited by E. R. Dodds. Oxford: Clarendon Paperbacks, 1990.

Doyle, James. "Desire, Power, and the Good in Plato's *Gorgias*." In *Moral Psychology*, edited by Sergio Tenenbaum, 15–36. Poznań Studies in the Philosophy of the Sciences and the Humanities, 94. Amsterdam: Rodopi, 2007.

Elster, Jan. "Accountability in Athenian Politics." In *Democracy, Accountability, and Representation*, edited by Adam Przeworski, Susan C. Stokes, and Bernard Manin, 253–78. Cambridge: Cambridge University Press, 1999.

———. Introduction to *Deliberative Democracy*, edited by Jan Elster, ix–xxx. Cambridge: Cambridge University Press, 1998.

———. "The Market and the Forum: Three Varieties of Political Theory." In *Deliberative De-*

mocracy: Essays on Reason and Politics, edited by James Bohman and William Rehg, 3–33. Cambridge, MA: MIT Press, 1997.

Euben, Peter. *Corrupting Youth: Political Education, Democratic Culture, and Political Theory.* Princeton, NJ: Princeton University Press, 1997.

———. "Democracy and Political Theory: A Reading of Plato's *Gorgias.*" In *Athenian Political Thought and the Reconstruction of American Democracy*, edited by J. P. Euben, J. R. Wallach, and J. Ober, 198–226. Ithaca: Cornell University Press, 1994.

Euripides. *Helen. Phoenician Women. Orestes.* Edited and translated by David Kovacs. Loeb Classical Library. Cambridge, MA: Harvard University Press, 2002.

Finley, Moses. "Athenian Demagogues." *Past and Present* 21 (1962): 3–24.

Fishkin, James. "Deliberative Democracy." In *The Blackwell Guide to Social and Political Philosophy*, edited by Robert L. Simon, 221–38. Malden, MA: Blackwell, 2002.

———. *When the People Speak.* Oxford: Oxford University Press, 2009.

Forsdyke, Sara. "Athenian Democratic Ideology and Herodotus' *Histories.*" *American Journal of Philology* 122 (2001): 329–58.

———. *Exile, Ostracism, and Democracy: The Politics of Expulsion in Ancient Greece.* Princeton, NJ: Princeton University Press, 2005.

———. "Herodotus, Political History and Political Thought." In *The Cambridge Companion to Herodotus*, edited by Carolyn Dewald and John Marincola, 224–41. Cambridge: Cambridge University Press, 2006.

———. *Slaves Tell Tales: And Other Episodes in the Politics of Popular Culture in Ancient Greece.* Princeton, NJ: Princeton University Press, 2012.

———. "The Uses and Abuses of Tyranny." In *A Companion to Greek and Roman Political Thought*, edited by Ryan K. Balot, 231–46. Malden, MA: Wiley-Blackwell, 2009.

Foucault, Michel. *Fearless Speech.* Edited by Joseph Pearson. Los Angeles: Semiotext(e), 2001.

Fowler, Anthony, and Andrew Hall. "Do Shark Attacks Influence Presidential Elections? Reassessing a Prominent Finding on Voter Competence." *Journal of Politics* 80 (2018): 1423–37.

Gagarin, Michael. "Background and Origins: Oratory and Rhetoric before the Sophists." In *A Companion to Greek Rhetoric*, edited by Ian Worthington, 27–36. Oxford: Blackwell, 2007.

Garsten, Bryan. *Saving Persuasion.* Cambridge, MA: Harvard University Press, 2006.

Glowacki, Kevin. "A Personification of Demos on a New Attic Document Relief." *Hesperia* 72, no. 4 (2003): 447–66.

Gomme, A. W. *An Historical Commentary on Thucydides.* Vol. 2. Oxford: Oxford University Press, 1956.

Gray, Vivienne. "Herodotus and Images of Tyranny: The Tyrants of Corinth." *American Journal of Philology* 117 (1996): 361–89.

———. "Short Stories in Herodotus' *Histories.*" In *Brill's Companion to Herodotus*, edited by Egbert J. Bakker, Irene J. F. De Jong, and Hans Van Wees, 291–320. Leiden, Netherlands: Brill, 2002.

Grote, George. *A History of Greece from the Time of Solon to 403 B.C.* Edited and condensed by J. M. Mitchell and M. O. B. Caspari. London: Routledge, 2002.

Guerrero, Alexander. "Against Elections." *Philosophy and Public Affairs* 42 (2014): 135–78.

Gutmann, Amy, and Dennis Thompson. *Democracy and Disagreement.* Cambridge, MA: Harvard University Press, 1996.

———. *Why Deliberative Democracy?* Princeton, NJ: Princeton University Press, 2004.

Halliwell, Stephen. "Comic Satire and Freedom of Speech in Classical Athens." *Journal of Hellenic Studies* 111 (1991): 48–70.

Hamel, Debra. *The Battle of Arginusae*. Baltimore: Johns Hopkins University Press, 2015.

Hammer, Dean. "Plebiscitary Politics in Archaic Greece." *Historia: Zeitschrift für Alte Geschichte* 54 (2005): 107–31.

Hansen, Mogens Herman. *The Athenian Assembly in the Age of Demosthenes*. New York: Blackwell, 1987.

———. *The Athenian Democracy in the Age of Demosthenes*. Norman: University of Oklahoma Press, 1991.

———. "The Athenian 'Politicians,' 403–322 B.C." *Greek, Roman, and Byzantine Studies* 24 (1983): 33–55.

———. *Eisangelia: The Sovereignty of the People's Court in Athens in the Fourth Century B.C. and the Impeachment of Generals and Politicians*. Odense: Odense University Press, 1975.

———. *The Sovereignty of the People's Court in Athens in the Fourth Century B.C. and the Public Action against Unconstitutional Proposals*. Odense: Odense University Press, 1974.

Harris, Edward. *Democracy and the Rule of Law in Classical Athens*. Cambridge: Cambridge University Press, 2006.

———. "How to Address the Athenian Assembly: Rhetoric and Political Tactics in the Debate about Mytilene (Thuc. 3.37–50)." *Classical Quarterly* 63, no. 1 (2013): 94–109.

———. "The Rule of Law in Athenian Democracy: Reflections on the Judicial Oath." *Ethics & Politics* 9 (2007): 55–74.

Harris, Edward, and Lene Rubinstein. Introduction to *The Law and the Courts in Ancient Greece*, edited by Edward Harris and Lene Rubinstein, 1–18. London: Duckworth, 2004.

Harris, William V. *Dreams and Experience in Classical Antiquity*. Cambridge, MA: Harvard University Press, 2009.

Harrison, Thomas. "The Persian Invasions." In *Brill's Companion to Herodotus*, edited by Egbert J. Bakker, Irene J. F. De Jong, and Hans Van Wees, 551–78. Leiden, Netherlands: Brill, 2002.

Heath, Malcolm. "Response to Burian, Hesk, and Barker." In *Why Athens? A Reappraisal of Tragic Politics*, edited by D. M. Carter, 163–74. Oxford: Oxford University Press, 2011.

Henderson, Jeffrey. "Attic Old Comedy, Frank Speech, and Democracy." In *Democracy, Empire, and the Arts in Fifth-Century Athens*, edited by Deborah Boedeker and Kurt Raaflaub, 255–74. Cambridge, MA: Harvard University Press, 1998.

———. "Demos, Demagogue, Tyrant in Attic Old Comedy." In *Popular Tyranny: Sovereignty and Its Discontents in Ancient Greece*, edited by Kathryn Morgan, 155–80. Austin: University of Texas Press, 2003.

Herodotus. *Histories*. Translated by A. D. Godley. Loeb Classical Library. 4 vols. Cambridge, MA: Harvard University Press, 1981–82.

———. *The Landmark Herodotus: The Histories*. Edited by Robert Strassler. Translated by Andrea L. Purvis. New York: Anchor Books, 2007.

Hesk, Jon. *Deception and Democracy*. Cambridge: Cambridge University Press, 2000.

———. "Types of Oratory." In *The Cambridge Companion to Ancient Rhetoric*, edited by E. Gunderson, 145–61. Cambridge: Cambridge University Press, 2009.

Hobbes, Thomas, trans. *Eight Bookes of the Peloponnesian Warre*, by Thucydides. 1629.

———. *Elements of Law*. 1640.

Hoekstra, Kinch. "Athenian Democracy and Popular Tyranny." In *Popular Sovereignty in His-*

torical Perspective, edited by Richard Bourke and Quentin Skinner, 15–51. Cambridge: Cambridge University Press, 2016.

Hoekstra, Kinch, and Mark Fisher. "Thucydides and the Politics of Necessity." In *The Oxford Handbook of Thucydides*, edited by Ryan Balot, Sarah Forsdyke, and Edith Foster, 373–90. Oxford: Oxford University Press, 2017.

Hohti, Paavo. "Freedom of Speech in Speech Sections in the *Histories* of Herodotus." *Arctos* 8 (1974): 19–27.

Holton, John. "*Philanthropia*, Athens, and Democracy in Diodorus Siculus: The Athenian Debate." In *The Hellenistic Reception of Classical Athenian Democracy and Political Thought*, edited by Mirko Canevaro and Benjamin Gray, 177–208. Oxford: Oxford University Press, 2018.

Hornblower, Simon. *A Commentary on Thucydides*. Vols. 1–2. Oxford: Clarendon Press, 1991–96.

Hunt, Peter. "The Slaves and the Generals of Arginusae." *American Journal of Philology* 122 (2001): 359–80.

Isocrates. *Isocrates I*. Translated by David Mirhady and Yun Lee Too. Austin: University of Texas Press, 2000.

———. *Isocrates II*. Translated by Terry L. Papillon. Austin: University of Texas Press, 2004.

———. *Works*. Vol. 1–2, translated by George Norlin. Vol. 3, translated by La Rue Van Hook. Loeb Classical Library. 3 vols. Cambridge, MA: Harvard University Press, 1954–56.

Jaffe, Seth. *Thucydides on the Outbreak of War: Character and Contest*. Oxford: Oxford University Press, 2017.

Johnson, David M. "Herodotus' Storytelling Speeches: Socles (5.92) and Leotychides (6.86)." *Classical Journal* 97 (2001): 1–26.

Johnstone, Steven. *A History of Trust in Ancient Greece*. Chicago: University of Chicago Press, 2011.

Jones, A. H. M. *Athenian Democracy*. Baltimore: Johns Hopkins University Press, 1957.

———. "Athenian Democracy and Its Critics." *Cambridge Historical Journal* 11 (1953): 1–26.

Kahn, Charles. "Drama and Dialectic in Plato's *Gorgias*." *Oxford Studies in Ancient Philosophy* 1 (1983): 75–121.

Kallet, Lisa. "*Demos tyrannos*: Wealth, Power, and Economic Patronage." In *Popular Tyranny: Sovereignty and Its Discontents in Ancient Greece*, edited by Kathryn Morgan, 117–54. Austin: University of Texas Press, 2003.

Kallet-Marx, Lisa. "Money Talks: Rhetor, Demos, and the Resources of the Athenian Empire." In *The Athenian Empire*, edited by Polly Low, 185–210. Edinburgh: Edinburgh University Press, 2008.

Kantzios, Ippokratis. "The Politics of Fear in Aeschylus' *Persians*." *Classical World* 98 (2004): 3–19.

Kennedy, George. *A New History of Classical Rhetoric*. Princeton, NJ: Princeton University Press, 1994.

Keum, Tae-Yeoun. "Why Did Socrates Conduct His Dialogues before an Audience?" *History of Political Thought* 37, no. 3 (2016): 411–37.

Kirkwood, G. M. "Thucydides' Words for 'Cause.'" *AJP* 73 (1952): 37–61.

Kock, Theodorus. *Comicorum atticorum fragmenta*. Vol. 2. Leipzig, Germany: Teubner, 1874.

Konstan, David. *Friendship in the Classical World*. Cambridge: Cambridge University Press, 1997.

———. *Greek Comedy and Ideology*. New York: Oxford University Press, 1995.

Laks, André, and Glenn W. Most, ed. *Sophists, Part 2*. Vol. 4 of *Early Greek Philosophy*. Loeb Classical Library. Cambridge, MA: Harvard University Press, 2016.

Landauer, Matthew. "Democratic Theory and the Athenian Public Sphere." *Polis* 33, no. 1 (2016): 31–51.

———. "*Parrhesia* and the *Demos Tyrannos*: Frank Speech, Flattery, and Accountability in Democratic Athens." *History of Political Thought* 33, no. 2 (2012): 185–208.

Lane, Melissa. "The Origins of the Statesman-Demagogue Distinction in and after Ancient Athens." *Journal of the History of Ideas* 73, no. 2 (2012): 179–200.

———. "Popular Sovereignty as Control of Office-Holders: Aristotle on Greek Democracy." In *Popular Sovereignty in Historical Perspective*, edited by Richard Bourke and Quentin Skinner, 52–72. Cambridge: Cambridge University Press, 2016.

Lanni, Adriaan. *Law and Justice in the Courts of Classical Athens.* Cambridge: Cambridge University Press, 2006.

———. "Spectator Sport or Serious Politics? *Hoi Periestēkotes* and the Athenian Lawcourts." *Journal of Hellenic Studies* 117 (1997): 183–89.

Lateiner, Donald. "No Laughing Matter." *Transactions of the American Philological Association* 107 (1977): 173–82.

Lattimore, Richmond. "The Wise Adviser in Herodotus." *Classical Philology* 34 (1939): 24–35.

Lebow, R. N. "Thucydides and Deterrence." *Security Studies* 16, no. 2 (2007): 163–88.

Lewis, J. D. "*Isēgoria* at Athens: When Did It Begin?" *Historia* 20 (1971): 129–41.

Lewis, Sian. *Greek Tyranny.* Bristol, UK: Phoenix Press, 2009.

Lombardini, John. "*Isonomia* and the Public Sphere in Democratic Athens." *History of Political Thought* 34, no. 3 (2013): 408–12.

London, Jennifer. "How to Do Things with Fables: Ibn al-Muqaffaʻ's Frank Speech in Stories from *Kalila Wa Dimna*." *History of Political Thought* 29 (2008): 189–212.

Loraux, Nicole. *The Divided City: On Memory and Forgetting in Ancient Athens.* Translated by Corinne Pache with Jeff Fort. New York: Zone Books, 2002.

Luraghi, Nino. "Anatomy of the Monster: The Discourse of Tyranny in Ancient Greece." In *Antimonarchic Discourse in Antiquity*, edited by Henning Börm, 67–84. Stuttgart, Germany: Franz Steiner Verlag, 2015.

———. "Ruling Alone: Monarchy in Greek Politics and Thought." In *The Splendors and Miseries of Ruling Alone: Encounters with Monarchy from Archaic Greece to the Hellenistic Mediterranean*, edited by Nino Luraghi, 11–24. Stuttgart, Germany: Franz Steiner Verlag, 2013.

———. "To Die like a Tyrant." In *The Splendors and Miseries of Ruling Alone: Encounters with Monarchy from Archaic Greece to the Hellenistic Mediterranean*, edited by Nino Luraghi, 49–71. Stuttgart, Germany: Franz Steiner Verlag, 2013.

Lycurgus, Dinarchus, Demades, and Hyperides. *Minor Attic Orators.* Translated by J. O. Burtt. Loeb Classical Library. 2 vols. Cambridge, MA: Harvard University Press, 1954.

Lysias. Translated by W. R. M. Lamb. Loeb Classical Library. Cambridge, MA: Harvard University Press, 1930.

MacDowell, Douglas. *The Law in Classical Athens.* Ithaca: Cornell University Press, 1978.

Mackil, Emily. *Creating a Common Polity: Religion, Economy, and Politics in the Making of the Greek Koinon.* Berkeley: University of California Press, 2013.

MacLeod, C. W. "Reason and Necessity: Thucydides III 9–14, 37–48." *Journal of Hellenic Studies* 98 (1978): 64–78.

Manin, Bernard, Adam Przeworski, and Susan C. Stokes. Introduction to *Democracy, Accountability and Representation*, edited by Adam Przeworski, Susan C. Stokes, and Bernard Manin, 1–26. Cambridge: Cambridge University Press, 1999.

Markovits, Elizabeth. *The Politics of Sincerity: Plato, Frank Speech, and Democratic Judgment.* University Park: Pennsylvania State University Press, 2008.

McGlew, James F. *Tyranny and Political Culture in Ancient Greece*. Ithaca: Cornell University Press, 1993.

McKim, Richard. "Shame and Truth in Plato's *Gorgias*." In *Platonic Writings, Platonic Readings*, edited by C. L. Griswold Jr., 34–48. New York: Routledge, 1988.

Mitchell, Lynette. "Tyrannical Oligarchs at Athens." In *Ancient Tyranny*, edited by Sian Lewis, 178–87. Edinburgh: Edinburgh University Press, 2006.

Monoson, S. Sara. *Plato's Democratic Entanglements*. Princeton, NJ: Princeton University Press, 2000.

Moore, J. M. *Aristotle and Xenophon on Democracy and Oligarchy*. Berkeley: University of California Press, 1975.

Morgan, Kathryn. Introduction to *Popular Tyranny: Sovereignty and Its Discontents in Ancient Greece*, edited by Kathryn Morgan, ix–xxvii. Austin: University of Texas Press, 2003.

———. *Pindar and the Construction of Syracusan Monarchy in the Fifth Century BC*. Oxford: Oxford University Press, 2015.

———. "The Tyranny of the Audience in Plato and Isocrates." In *Popular Tyranny: Sovereignty and Its Discontents in Ancient Greece*, edited by Kathryn Morgan, 181–214. Austin: University of Texas Press, 2003.

Morrow, Glenn. *Plato's Cretan City*. Princeton, NJ: Princeton University Press, 1960.

Moss, Jessica. "The Doctor and the Pastry Chef: Pleasure and Persuasion in Plato's *Gorgias*." *Ancient Philosophy* 27 (2007): 229–49.

Munson, Rosaria Vignolo. "Artemisia in Herodotus." *Classical Antiquity* 7 (1988): 91–106.

———. "The Madness of Cambyses: (Herodotus 3.16–38)." *Arethusa* 24 (1991): 43–65.

Ober, Josiah. *The Athenian Revolution*. Princeton, NJ: Princeton University Press, 1998.

———. *Democracy and Knowledge*. Princeton, NJ: Princeton University Press, 2008.

———. *Demopolis: Democracy before Liberalism in Theory and Practice*. Cambridge: Cambridge University Press, 2017.

———. *Mass and Elite in Democratic Athens: Rhetoric, Ideology, and the Power of the People*. Princeton, NJ: Princeton University Press, 1989.

———. *Political Dissent in Democratic Athens: Intellectual Critics of Popular Rule*. Princeton, NJ: Princeton University Press, 1998.

———. "Tyrant Killing as Therapeutic *Stasis*: A Political Debate in Images and Texts." In *Popular Tyranny: Sovereignty and Its Discontents in Ancient Greece*, edited by Kathryn Morgan, 215–50. Austin: University of Texas Press, 2003.

Olson, S. Douglas. "Politics and Poetry in Aristophanes' *Wasps*." *Transactions of the American Philological Association* 126 (1996): 129–50.

Orwin, Clifford. "Democracy and Distrust: A Lesson from Thucydides." *American Scholar* 53, no. 3 (1984): 313–25.

———. *The Humanity of Thucydides*. Princeton, NJ: Princeton University Press, 1994.

Osborne, Robin. "Changing the Discourse." In *Popular Tyranny: Sovereignty and Its Discontents in Ancient Greece*, edited by Kathryn Morgan, 251–72. Austin: University of Texas Press, 2003.

Ostwald, Martin. *From Popular Sovereignty to the Sovereignty of Law: Law, Society, and Politics in Fifth-Century Athens*. Berkeley: University of California Press, 1986.

Pelling, Christopher. "Educating Croesus: Talking and Learning in Herodotus' Lydian Logos." *Classical Antiquity* 25 (2006): 141–77.

———. "Herodotus and Samos." *Bulletin of the Institute of Classical Studies* 54 (2011): 1–18.

———. "Speech and Action: Herodotus' Debate on the Constitutions." *Proceedings of the Cambridge Philological Society* 48 (2002): 123–58.

———. "Speech and Narrative in the *Histories*." In *The Cambridge Companion to Herodotus*, edited by Carolyn Dewald and John Marincola, 103–21. Cambridge: Cambridge University Press, 2006.

———. "Thucydides' Archidamus and Herodotus' Artabanus." In *Georgica: Greek Studies in Honour of George Cawkwell*, edited by Michael A. Flower and Mark Toher, 120–42. London: University of London, Institute of Classical Studies, 1991.

Penner, Terry. "Desire and Power in Socrates: The Argument of *Gorgias* 466A–468E That Orators and Tyrants Have No Power in the City." *Apeiron* 24, no. 3 (1991): 147–202.

Perlman, Shalom. "The Politicians in the Athenian Democracy of the Fourth Century BC." *Athenaeum* 41 (1963): 327–55.

Perry, Ben. *Aesopica*. Urbana: University of Illinois Press, 1952.

Philp, Mark. "Delimiting Democratic Accountability." *Political Studies* 57, no. 1 (2009): 28–53.

Plato. *Complete Works*. Edited by John M. Cooper. Indianapolis: Hackett, 1997.

———. *Gorgias*. Translated by James H. Nichols Jr. Ithaca: Cornell University Press, 1998.

———. *Opera*. Edited by John Burnet. 5 vols. Oxford: Clarendon Press, 1900–1907.

Plutarch. *Lives*. Vols. 1–11. Translated by Bernadotte Perrin. New York: Macmillan, 1914–26.

———. *Moralia*. Vol. 10. Translated by Harold North Fowler. Loeb Classical Library. Cambridge, MA: Harvard University Press, 1936.

Pope, Maurice. "Thucydides and Democracy." *Historia: Zeitschrift für Alte Geschichte* 37 (1988): 276–96.

Przeworski, Adam, Susan Stokes, and Bernard Manin. *Democracy, Accountability, and Representation*. Cambridge: Cambridge University Press, 1999.

Raaflaub, Kurt. "Democracy, Oligarchy, and the Concept of the 'Free Citizen' in Late Fifth-Century Athens." *Political Theory* 11 (1983): 517–44.

———. *The Discovery of Freedom in Ancient Greece*. Chicago: University of Chicago Press, 2004.

———. "Philosophy, Science, Politics: Herodotus and the Intellectual Trends of His Time." In *Brill's Companion to Herodotus*, edited by Egbert J. Bakker, Irene J. F. De Jong, and Hans Van Wees, 149–86. Leiden, Netherlands: Brill, 2002.

———. "*Polis Tyrannos*: Zur Entstehung einer politischen Metapher." In *Arktouros: Hellenic Studies Presented to B. M. W. Knox*, edited by Glen Bowersock, Walter Burkert, and Michael Putnam, 237–52. Berlin: Walter de Gruyter, 1979.

———. "Stick and Glue: The Function of Tyranny in Fifth-Century Athenian Democracy." In *Popular Tyranny: Sovereignty and Its Discontents in Ancient Greece*, edited by Kathryn Morgan, 59–94. Austin: University of Texas Press, 2003.

Redfield, James. "Herodotus the Tourist." *Classical Philology* 80 (1985): 97–118.

Rhodes, P. J. "Demagogues and *Demos* in Athens." *Polis: The Journal for Ancient Greek Political Thought* 33, no. 2 (2016): 243–64.

———. "Keeping to the Point." In *The Law and the Courts in Ancient Greece*, edited by Edward Harris and Lene Rubinstein, 137–58. London: Duckworth, 2004.

———. "Nothing to Do with Democracy: Athenian Drama and the *Polis*." *Journal of Hellenic Studies* 123 (2003): 104–19.

———. "Thucydides on the Causes of the Peloponnesian War." *Hermes* 115, no. 2 (1987): 154–65.

Roberts, Jennifer Tolbert. *Accountability in Athenian Government*. Madison: University of Wisconsin Press, 1982.

———. *Athens on Trial: The Antidemocratic Tradition in Western Thought*. Princeton, NJ: Princeton University Press, 1994.

Roberts, William Clare. *Marx's Inferno: The Political Theory of Capital*. Princeton, NJ: Princeton University Press, 2017.

Robinson, Eric. *Democracy beyond Athens: Popular Government in the Greek Classical Age*. Cambridge: Cambridge University Press, 2011.

Rogkotis, Zacharias. "Thucydides and Herodotus: Aspects of Their Intertextual Relationship." In *Brill's Companion to Thucydides*, edited by Antonis Tsakmakis and Antonios Rengakos, 57–86. Leiden, Netherlands: Brill, 2006.

Rood, Tim. "Thucydides' Persian Wars." In *The Limits of Historiography: Genre and Narrative in Ancient Historical Texts*, edited by C. S. Kraus, 141–68. Mnemosyne Supplement 191. Leiden, Netherlands: Brill, 1999.

Rousseau, Jean-Jacques. *The Social Contract and Discourses*. Translated by G. D. H. Cole. London: J. M. Dent and Sons, 1923.

Rubinstein, Lene. "The Political Perception of the *Idiōtēs*." In *Kosmos: Essays in Order, Conflict and Community in Classical Athens*, edited by Paul Cartledge and Paul Millett, 125–43. Cambridge: Cambridge University Press, 1998.

Saxonhouse, Arlene W. *Athenian Democracy: Modern Mythmakers and Ancient Theorists*. Notre Dame, IN: University of Notre Dame Press, 1996.

———. "Deciding to Go to War: Who Is Responsible?" In *Our Ancient Wars: Rethinking War through the Classics*, edited by Victor Caston and Silke-Maria Weineck, 167–83. Ann Arbor: University of Michigan Press, 2016.

———. *Free Speech and Democracy in Ancient Athens*. Cambridge: Cambridge University Press, 2006.

Schlosser, Joel. "Hope, Danger's Comforter: Thucydides, Hope, Politics." *Journal of Politics* 75, no. 1 (2013): 169–82.

———. *What Would Socrates Do? Self-Examination, Civic Engagement, and the Politics of Philosophy*. Cambridge: Cambridge University Press, 2014.

Schofield, Malcolm. *Plato: Political Philosophy*. Oxford: Oxford University Press, 2006.

Sealey, Richard. "Thucydides, Herodotos, and the Causes of War." *Classical Quarterly* 7, no. 1–2 (1957): 1–12.

Shapiro, Susan O. "Learning through Suffering: Human Wisdom in Herodotus." *Classical Journal* 89 (1994): 349–55.

Simonton, Matthew. *Classical Greek Oligarchy: A Political History*. Princeton, NJ: Princeton University Press, 2017.

Sinclair, R. K. *Democracy and Participation in Athens*. Cambridge: Cambridge University Press, 1988.

Skinner, Quentin. *Hobbes and Republican Liberty*. Cambridge: Cambridge University Press, 2008.

Stahl, Hans Peter. "Learning through Suffering? Croesus' Conversations in the History of Herodotus." In *Yale Classical Studies*, vol. 24, edited by Donald Kagan, 1–36. Cambridge: Cambridge University Press, 1975.

Stauffer, Devin. *The Unity of Plato's "Gorgias": Rhetoric, Justice, and the Philosophic Life*. Cambridge: Cambridge University Press, 2006.

Staveley, E. S. *Greek and Roman Voting and Elections*. Ithaca: Cornell University Press, 1972.

de Ste. Croix, G. E. M. *The Origins of the Peloponnesian War*. London: Duckworth, 1972.

Stokes, Susan. "Accountability for Realists." *Critical Review* 30 (2018): 130–38.

Strauss, Leo. *On Tyranny*. Chicago: University of Chicago Press, 2000.

Tacon, Judith. "Ecclesiastic 'Thurobos': Interventions, Interruptions, and Popular Involvement in the Athenian Assembly." *Greece and Rome* 48 (2001): 173–92.

Tarnopolsky, Christina. "Plato on Shame and Frank Speech." In *Bringing the Passions Back In*, edited by Rebecca Kingston and Leonard Ferry, 40–59. Vancouver: UBC Press, 2008.

———. *Prudes, Perverts, and Tyrants*. Princeton, NJ: Princeton University Press, 2010.

Thomas, Rosalind. *Herodotus in Context: Ethnography, Science, and the Art of Persuasion*. Cambridge: Cambridge University Press, 2000.

Thucydides. *History of the Peloponnesian War*. Translated by Charles Forster Smith. Loeb Classical Library. 2 vols. Cambridge, MA: Harvard University Press, 1965–69.

———. *The War of the Peloponnesians and the Athenians*. Edited and translated by Jeremy Mynott. Cambridge: Cambridge University Press, 2013.

Timmerman, David, and Edward Schiappa. *Classical Greek Rhetorical Theory and the Disciplining of Discourse*. Cambridge: Cambridge University Press, 2010.

Too, Yun Lee. *The Rhetoric of Identity in Isocrates: Text, Power, Pedagogy*. Cambridge: Cambridge University Press, 1995.

Usher, Stephen. *Greek Oratory: Tradition and Originality*. New York: Oxford University Press, 1999.

———. "Symbouleutic Oratory." In *A Companion to Greek Rhetoric*, edited by Ian Worthington, 220–35. Oxford: Blackwell, 2007.

Vegetti, Mario. "Culpability, Responsibility, Cause: Philosophy, Historiography, and Medicine in the Fifth Century." In *The Cambridge Companion to Early Greek Philosophy*, edited by A. A. Long, 271–89. Cambridge: Cambridge University Press, 1999.

Waldron, Jeremy. *Political Political Theory*. Cambridge, MA: Harvard University Press, 2016.

———. "The Wisdom of the Multitude: Some Reflections on Book 3, Chapter 11 of Aristotle's *Politics*." *Political Theory* 23 (1995): 563–84.

Wallace, Robert W. "Greek Oligarchy, and the Pre-Solonian Areopagos Council in [Aristotle] *Ath. Pol.* 2.2–8.4." *Polis* 31 (2014): 191–205.

———. "The Power to Speak—and Not to Listen—in Ancient Athens." In *Free Speech in Classical Antiquity*, edited by Ineke Sluiter and Ralph M. Rosen, 221–32. Leiden, Netherlands: Brill, 2004.

Wallach, John. *The Platonic Political Art*. University Park: Pennsylvania State University Press, 2001.

———. "Platonic Power and Political Realism." *Polis* 31 (2014): 28–48.

Westlake, H. D. "The Commons at Mytilene." *Historia: Zeitschrift für Alte Geschichte* 25, no. 4 (1976): 429–40.

Wilson, Peter. "Demosthenes 21 (against Meidias): Democratic Abuse." In *Proceedings of the Cambridge Philological Society* 37 (1991): 164–95.

Wohl, Victoria. *Love among the Ruins: The Erotics of Democracy in Classical Athens*. Princeton, NJ: Princeton University Press, 2002.

Worthington, Ian. "Rhetoric and Politics in Classical Greece: Rise of the Rhetores." In *A Companion to Greek Rhetoric*, edited by Ian Worthington, 255–71. Oxford: Blackwell, 2007.

Xenophon. *The Hellenica (Greek History) of Xenophon of Athens*. Translated by Donald F. Jackson and Ralph E. Doty. Lewiston, NY: Edwin Mellen Press, 2006.

———. *The Landmark Xenophon's Hellenika*. Edited by Robert Strassler. Translated by John Marincola. New York: Anchor Books, 2010.

Yack, Bernard. "Rhetoric and Public Reasoning: An Aristotelian Understanding of Political Deliberation." *Political Theory* 34 (2006): 417–38.

Yunis, Harvey. "The Constraints of Democracy and the Rise of the Art of Rhetoric." In *Democracy, Empire, and the Arts in Fifth-Century Athens*, edited by Deborah Boedeker and Kurt
Raaflaub, 223–40. Cambridge, MA: Harvard University Press, 1998.

———. Introduction to *Speeches 18 and 19*, by Demosthenes. Translated by Harvey Yunis, 23–31.
Austin: University of Texas Press, 2005.

———. "Law, Politics, and the *Graphe Paranomon* in Fourth-Century Athens." *Greek, Roman,
and Byzantine Studies* 29 (1988): 361–82.

———. *Taming Democracy: Models of Political Rhetoric in Classical Athens*. Ithaca: Cornell University Press, 1996.

Zumbrunnen, John. "Fantasy, Irony, and Economic Justice in Aristophanes' *Assemblywomen* and
Wealth." *American Political Science Review* 100 (2006): 319–33.

———. *Silence and Democracy*. University Park: Pennsylvania State University Press, 2008.

Index

Wilson, Peter, 197n112
Wohl, Victoria, 64, 75, 218n28

Xanthias (in Aristophanes' *Wasps*), 70
Xenophon, 180; on Boeotian politics, 36; *Hellenica*, 76–80, 81–82, 180, 221n71; *Hiero*, 15
Xerxes: in Aeschylus' *Persians*, 63; in Herodotus' *Histories*, 89, 94–101, 125–26, 135

Yack, Bernard, 8
Yunis, Harvey, 6, 17–18, 42, 80

Zopyrus, 87